Praise for *How to Be a Geek Goddess*

This book proves beyond a shadow of a doubt that Christina Tynan-Wood totally "gets" where men and women divide in terms of technology. If you're of the XX-chromosome persuasion and want a comprehensive, easy-to-understand guide to using today's tech to get organized, connect with your loved ones, streamline the day-to-day running of your household, and more, buy this book now. You'll thank me later.
—Jonna Gallo Weppler, senior editor, *Family Circle* magazine

Unlike our digital native kids, many of us women find ourselves lost as digital immigrants, navigating the ever-morphing ins and outs of a wired lifestyle. Thankfully, Christina Tynan-Wood does the hard work for us: *How to Be a Geek Goddess* offers clear, comprehensive solutions to every woman's tech troubles.
—Stacy DeBroff, national mom expert and CEO of *www.MomCentral.com*

This is the book every guy should give to his girlfriend, wife, mistress, mother, grandmother, female friend, or any other woman who nags him to fix her computer when he'd rather be watching the ballgame.
—Steve Fox, editorial director, *PC World* magazine

D1217783

how to be a

GEEK
GODDESS

practical advice for using computers
with smarts and style

Christina Tynan-Wood

**no starch
press**

San Francisco

11 10 09 08   1 2 3 4 5 6 7 8 9

ISBN-13: 978-1-59327-187-9

ISBN-10: 1-59327-187-5

Publisher: William Pollock
Production Editor: Megan Dunchak
Cover Design: Gregg Kulick
Interior Design: Octopod Studios
Developmental Editor: Tyler Ortman
Copyeditor: Kathleen Mish
Compositor: Riley Hoffman
Proofreader: Rachel Kai
Indexer: John Hulse

For information on book distributors or translations, please contact No Starch Press, Inc. directly:

No Starch Press, Inc.

555 De Haro Street, Suite 250, San Francisco, CA 94107

phone: 415.863.9900; fax: 415.863.9950; info@nostarch.com; http://www.nostarch.com/

Library of Congress Cataloging-in-Publication Data

Tynan-Wood, Christina.

  How to be a geek goddess : practical advice for using computers with smarts and style / Christina Tynan-Wood. -- 1st ed.

    p. cm.

  Includes index.

  ISBN-13: 978-1-59327-187-9

  ISBN-10: 1-59327-187-5

  1. Computers and women. I. Title.

  QA76.9.W65T95 2008

  004.082--dc22

                2008042964

BRIEF CONTENTS

contents in detail

a note for men

I'm writing this foreword for guys who've stumbled
onto this title and are wondering why the hell they're
reading something called *How to Be a Geek Goddess*.
If you're a woman who can't abide yet another male
of the species being a pompous ass about technology,
skip to Christina's introduction, where she gives me a
hard time for being a pompous ass about technology.
(Yes, I'm Christina's husband. You'll be hearing more
about me later. Don't believe everything you read.)

The core idea of this book is that men and women
are fundamentally different in how they think about
and use technology. Of course, you could probably say
the same thing about practically anything. It's just the
way we're wired. Don't blame us, blame our DNA.

Not much has changed since man crawled out from the primordial ooze 20 million years ago looking for someone to bring him a beer and a sandwich. We've always been all about the tech. Back then it was rocks and sticks; today it's cell phones and TV remotes. We also like to puff up our chests and talk, show off our expertise (or lack thereof), and get into arcane arguments involving lots of TLAs (three-letter acronyms) while we grunt and scratch ourselves. It's part of what women secretly like about us, which is why they complain so bitterly about it.

Women approach technology a little differently. They don't understand why men paint huge pictures of The Hunt on the walls of their caves (the first big-screen TVs) when they could be out slaying another mastodon. They don't want to hear about the advantages of using flint instead of bone in an arrowhead; they just want something that will put food on the table, giving them more time to raise the kids, tend the crops, and rub flowers and berries on their skins so they can compete with those cute cave girls in the village across the river. (Not that I noticed them or anything.)

Generally speaking, women care more about function and aesthetics than acronyms and specs. But it's not a point of view you often hear, because 98 percent of all articles, websites, and books about technology are written by guys. Which is why a book called *How to Be a Geek Goddess* is not merely a clever idea, but also a necessary one.

I can think of no person better qualified to write this book than Christina, and I am not just saying that simply because I'd like to keep having sex with her. Christina is the real deal. She's been writing and reporting about technology for longer than I'm allowed to say. She was one of the first to bring investigative reporting to the tech beat (and she's got a drawer full of awards to show for it). She's the only woman to write columns for the two major magazines with *PC* in their title. She's covered technology for mainstream publications whose editors (even the men) are secretly terrified of TLAs.

But being married to a geek goddess isn't easy, especially when she's using you as Exhibit A in her rant against men and their domination of all things geeky. So I'd like to state, for the record, that though I try to use flashlights in new and exciting ways every day, I have never stood in the middle of our living room using one to figure out the range of our Wi-Fi router (see Chapter 7). That's just stupid. And despite what it says in Chapter 12, I don't leave the toilet seat up at night or watch too much football, though I do snore and leave my socks under the dining room table. That way I always know where they are.

If you're the kind of guy who sees the words *geek goddess* and immediately wants to sneak off to the bathroom to search for the naughty bits, just skip the rest of this foreword and go straight to Chapter 12. It has what you're looking for. Trust me.

If you want to know how women think, both about technology and about the men in their life, you want to read this book. And you should commit it to memory, destroy it, and buy another copy—because frankly, we could use the cash, but also because you're not likely to find this kind of information anywhere else. It's the kind of book to buy your wife, your techno-phobe sister-in-law, and that old high school sweetheart who keeps calling when you're watching the ballgame to ask you where the "any" key is. (I swear, honey, that's all she's calling about. Really.)

They call it *empowerment*. I call it *getting them out of my hair*. Either way, it works for me. And it will for you too.

Dan Tynan
North Carolina
August 2008

Longtime tech journalist Dan Tynan is a contributing editor for *PC World*, Infoworld.com, and *US Airways* magazine; he has written for *Family Circle*, *Newsweek*, *Wired*, Playboy.com, and many other publications too geeky to name. He blogs at *http://www.dantynan.com/*.

INTRODUCTION

My husband is a pompous ass. I say that with great affection, and he freely admits it. In fact, he looks proud when I say it and even puts *p.a.* after his name on business cards. If you aren't married to a tech-know-it-all, chances are pretty good you have one of these men in your life. Maybe he's your brother, coworker, or father. In fact, I think it is the rare man who doesn't have a tendency to puff up his chest and pontificate—even on subjects he knows little or nothing about. And because technology is a subject that is both vast and ever changing, it is a topic that brings out male bluster in full force.

Even though bluster is a completely harmless side effect of testosterone, I think it has conspired with a few other factors in the modern woman's life—overwork, stress, information overload—to cause a negative reaction. Because men act so confident on the subject, and it's such a slippery topic, women react with apathy toward the world of technology. It's an apathy that's often mixed with regret, anxiety, and a desperate feeling of incomprehension. I would like to offer this book as a prescription for this reaction.

Every woman can be a geek goddess. Becoming one does not in any way resemble becoming a pompous ass or behaving like a man. It doesn't require learning absurd acronyms or caring about things that don't interest you. It is simply a matter of embracing the incredible innovation that's going on in our times and harnessing it for our own purposes. Men have their way of relating to technology, and we have ours. I propose we live and let live.

I write geeky magazine articles for a living, have consulted with a major national retailer on what gadgets to carry in its stores, write a blog on technology, and have a constant stream of geeky gear and software running in my little home office. I like the stuff. I can hold my own in the geekiest company but see no reason for all the acronyms, a dorky array of gadgets worn on the belt, or time wasted time on technologies that don't do anything useful. I like tools that help me work more efficiently, that help me keep in touch with friends and family, that help my kids become smarter, and that allow me to spend time with my family instead of traveling or working. I think that makes me a pretty typical woman—even if I am a geek.

Since I'm a female geek, my girlfriends (and often women I just met in the line at the supermarket) come to me with technical questions. A lot of these questions are basic, some are difficult, and others are fascinating. They are almost always excellent questions but are frequently followed with an apology that sounds approximately like, "I'm sorry to be so clueless." I find this upsetting. These women are rarely clueless. In fact, they are often more well informed than a guy who is willing to pontificate at length on the subject.

I also hear, in these questions, a plea for information. And—between the lines of each specific question—that plea sounds something like: "Could someone just tell me what I need to know without trying to convince me that I need the latest gadget, assuming I have all the time in the world to trudge through geek speak, and wasting my time with a lengthy explanation of how it all works? I'm busy. I want to use technology, but I don't love it for its own sake." That plea is why I decided to write this book.

I also understand the feeling that there is simply too much to know about technology and that even beginning to sort it all out is overwhelming. It's true that there is a lot to know. In fact, there is so much to know that no one person can understand it all. I spend every day immersed in the stuff, and it's always like being an explorer. Every day there's a new discovery, a new invention, a new tool to find that I will love (or hate). And I have been in enough conversations with super-geeks—the ones with incomprehensible job titles who sold a couple of startups to mega-corps and who can speak entirely in acronyms if necessary—and I've learned that they love technology for the same reason I do: the prospect of discovery. This stuff is being invented right now. Why should you be expected to know anything about it when everyone is just discovering it? In fact, knowing nothing—and so making no assumptions—is an advantage. That's why children embrace technology so quickly.

There has never been a better time for a woman to decide that instead of being overwhelmed she will take arms and become a geek goddess. The technology that's emerging these days serves all of the things women love: communicating, capturing memories, learning, teaching children, keeping a handle on our busy lives, meeting women (and men) with similar interests, discovering ourselves, and finding love. You don't have to learn all the acronyms or be afraid to ask questions. You simply have to decide you are in control and that technology is there to serve you, not overwhelm you.

A QUICK TOUR OF GODDESS LAND

Because it's impossible to predict where you are in your particular exploration into technology, I cover a lot of bases in this book. You may be all that when it comes to social networks yet feel lost working a Windows PC. You may know how to surf the Web like Gidget but balk at installing a wireless network. You may be handy with a PC and a network but be wondering what the heck virtual sex is. Feel free to jump in wherever you like, but I have tried to include a bit of basic information and some elements that I hope you will consider a discovery in every chapter.

Shopping for a computer is a great learning experience. I do it frequently to keep up with what's new. So that's where this book starts—with computer shopping (Chapter 1, "Getting a Smooth Ride, New or Used"). When men shop for computers they focus on speed, specs, and price. Women care about these things too. But we also care about fitting the computer into our home and into our sense of style. I think form is just as important as function, so I've devoted a chapter (Chapter 2, "Housebreaking") to choosing the right computer for your lifestyle.

Next comes the fun part: accessorizing. So Chapter 3, "Getting in Touch with Your Software Side," is about software—how and where to shop for it, how it can get you organized, how to get great software for free, and pretty much everything you need to know to trick out a PC. Then we will connect it to the Internet (Chapter 4, "Hook it Up"), go on a serious online shopping spree (Chapter 5, "Where the Stores Never Close"), and master the world of Internet phones, webcams, and instant messaging (Chapter 6, "Hello, Operator").

Once you get to the second half of the book, you will have picked up some lingo, tips, and most importantly, a little goddess attitude. We'll then tackle the intimidating but oh-so-simple task of setting up and securing a Wi-Fi network in your home (Chapter 7, "The Wireless Home"). And now that you are getting seriously geeky, we'll take the time to understand one of life-in-the-Internet-age's unfortunate necessities: your safety and security (Chapter 8, "Keeping It Safe") and the online safety of your children (Chapter 9, "Geek Parenting").

Next up, we will visit that male bastion of belt clips and remote controls and explore small electronics, cameras, and home entertainment from a female perspective (Chapter 10, "Groovy Gear and Gadgets"). Lots of gear is marketed to men, and it is my belief that you cannot trust your man to purchase these gadgets on his own. Men are blinded by gadget lust and are trying to turn your beautiful home into a cave. Arm yourself with knowledge.

And, of course, I have saved the best topics for last. Chapter 11, "Your 200 Closest Friends," explores online social networks and the many tools women use to connect with friends and family, build businesses from their homes, and reach across the world for friends and work associates. Chapter 12, "The Sexy Geek," explores the fascinating and titillating ways women are using technology to find love, make love, and explore their own sexuality.

WHEN YOU ARE A GEEK GODDESS

When you get to the end of this book—or even before—come visit your fellow geek goddesses at my blog (*http://www.geekgirlfriends.com/*). Maybe you have a technical question, want to help other women when they run into snags, or just want to find out what we are currently discovering about technology. Throughout this book I use actual products as examples of what's available rather than as particular product recommendations. Technology changes much faster than books do. But at GeekGirlfriends.com I review current products when—or sometimes before—they hit the market.

If you find, as you get to the end of this book, that you know more about technology than the (pompous) man in your life, please be kind. The male ego is fragile. And having a pompous know-it-all around can be useful. As more and more technology becomes part of our homes, some of this technical stuff—upgrading software and hardware, fixing gadgets as they break—becomes yet another domestic chore.

If your husband likes fixing things, by all means let him tinker with the computers. Men like to feel needed. And sometimes it's fun to have them take care of things. We women can't be expected to do everything.

<table>
<tr><td>

1

</td><td>

GET A SMOOTH RIDE, NEW OR USED

</td></tr>
</table>

When I was a kid, my mother deferred all automotive decisions to my father and barely bothered to learn to drive. As a result, we rode in a series of unsuitable vehicles—a Volkswagen with an unpredictable gear shift that provoked a stream of shocking expletives from my father, a sedan that required us kids to pile up in the backseat like a litter of snarling puppies, and a sporty number that, even in an era when seating capacity was measured by the mass of the passengers rather than the number of available seat belts, was inadequate for the size of my family. To make matters worse, my father got fleeced on every purchase.

Most people would agree with me that my father was ill-suited to the car-buying chore, but neither he nor my mother ever questioned his authority. He was supremely confident and willfully bandied about the jargon of the automobile industry to create a smokescreen of impenetrable male bluster. My mother fell for it.

Stereotypical role definitions like may this seem comical to a generation of women who purchase 65 percent of all new cars and influence 95 percent of all auto purchases. When it comes to technology, though, women are often in the same boat as my mother. In fact, though women control the domestic budget almost completely, technology has remained, until recently, the last male stronghold. Technology possesses all the jargon, dizzying specs, and speed claims that once made cars so much fun for men and so tiresome for women. Electronics stores are designed to appeal mainly to 12-year-old boys, and the products themselves have been largely designed for speed and power, with little concern for beauty or safety.

Fortunately, for women anyway, the technology industry has begun to change. That's because, like the automobile industry before it, it has noticed that women have money. Recent statistics from the Consumer Electronics Association show that women now spend $68 billion annually on consumer electronics products and influence 89 percent of all purchases. This is beginning to change the lay of the land. We are beginning to see more products that appeal to women (and not just pink ones) and the places we go to buy them are beginning to calm the testosterone-fueled atmosphere in order to appeal to shoppers who sport a bit more estrogen.

But, like my mother, who went solo buying a car for the first time at age 60, many women are playing catch-up on a subject that changes quickly, involves enormous technical detail, and is saddled with enough specialized jargon to launch a foreign language class.

There are a fair number of women who adore technology in the same way other women like purses and shoes, though. We don't love the male bluster that so often comes with the subject any more than the next girl, but we have penetrated the jargon and can make sense of it. We call ourselves geeks, but we aren't people who love technology for its own sake. We like it because it can make our lives easier and our days go better. If you are a woman who is playing catch-up and is tired of trying to sort out what you want to know from the world of guys who like to hear themselves talk, I would like to help. I can't stop your man from delivering pompous technical lectures or wearing a phone, PDA, and MP3 player clipped to his belt at the same time (sorry), but I can help you get up to speed on the technologies you will love.

Let's start with shopping for a new computer, because that's a good way to get your bearings. (You learned the difference between a pump and a mule shopping at your mother's side, right? This isn't much different.) If you already have a computer and would like to rejuvenate it so you can get another season of use out it, we'll get to that later in this chapter.

THE BIG PURCHASE

Buying technology can be daunting. You can't blindly trust the salespeople, the ads, the marketplace, or anyone from the home-audio department. According to my girlfriend Karen Henke, who donates her free time to noble causes like wiring schools for the Internet, "The only person you should trust is an IT consultant, one who isn't getting a commission." I actually think that's generous. I've gotten some bad advice from consultants.

Don't get me wrong. Salespeople, consultants, the IT guy at work, even husbands and boyfriends often know their stuff and can be excellent resources, especially when you are buying a new computer. Technology changes so fast that unless you shop weekly, it's hard to keep up—so a good salesperson or reliable geek can save you a lot of time.

Jamye Chambers, a Dell account executive, suggests that before you shop for a computer, you should shop for a computer salesperson. "Look for someone who is consultative," she suggests. "You will know who she is because she will ask you a lot of questions about how you plan to use the computer." When you interview salespeople, keep in mind one thing about the difference between many men and women. My girlfriend Melissa Lavengood, an erstwhile computer consultant, put it best: "When a woman doesn't know the answer to something, she will say, 'Hold on, I'll research that and get back to you.' When a man doesn't know, he'll use a lot of jargon and an authoritative tone of voice and make something up."

That doesn't mean you should avoid male salespeople. Some of them are good. I went shopping for a computer recently at Best Buy and a polite and knowledgeable (and even cute) young man asked me what I wanted to use it for, if there were other people in the family who would use it, if it would be the only computer in the house, did anyone plan to play games on it, and a bunch of other great questions like that. Then he proceeded to give me a tour of my options—laptop or desktop, low-end eMachine, middle-of-the-pack Hewlett-Packard, or high-end Sony—with very little jargon and a thorough survey of the important features, choices, and considerations along the way. He gave the entire tour in less than 20 minutes and didn't give me a bit of bad advice. But I've also had salespeople talk to me like I'd be more comfortable in the toy section. I've been patronized and ignored (because my husband was there), and I've had salespeople read aloud (poorly) from the sign in front of the computer. So you see, buying a computer is just like buying tools, a lawnmower, or any other product that appeals to the testosterone set. You have to learn to spot male bluster.

There are reasons in addition to male bluster that should prompt you to weigh a salesperson's recommendations carefully, though. Even if he grasps the technology and asks the right questions, he might have a quota or recommend one item over another because he gets a cash bonus (called a *spiff*) from the manufacturer. Or maybe he is just in a hurry to sell you something, even if he knows it's not the right machine for you, simply because it's in stock. Maybe he's more concerned with paying his rent than with helping you find the perfect computer.

Jamye—from her insider perspective at Dell—has seen some grievous examples of what can go wrong if you trust a salesperson too much. "I know of one case, and I'm not naming the company, where a salesperson sold a bunch of average home users high-end servers when all they needed was basic desktop PCs," she says. "Servers are huge and very expensive, but he'd convinced these poor people they were great and that the service was better." Why would he do this? "He had a server quota to meet."

Heck, even if the salesperson is Andy Stitzer (the virgin in *The 40-Year-Old Virgin*), knows the technology inside and out, and has only your best interests at heart, he isn't perfect. Would you wear the shoes he's wearing? Maybe you don't want the computer he likes either.

The gist? You have to get at least halfway to knowing what you want all by yourself.

You Are the Most Important Component

Before you try to decipher the list of specs listed next to any particular computer at the store, turn your attention inward. Know thyself and the rest will become clear. Ask yourself, as my nice-guy salesman did, "Why do I want a computer? What do I plan to do with it?"

Your answer will depend on a lot of factors, from the size of your home to the number of people in your family to your interests. Are you launching a small business? Do the kids want to play computer games? Do you want to communicate with far-flung family and friends? Are you planning a European hiatus and want to stay in touch with people back home? Do you have a room set aside for the computer or do you plan to prop yourself up in bed to use it? Or maybe you already have a laptop but want something more powerful. Or you have a desktop and want something more portable. These lifestyle issues are much more pertinent to finding the right computer than knowing what a terabyte or TCP/IP is.

A lot of women I talk to know right away that they want a laptop. "I can't imagine buying a desktop," says my girlfriend Angela Freeman, who is a web editor for Stanford University. But desktops do have their place. You can get an enormous amount of computing power for very little money with a desktop. So if I'm buying a computer for the kids to play games on, they are likely to get a desktop because a laptop with the same power would be much more expensive. (And do I want them taking it out of the house, anyway?) If you have the space for it, you can stash the big, ugly, boxy part of a desktop under the desk or in a cabinet where you will never have to look at it.

If you have your heart set on a laptop because you think they are cute, you might want to do the math—and take a close look at your personal situation—before you drop the coin. Maybe what you want is a high-powered desktop with a lovely monitor *and* a slick PDA (a personal digital assistant that will fit in your purse, like a Treo or LifeDrive—see Chapter 10 for more on these), which you could easily have for less than the price of a laptop. If you plan to travel, want to bring your computer to cafés or to school, have a job that takes you all over town, have space limitations in your home, or anything like that, you do need a laptop.

But if you plan to sit at your desk most of the time or park it in the family room for web surfing, that dinky laptop keyboard and glide pad will feel inadequate and irritating pretty quickly, and you will grow weary of squinting at a tiny screen. You will have to raise the whole thing to eye level somehow, unless you want to hunch over it and peck like a chicken, and then the keyboard will be way too high, making you look like a little dog sitting up to beg. There are ways to fix all these things (see "Perilous Positions" on page 50) but laptops—as they come out of the box—are hard on the body because the keyboard and screen are too close together for comfort.

Another reason to think about buying a desktop is that they have more options when it comes to upgrading parts. Down the road, you may decide you want more memory, better graphics, or some other extra that you didn't think about or that wasn't available when you bought the computer. (This is especially true if you have young gamers in the house; their gaming demands will grow right along with them.) Instead of replacing the whole shebang, a desktop lets you replace key parts. Just think about it. That's all I'm saying.

If you have narrowed your choices down to a laptop, you need to focus on how you are going to use it before you can settle on which laptop to buy. A laptop that's "only seven pounds" will feel very heavy after you've hauled it through the airport once or twice. But a very light one will either be more expensive or have much less power, and it will have a small screen and keyboard. This is a dance you will have to do with yourself, determining what makes the most sense in terms of weight and usability.

If you move a lot, have a small house, or just want to be able to wander from room to room with your computer, consider a big, less mobile laptop. Laptops get more expensive as they get smaller and lighter. So a big one—even though it has a huge screen and a standard-sized keyboard—will have a lower price than a light, portable one. A big laptop may be too heavy to lug around campus or to travel with on a regular basis (although it can be done), but it will fold up and move out of the way if your dining room table is doubling as a desk.

My girlfriend Melissa got a Dell laptop with a 17-inch screen recently and loves it. "I wanted to be able to surf and shop while in bed," she says. But she didn't want to carry it around the world or even around town. She just wanted to be able to move it from the bedroom to the couch or move it out of the way when her toddler starts flinging fingerpaint. So for her purposes, a bigger laptop is fine. It is not a good travel computer though. "My husband and I are going to Mexico," Melissa told me recently. "We are debating not taking the laptop because we don't want to lug it, but we've been told our cell phones are useless there, and our hotel has Internet access so we want it take it to stay in touch. It's the only time I hate having that 17-inch screen!"

On the other hand, I recently took a two-pound Gateway laptop on vacation and it was life changing. I brought it everywhere and used it frequently. I worked while the kids frolicked on playgrounds, filed articles from cafés, and never minded having it in my little backpack since it was lighter than a couple of magazines and offered a lot more entertainment per pound. But it has a tiny screen, puny keyboard, and cost twice as much as Melissa's big laptop did. If puny sounds good to you, though, you might want to consider a sub-compact or mini computer. These are built as highly portable Internet appliances, not as powerful computers, and they are both tiny and inexpensive. But if all you want to do is check email and surf the Web, this could be the way to do it from wherever life takes you.

Apple or Windows?

Deciding between an Apple computer (or Mac; Apple is the company, and its computers are called *Macs*) and a Windows PC is more personal than technical. If you like the look of Apple, if you identify with the hip, friendly image the company has nurtured, if you are intimidated by Windows, or if you are a graphics, music, or web professional and everyone you work with uses a Mac, get one. If you like plenty of options and support from your friends and neighbors, a Windows PC might be more your style. Tonya Engst, editor-in-chief of ebook publisher Take Control Books, suggests that you "buy the [operating system] that your most technically competent friends use, so you can share files, gadgets, and know-how. One of my best friends uses Windows and we end up sniping at each other instead of sharing [because I'm on a Mac]," she admits. This might be a good time to tell you that I (and most of the women I consulted for this book) use a Windows PC. So in areas where we talk about how to use your computer or software, we will be talking about Windows PCs. For the most part, the content in this book will be relevant even if you do have a Mac, but you might want to take a look at *My New Mac* by Wallace Wang (No Starch Press, 2008) as well.

I suspect Mac owners swear at their computers less than we Windows PC owners do. Perhaps they were driven to buy their Macs by a romantic feeling of attraction and are therefore more tolerant. Romance is powerful. How long do women stay with husbands they were driven to for the same reason, despite their shortcomings? I have noticed that Mac owners tend to hug their computers or beam beatifically at them. That sort of affection is achieved through design, branding, and prettiness of interface, though, not by anything as mundane as price, processor speed, or upgradeability. People who buy cars because they are adorable, sexy, or evoke a feeling of luxury probably love those cars more than people who buy cars for cost-effectiveness. And it is that sort of emotional appeal that differentiates the Mac from many PCs (though I have gotten pretty fond of a few computers in my time), not anything particularly technical. The main difference between an Apple computer and a Windows PC is the operating system. Macs runs Mac OS X and a Windows PC runs some version of Windows. But the operating system is fundamental. Without one, the computer won't do much unless you can speak to it in ones and zeros. So your choice of operating system not only determines your user interface (what's on the screen), but also dictates which software programs and hardware accessories will work with your computer.

If you use Windows and develop a loathing for the calendar software that came with it, for example, you can hit the Internet or visit a retailer and find something you like better. You will have a mind-boggling number of choices from a seemingly infinite number of companies and even individuals. Microsoft's operating system dominates the market, with about 90 percent of all desktops computers running Windows. The top computer makers (such as Dell, HP, and Lenovo) sell Windows machines. Apple, on the other hand, is the only company selling Macs, and it grabs only a small share of the computer market. So, when some brilliant teen takes up programming or an electronics company builds computer accessories, they go for the big market. The result for you Mac coveters is fewer choices. "You will definitely have to look harder for Mac software and hardware," agrees Tonya.

That being said, there are reasons why Macheads are so devoted to their machines. As I've said, they love them. And love is illogical. In addition, the exterior and the operating system are very pretty. Beauty is intangible, but it evokes great devotion. Many beautiful Windows PCs have hit the market in the past couple of years, and the latest version of Windows—Vista—is also lovely. Mac users claim Macs are less often the target of viruses and other security problems. Windows PCs do get hit more often by viruses, but that is not necessarily because Windows (especially Vista) is less secure, as Mac users are fond of saying (so fond that I'll be getting angry letters about this statement). Windows machines could get hit by viruses more often because they are more widely used. Malicious hackers, like software developers and component builders, go for the bigger market.

It is certain that Macs appeal to a certain kind of buyer. That buyer often feels drawn toward the Mac and can't be dissuaded from that course. I don't want to suggest that you should fight that urge if I am describing you here. To thine own self be true.

Buying a Mac is pretty straightforward: one company, a finite line of products. Go to *http://www.apple.com/* and choose the machine targeted at the kind of computer user you are (or plan to be). Expect to pay a bit more for comparable performance. One caveat: If you or anyone who plans to use this computer intends to play games, step back and rethink. Most game developers build first

HOW TECH GEAR IS PRICED

Technology is a moving target. Higher-speed processors and updated software appear faster than mosquitoes at dusk. But there are a few universal rules when it comes to how things are priced.

* The price always goes down. No matter what, the exact computer you buy today won't be available in a year, and a newer version with twice the power will cost the same. That's no reason to wait a year to buy, though, because this will always be true. Pick your time and find the best deal. We live in wild times. Enjoy.

* Having current features makes a computer more expensive. Buying the hottest new processor or a larger-than-standard monitor pushes you into a luxury model. A nice preinstalled software bundle also drives up the price. But while bargains do exist, be careful of what you're really getting. Retailers cut corners to make low prices possible; you may later regret having sacrificed software, memory, or a useful support staff to save a few bucks up front. You know perfectly well when you are shopping for a car that there is good reason for the price disparity between last year's Daewoo and this year's Lexus. It's no different with computers, even if the brand distinctions aren't as familiar to you.

* A big, slick, state-of-the-art monitor costs a lot but is usually worth it. There are few things finer (in computing, anyway) than a nice, crisp, flat-panel display. It's pleasant to look at and looks good on your desk. Also, the monitor becomes your virtual desk, and it's nice to spread out and do a bunch of things at once on the screen. This is not money you will regret unless you never use the computer. Maybe you should skip that Kate Spade purse and spring for the 24-inch monitor. You could always download a picture of the purse and use it as wallpaper.

* Tiny and cute costs more than roomy and functional. (Isn't this also true of underwear?) A small but powerful desktop costs more than a large one with the same power, a laptop costs more than a desktop, a bitty laptop costs more than a beefy one with the same features, and a really cute miniscule laptop costs more than a diminutive but hideous one. This is one of life's elemental defining truths. Accept it. Sure, it's going to break your heart deciding between that plum-colored $1,000 Sony VAIO that fits in your purse and comes with your favorite Zen saying engraved on it versus a bulky $400 desktop with the same computing ability. Life is hard.

* If you want to do any video editing or hope to design your next house in AutoCAD—or plan to do anything else that will put graphical demands on your system—don't skimp on hardware. And if you or anyone you intend to share the computer with will use it to play games, spend more money. Way more money.

for the PC; your choice of Mac-compatible games will be limited. And it's not just games: Some other software categories are not well represented on the Mac. If you *need* a particular piece of software for your job, such as Autodesk's AutoCAD, or for your favorite hobby, check to see if there's a Mac version before you commit the next few years of your life to Apple. You may have heard talk about a new line of Macs that can run Windows too, but this isn't really a beginner activity and shouldn't drive your purchasing decision.

Basic Research

If it were possible for me to tell you exactly which computer to get, that's what I'd do, but you know I can't. I have bought a lot of computers, though, and it is a new experience every time. After identifying what I'm buying (desktop, laptop, handheld), I go through the same basic process:

1. If you have access to a computer, go online. Read some computer reviews at *PC World* (*http://www.pcworld.com/*), *PC Magazine* (*http://www.pcmag.com/*), and CNET (*http://www.cnet.com/*). If those are too daunting, you could stick with the advice of the technology columnist in your local paper or in a magazine. But the geeky publications review a lot of computers, and they do all kinds of fancy tests and reliability and service surveys that the mainstream media would never attempt. If you can stomach the jargon, you'll get good information. You don't have to read every word. This is like doing crunches: no fun, but good for you. Expose yourself to the terminology, get current information on the latest exhilarating thing, and familiarize yourself with the brand names.

2. When reading reviews, I find it more useful to look at what the reviewer likes about a computer, rather than jotting down a specific model number and running out to buy it. These guys tend to use expressions like "blazingly fast," which seems patently silly to the rest of us when we realize that the writer used a stop watch to determine that one computer ran a test four seconds faster than another. To choose the "best" system, these reviewers weigh test results like that against price and other specs, plug them into a spreadsheet, and the winner takes first place in their ranking system. But the editors' criteria for "best" may not reflect what you want in a computer, and it's very hard to put a number ranking on something like "really cute." (Try to imagine—if you dare—the shoes this computer lab guy is wearing. Do you care what he thinks qualifies as "really cute"?)

    Still, the attributes are useful to know. "Blazingly fast on a graphics test" might be very important to a gamer but doesn't mean a thing to you.

On the other hand, "crisp display" could mean the difference—to you—between happiness and a headache at the end of every day. These reviews are written by nerdy guys who do things like go to computer conventions where they covet the free t-shirts (I'm not kidding!), but they do know their stuff. If they seem over-excited by graphics controller cards, just avert your eyes. Spend as much time as you can reading computer reviews, but don't make yourself ill.

3.   Go to a couple of manufacturers' websites (check out *http://www.dell.com/*, *http://www.gateway.com/*, *http://www.hp.com/*, or *http://www.sonystyle.com/*) and look at the range of prices. This is a good place to see what sort of components you will have to choose.

4.   If you doubt your shopping skills or want a quick look at what's available out there, check out some of the nifty deal finders and shopping aggregators. These are sites that scan the online shopping universe and pull together the best deals for you. Some popular sites are FatWallet (*http://www.fatwallet.com/*), PriceGrabber (*http://www.pricegrabber.com/*), Shopping.com (*http://www.shopping.com/*), Yahoo! Shopping (*http://www.shopping.yahoo.com/*), and Slickdeals (*http://www.slickdeals.net/*). (See also Chapter 5.)

Just like when you're shopping for a car, you want to know what's considered luxury, midsize, and economy. Since technology changes fast, today's luxury computer will be tomorrow's economy model. You don't have to buy a computer from one of these websites, though you can if you want to. You are still warming up. If you really like something you see online, you'll want take the time to look at it in person, if possible.

5.   Go to the store and find a salesperson. This is a scouting mission, so don't feel any pressure to buy. Feel free to play dumb. It's fun. You want to see how the salespeople handle you at your most vulnerable to find out if you can trust them.

6.   Don't leave the store yet. After you've dealt with the salespeople, go put your hands and eyes on the equipment. This is your chance to touch the product; get a feel for what you like and what you don't. How it feels and looks to you is important. Touch the keyboard and mouse, look at the monitor, and ask the salesperson to open up some files so you aren't just looking at a snazzy screen saver. "If you're fussy like me about how your fingers feel when you're typing and mousing around," says Aoife McEvoy, who writes for *PC World*, "choose a keyboard and mouse that feel comfortable—even if they aren't the ones that come bundled with the computer." Is the computer aesthetically pleasing to you? You will touch this stuff, look at it a lot, and have it in your home. Don't let anyone tell you that the color, the way the

keys feel, or the look is unimportant. If these things matter to you, they are important. Because you can't change the physical interface of a laptop, be certain you're comfortable with its screen, pointing device, and keyboard.

7. If you are on a bargain hunt, go to one of the warehouse stores (or their websites) like Sam's Club or Costco. Now that you know what the market offers, see if these discounters have any great deals. Sometimes they do, sometimes they don't. I've bought a few computers this way and been happy with them. And since warranty services are usually offered through the manufacturer, not the retailer, buying a reputable brand from one of these low-service outlets shouldn't affect your support options. Sometimes the retailer has a more generous return policy than the manufacturer. But this stuff changes frequently, so be sure to ask about it. Just like everything else in these superstores, the selection is limited. If they have exactly what you want for the lowest possible price and you are comfortable with the complete lack of sales help, go for it. "But don't be cheap," advises Karen. "Don't buy something just because it's on sale or meets your minimum requirements. For a little bit more money, you might get a lot more benefit that you don't know about yet."

8. Sit down and review your notes—if you kept any—and reflect on what you saw, what you liked, and your budget. If you have narrowed your choices down to three, this is a good time to ask your husband (or the geek you have been bothering with your technical questions up till now) what he (or she) thinks. It will make him feel needed, demonstrate exactly how much—or how little—he actually knows, and give you someone to bounce ideas off of before you come to a decision. If you have it narrowed down to one or two models, go to the manufacturer's website to see if they are about to release a new upgrade that you will like better or that will save you a few bucks on the soon-to-be-older model. Then read Chapter 2, and you should be ready to buy a computer you will love.

9. You may not have the time or inclination for all that research and shopping around, and that's okay. If you refrain from buying things that don't suit you, that seem impossibly cheap or insanely expensive, or that you find personally distasteful, you've done pretty well. But I have to ask you to rally with your girlfriends here: If you get a salesperson who ogles you, barrages you with acronyms, or patronizes you, just walk away. These guys won't last long if we stick together. Even if it's the only store in town, there's always the Internet. And if you really want to buy from the store, ask for another salesperson.

Dear Geek Goddess,

This might seem like a basic question, but when I asked the geeky folks in my office, they got into an argument. I walked away. But I do want to know: Where does hardware end and software start?

Curious in Carlsbad

· · · · · · ·

Dear Curious,

It is sometimes the most basic questions that set people off. The question, "Where does the human body end and consciousness begin?" has the same effect. The thought, "A piece of chocolate would certainly be nice right now" is like software. But the hand that's reaching into that bag of truffles, the mouth that's chewing, and the tongue that's tasting are hardware. It's the same with computers. The hardware actually performs the processes thought up by the software.

Checklist of Features

Computers are pretty complicated devices. They have a lot of parts, and those parts are usually described in a language that comes from the bizarre and unfathomable world of engineers. Though most computers are packaged in a complete bundle targeted at a particular type of user, and you aren't likely to get home with an essential piece missing, understanding the options will help you understand which features are worth paying extra for and which aren't.

OPERATING SYSTEM

The operating system is an elemental bit of software and is usually installed at the factory. It makes the computer capable of interacting with you, its components, the outside world, and other software. Without it, your computer is rather useless. The operating system (OS) defines the class of computer you are buying. Macs come with a version of OS X. In the PC universe, the operating system is most likely some version of Windows. (There are other operating systems—Linux, for example—but most are not yet the sort of thing typical home users are ready to embrace, though this could change very soon.) For many years, most home computers ran on Windows XP, but now you will likely choose a version of the newer Windows Vista. It comes in four editions: Home Basic, Home Premium, Business, and Ultimate. Home Basic likes a fairly powerful computer, but the tricked-out Ultimate needs even more power under the hood. If you aren't planning to play graphics-intensive games or watch movies on the computer, you can get away with Home Basic. If this is a PC you plan to use as your entertainment center or if a gamer will be using it, you might want to spring for Home Premium. Business offers networking, backup and recovery, and web server support (along with other business stuff). The Business Edition doesn't have the media support of Home Premium, so it's really only worthwhile if you plan to use it only for business purposes. Ultimate is targeted at seriously geeky gamers and offers all the enterprise tools of the business edition as well as the media support of the Home Premium edition. You will want some serious power under the hood if you go this route. Your choice here will affect all the choices that follow. Choose your OS carefully, as it is important and, while you can change it later, it's not a fun project.

Dear Geek Goddess,

I was gabbing happily with my friends the other day when the question, "What version of Windows are you running?" was suddenly directed squarely at me. Are there versions? Is this a multiple choice question? Help!

Stalling in Seattle

· · · · · · ·

Dear Stalling,

Don't worry, this is easy—at least the technical part. Socially, I recommend sighing to indicate how bored you are by these mundane questions and then quickly changing the subject to sex. But when you are back at your computer, click the **Start** button, then **My Computer** (if it says only Computer, you are running some version of Windows Vista). Under System Tasks, click **View System Information** and choose the **General** tab. The version of Windows you are using should be displayed, along with all sorts of information about your computer. If you want to know what version of any other program you have (Microsoft Word or Internet Explorer, for example), click **Help** on the menu bar and choose **About**. This will tell you the version, who the software is registered to, and all sorts of other useful information.

CPU

CPU stands for *central processing unit*, which is essentially the brain of the computer. It is also often called simply the *processor*. It is a small but essential element of the mother-board and determines not only the power of your computer but, since it is usually the most expensive portion and the hardest to replace, the price. Make a careful choice here.

Photo courtesy of AMD
AMD Athlon 64 FX-70 series
processor

To protect yourself against a hankering for a computer upgrade in the near future, don't skimp by buying last year's model. Current processors are so powerful these days that I doubt very much you need anything top of the line. (Gamers are, as ever, an exception here.)

MEMORY, AKA RAM

As a rule, when it comes to RAM, more is better. You want more of it for the same reason you want more short-term memory for your brain. It allows your computer to think about more things at once, which means you can do more things at once without causing the computer to slow down or crash. If you can throw more money at a new PC purchase, this is a great place to put it. (Ask the salesperson about upgrading later, since the options vary by machine.) If you are shopping for Vista Home, you might read (at Microsoft's site and on the package) that it requires 512MB of RAM. I suspect men wrote those "requirements" because they are much more willing than I am to make accommodations for too little RAM. Go for a gigabyte or more if you'll use your computer for anything more than the basics.

HARD DRIVE

If RAM is like your short-term memory, the hard drive is like your long-term memory. When data is stored here, you can turn the computer off and the data will still be there when you turn it on again. How much hard drive space you need depends on the sort of things you want to store on it. Planning to store and edit home movies on your computer, use it as a digital video recorder, or digitize an enormous music collection? Get the biggest hard drive you can afford. Just planning to send email, surf the Internet, and write a dozen novels? You can skimp on the hard drive. Text files—even very large ones—don't take up much space. Anything with images, sound, or especially both, takes up lots. Most hard drives are so huge these days you'll probably never max yours out unless you plan to edit video. In any case, this isn't a deal breaker since you can always buy an external hard drive later if you run out of memory.

Dear Geek Goddess,

I have no head for names—or acronyms—but I keep hearing the terms (or names?) ROM and RAM. Who are they?

Not Paying Attention in Newark

. . . .

Dear Not Paying Attention,

With names like this, they should be demons from Greek myths, but these are merely terrible acronyms that have taken up residence in the daily vernacular. ROM stands for read only memory *and RAM for* random access memory. *An audio CD, for example, is read only because you can read it but not store anything on it. Fortunately, sane people have stopped using that term, and the term CD is now acceptable. RAM, though, is still with us. It refers most often to a computer's memory. How much RAM you get when you buy a computer deeply affects your future relationship with that machine. (Though, if you find out later that it doesn't have enough RAM, you can add more. Are you starting to like computers yet?)*

PORTS

The term *ports* refers universally to any of the places on your computer where you plug in accessories. The monitor, printer, mouse, and keyboard each get their own port. Almost everything else—your camera, headphones, Internet phone, personal digital assistant, MP3 player, keychain drives, external drives, and a host of other weird devices (like heart monitors, fans, and mood lighting)—plugs into the USB port. In fact, you can get a USB version of your keyboard, printer, and mouse if you like. The gist: You want a lot of USB ports. Four, six, eight, ten . . . the more the merrier. (You can get a USB hub, a device like an extension cord, to add more USB ports later, but some devices don't run well off of these.) It's convenient if some of your USB ports are on the front of the computer. Some PCs (and most Macs) come with a FireWire port, which is used for plugging in video cameras and other video devices.

MONITOR

The monitor is essentially the screen. This is a very important part of your purchase because it affects how you interact with your computer. When you compare desktops, confirm that the price includes the monitor, since that isn't always the case. Flat panel monitors are pretty and versatile and have become standard.

Dear Geek Goddess:

My son wants a digital camera. But every one I see—and every other gadget too—says "USB" on the box. I looked up what the acronym stands for (Universal Serial Bus), which didn't help much, since I'm pretty sure this has nothing to do with space travel. Can you tell me what it means before my son notices I don't know?

Embarrassed in Exeter

. . . . . .

Dear Embarrassed,

Your secret is safe with us. Before the USB port was invented, it was even more annoying to attach gadgets to your computer than it is now. Each one had to carefully installed and uninstalled before you could use it or before you could use the port for something else. The people who came up with the idea of one port that all gizmos would use and that would be smart enough to know when things were being plugged in and unplugged also came up with a great name for the concept: hot docking. (It came out just before the USB, but it was the dawn of the idea.) Unfortunately, no one could say that without sniggering, so it fell out of use and we are stuck with the puzzling engineering moniker and the equally dull acronym.

Every USB port or plug has a symbol on it so you can identify it. The symbol looks like this:

The bigger the monitor, the more you will pay for it and the more you will be able to multitask on it. But big monitors also take up more space. There are other features that are nice, such as the ability to move the monitor up, down, and side to side, but these features usually cost more.

Sometimes you will see numbers like *1024 × 768* in the monitor description. This refers to the maximum screen resolution. Bigger numbers mean potentially higher resolution, and high resolution usually means greater clarity and detail. (It is something you can sometimes adjust, but a monitor that is capable of high resolution is nice. And if your eyes are bad, high resolution gives you more options for bumping up the font size while maintaining clarity.) Things look big and chunky on a low-resolution monitor.

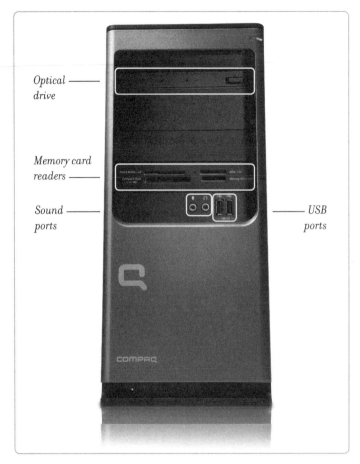

Optical drive

Memory card readers

Sound ports

USB ports

Photo courtesy of HP

Trust your eyes and consider what you want to do with your monitor. If you are getting a media PC that you intend to use to watch movies, you should consider springing for a high-definition monitor. Look at a lot of monitors and choose one that looks good, fits your budget, and suits the computer's intended usage. In a laptop, this is an essential part of your decision because you can't change the built-in monitor (though you can connect the laptop to a second monitor). With a desktop, changing the monitor is a matter of unplugging the old one and plugging in the new one, but monitors are often sold as a package, with speakers or other functional features built in. A nice monitor is worth the money. If you buy a scrumptious monitor, you will love it, and if you upgrade the computer later, you can keep the monitor. Don't go too crazy, though. This is technology, after all, so the prices on flat-panel monitors will continue to drop while the quality keeps going up.

GRAPHICS CARD

A *graphics card* is the bit inside the computer that makes the artsy stuff in games possible and allows you to display movies or other images. It's sometimes called the *video card* or *graphics controller*. All computers have some sort of graphics capability. Getting a high-end graphics card is an option you will often be presented with when you are shopping for a computer. It is often presented as a low-, middle-, or high-end choice with the particulars selected by the manufacturer. A high-end card will sport more onboard memory. Some people (gamers) get very particular about this choice, but you don't need to worry; just make your choice based on your needs and budget. (If you have a gaming teen in your life, he may be very knowledgeable about graphics cards. In fact, these make great Christmas presents for teens, but you'll do best if you ask him what he wants since he will have spent an absurd amount of time thinking about it.) If you encounter a computer that's billed as a media PC or that boasts about its ability to show movies (those on DVD as well as those you shoot yourself) or play games, it has a tricked-out graphics card and TV tuner. If you want a computer with better game or video performance, start with a good processor, bump up the RAM, and drop some money here.

Photo courtesy of AMD

ATI FireGL V7700 3D Graphics Accelerator Board

TV TUNER

Since PC manufacturers would like their machines to become the heart of your entertainment center, TV tuners in computers are the latest hot accessory. If playing games and watching TV on your computer appeals to you, go ahead and add one of these to your new computer, especially if you are buying for a teenager or college student, since they have embraced watching TV on computers, even laptops, wholeheartedly. If you are buying a computer and intend to let it serve as your entertainment center (and not merely toying with the idea of watching reruns of *House* while you

travel with your laptop), you would do best buying a Media Center PC. This will have a TV tuner, a DVR (digital video recorder like the one you can get from your cable company), a high-resolution monitor, and software and an operating system designed to run it all. A TV tuner will cost you about a hundred bucks.

OPTICAL DRIVES

Optical drives include CD, DVD, HD-DVD (high-definition), and Blu-ray (another high-definition format) drives. You can choose from drives that will not only read the contents of a CD or DVD, but that will also let you write (or *burn*) to one. Not all drives do all things, though increasingly you will see drives that read and write all formats (at least until someone comes out with a new format). Drives that burn HD formats are still pretty cutting edge. If you just want to install software from a CD, listen to music CDs, and watch the occasional movie on your laptop, pretty much any new computer will have you covered. If you are interested in burning things to CD or DVD, make sure you get a drive that can do this. Look for the term *burner* or the acronym *RW* after the name. RW stands for *rewriteable*, which means that it can burn to media that can be written on and erased to be used again another day. You certainly want to be able to burn data, photos, and music to CDs, but you may also want to burn DVDs. Burning movies isn't only for movie pirates. You might want to burn your home movies to a DVD so you can watch it on your television.

Photo courtesy of HP

MEMORY CARD READER

If you have or plan to buy a digital camera or a cell-phone camera, it's nice if your computer has a drive that reads the kind of memory card used by these devices. There are a plethora of formats available, each one slightly different in shape. Most are not compatible with each other. A card reader that reads them all (such as a 13-in-one media card reader) won't add much to the price of a desktop and will likely prove a convenience down the road. If you are buying a laptop and the one you like doesn't have a memory card reader, don't worry too much. You can buy a card reader that plugs into the USB port. It's convenient to pop the card out of your camera and into your computer to transfer photos without digging out any cables, but it's hardly a deal breaker.

Photo courtesy of HP

FLOPPY DRIVE

Floppy drives are named for the kind of disks that go into them, but that technology is old. and many new computers don't include them. The floppy drive is a good object lesson in storage media: It can change fast. Don't let anything that's important to you languish on a storage format that's dying out.

NETWORKING CARD

Having an Ethernet card is essential for hooking your computer up to a cable modem or to whatever you intend to use for broadband Internet access. (See Chapter 4.) But unless you are shopping at Joe's Really Old and Discount Computer Warehouse, any model you choose will most likely come with one.

WIRELESS NETWORK ADAPTER

Most laptops these days come with a wireless adapter built in. This is something you definitely want. You can easily add a wireless adapter later (see Chapter 7), but it's nice if your laptop already has one so you can set up shop in any Starbucks and surf the Internet. If you are buying a desktop, a wireless adapter will either be an option that is installed internally or an accessory that plugs into the USB port.

KEYBOARD, MOUSE, AND JOYSTICK

Most desktop computer packages come with a keyboard and mouse, but you can upgrade the included stuff at any time for $50 or so. This is much more important with laptops. It's easy to add a mouse (and you will probably want to) and second keyboard, but you will use the built-in ones a lot, so be sure you like them. A joystick is not nearly as sexy as it sounds. They give a little thrill to those who love playing car chase games, but that's about all they're good for.

Dear Geek Goddess,

The last time I shopped for a computer, I was told to make sure it had a floppy drive. But I recently went shopping and none of the computers I saw had one. What happened?

Troubled in Tuscaloosa

. . . . . .

Dear Troubled,

The floppy drive, I'm afraid, is going the way of the VHS tape because it doesn't hold much data. (If the novel you wrote five years ago is on a floppy disk, this would be a good time to correct that.) So how do you hand someone a copy of your resume on disk? Thankfully, the floppy has been replaced by something much better: the USB key drive. This is a tiny, keychain-sized doodad that plugs into any USB port and holds—usually—a lot more data than a floppy ever did. Of late, these key drives have gotten so cheap that companies give them away as marketing promos. They come in all shapes and sizes and look cute on a keychain or clipped to a purse. There are even some designed to look like pieces of jewelry (like the Petito drive, shown here, and the Kingston Data Traveler Mini) that I think would be very romantic if packed full of love letters and worn close to the bodice.

Photo courtesy of SanDisk

SanDisk Cruzer

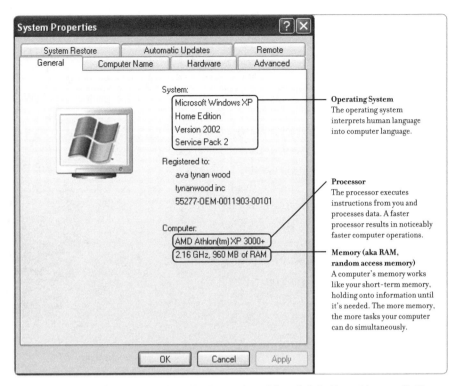

Operating System
The operating system interprets human language into computer language.

Processor
The processor executes instructions from you and processes data. A faster processor results in noticeably faster computer operations.

Memory (aka RAM, random access memory)
A computer's memory works like your short-term memory, holding onto information until it's needed. The more memory, the more tasks your computer can do simultaneously.

If you need further information, click the Hardware tab, and then click the Device Manager. You'll see all of your devices and all their number-y names. Who can remember that your DVD drive is model number 8820194-X, especially when it starts misbehaving? If you're having trouble with hardware, the Device Manager is also the place to begin troubleshooting.

PRINTER

Some merchants will throw a printer in for free when you buy a new computer because the printer manufacturers make their money on ink refills. If your needs are minimal, the free printer might work for you. Changing the printer— or adding a second or even a third—is easy. You will be faced with two main types: inkjet and laser. For the average home, an inkjet is a fine choice for documents. Inkjets are cheap to buy, though expensive to run. You'll quickly need to teach the kids to conserve ink and paper. If you plan on printing reams of documents, spring for a laser printer, which is more expensive to buy but cheaper to operate. A laser printer will usually print higher quality documents than an inkjet, often

Some people forget about the right button on the mouse. It holds the key to many secrets, Grasshopper. Use it wisely. Right-click your desktop, any

word in Microsoft Word, an email address in your email program, an icon on the desktop, or the menu bar in any program. Try it in a box. Try it with a fox. Try it on the train. Try it in the rain. Try it anywhere. There is often an entire menu of tools—directly related to the spot you clicked—hiding right there.

Left-click here.

Right-click by pressing here.

Scroll button

Photo courtesy of HP

at faster speeds. Look at the specs for how many pages-per-minute it prints and for features—such as a built-in scanner or fax machine—that you want. If you want to print photos from your digital camera, portable photo printers are a lot of fun at parties. They print directly from your camera or from its memory card, so you can take a picture and immediately embarrass the subject, just like with an old Polaroid. But they print only photo-sized creations, and like inkjets, they can be expensive to operate.

PREINSTALLED SOFTWARE

Think about which office productivity suite—the word processor, email program, web browser, and other basic tools you use every day—you want to use before you buy a new computer. For a little more money, you can get all the software you need neatly pre-installed and ready to go. The software offers vary by merchant and greatly affect the price of your computer, but if you want Microsoft Office, this can be an economical way to get it. See Chapter 3 for more on this choice.

THE EXTENDED WARRANTY

Computers are complex, prone to breaking down, and have expensive parts. Carrying a warranty on your computer is a good idea. But just like every other computer component, you have choices. I do not suggest automatically buying the warranty offered unless you have looked into your options first. The retailer wants to sell you a warranty guaranteeing that it will either service your computer itself or outsource the work. There is usually a grace period where you can decide if you want this type of warranty. The computer manufacturer also offers a warranty, and you should compare that one to the one offered by the retailer. (If you are buying directly from the manufacturer, you will have to go with its warranty.) The computer will automatically come with some sort of warranty—usually lasting a year. That's time you can use to weigh your options and see which warranty you like better. Go home and compare. Find out which parts are covered, if accidental damage is covered, how you would get your computer to the repair department and back again, and if there are guarantees on how long the work will take.

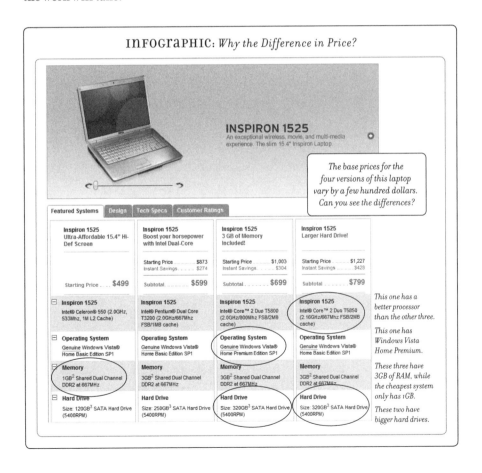

Dear Geek Goddess,

I downloaded a nifty software tool that tells me to click its icon in the system tray. I can't find anything anywhere with the name "system tray." Where is the darn thing?

Geekless in Geneva

• • • • • •

Dear Geekless,

This reminds me of Tony Randall's saying from the Odd Couple: "When you assume, you make an ass out of u and me." Everyone assumes we all know what the system tray is, but at one point, we all had to figure it out.

The system tray is the container on the bottom right portion of your screen in Windows. Icons for programs that are always running (your virus protection, media viewer, Internet connection, and a host of other things) hang out here. If the tray is overcrowded, it's a good bet your computer has a bad case of startup scum. Hover your mouse over an icon and be patient. A bubble will pop up telling you what the icon represents. Right-click an icon to get a menu of options that will allow you to close the program or make other changes.

REJUVENATE A TIRED FRIEND

If you are in the market for a new computer because the one you have is getting on your nerves, perhaps it (and you) need a spa day rather than a divorce. Maybe some understanding, affection, medical attention, and a few physical enhancements would put some pep back into your relationship. There is no such thing as Viagra for computers, but here are a few strategies that can breathe new life into a computer that's old, tired, or irritable.

Many software programs, even those you never use, load a small program or utility every time you start up your computer. You may not notice them, but they gum up the system, make your computer start and operate slowly, and cause it to crash frequently. I call this stuff *startup scum*.

* NOTE: *In Windows Vista the Start button no longer says* Start *on it but looks like this. It is usually located in the very bottom left-hand corner of the screen.*

Windows Vista has a charming tool that scrubs startup scum away. Click the Start button, then choose **Windows Defender** and click **Tools**. Now click **Software Explorer** to get an in-depth look at everything that starts up when your computer does. From here you can remove or disable anything you deem scum simply by clicking a button.

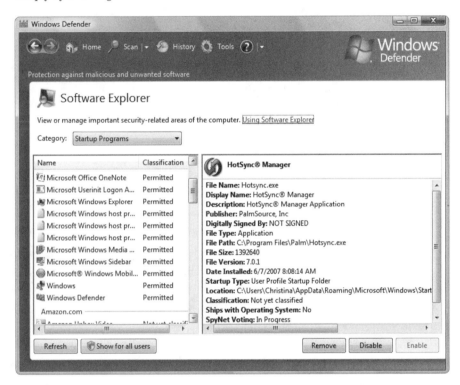

If you are using Windows XP, you have to use a little elbow grease to get rid of the startup scum. First, uninstall any programs you don't use anymore, especially if they run something at startup. (You will see a little icon in the bottom right of your screen if they do—even if you haven't used the program in ages.)

Click **Start**, then **Control Panel**, and look for Add or Remove Programs. You will see a menu like this:

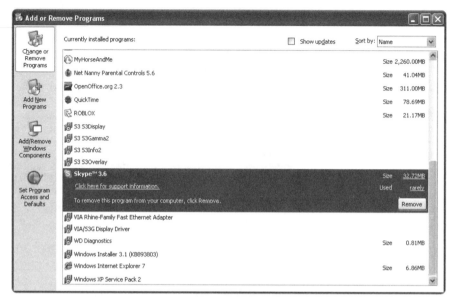

Simply click the name of the program you want to get rid of and click Remove. Windows will remove the software and all of its components—including the bit that is loading every time you turn on your computer.

As a last resort only, use the Microsoft System Configuration Utility. Click the **Start** button, choose **Run**, and then type (exactly as shown) msconfig in the window that pops up.

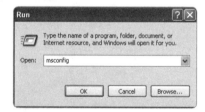

A dialog will appear. Click the **Startup** tab at the top.

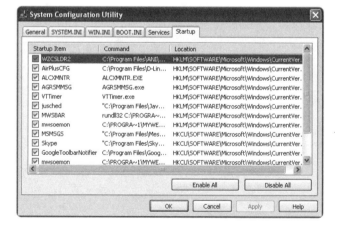

You—like most normal people—may have no idea what any of those file names mean, but just look how many there are. Most of that, right there, is startup scum. Disgusting. But you can get rid of it by simply unchecking the box next to the filename. The hard work is determining which of these files are useful and necessary and which are just dirt and grime. No two computers are the same because the grunge that accumulates depends on the software you have installed (or failed to uninstall) since you bought the computer. Some common, non-essential ones include qttask (part of QuickTime) and realsched (part of RealPlayer).

You might recognize some filenames that contain the title of a game your 10-year-old kid installed last year or the cute greeting card creator you forgot you had. By all means, uncheck those boxes. Leave alone anything that looks like it might have to do with your antivirus program, firewall, mouse, printer, or other essentials. Those that are so cryptic you can't begin to guess, go online and look them up at *http://www.processlibrary.com/*. Just type the filename into the search engine to learn more than you ever wanted to know about your startup scum.

When you are done cleaning up here, restart your computer. A message will appear when your computer is starting, telling you have just used System Configuration. Check the box that says *Don't show this message or launch the System Configuration Utility when Windows Starts*. Now, I'll bet your computer runs a lot smoother, doesn't it?

Clear Away Clutter

Next we are going to clean out the closets. Windows uses your computer's hard drive to help it remember things and complete tasks you ask it to do. If your hard drive is cluttered with games you never play, blurry photos of you with your eyes closed, and other junk, it will be always tripping over stuff when it's trying to work. This causes it to slow down or even crash. It's time for the digital equivalent of a trip to the dump.

Click the **Start** button and choose **My Computer** (or **Computer** in Vista). Then choose **Add or Remove Programs** (or in Vista, **Uninstall or Change Programs**). You will be looking at a complete list of the programs currently installed on your computer. See anything you never use, don't want, or have never heard of? Click it and then click the **Uninstall** button. Keep going. Don't remove anything you might want someday unless you are sure you have the CD it came on or know where the installation file is. The goal here is to get rid of junk—especially if it is taking up a lot of room.

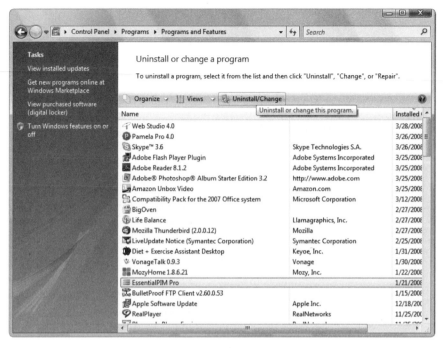

Here is how the Uninstall menu looks in Vista. Look for big, useless programs to uninstall.

Windows also offers some tools that will automate disk cleanup. Click the **Start** button, then in the **All Programs** menu, look for **Accessories**. In that list, you will find a collection called **System Tools**. Select **Disk Cleanup**. It is often very slow, but it gets rid of old junk you aren't likely to find on your own.

Grime with Mass

If you have a desktop computer, do some real-world cleaning. A computer is a delicate machine. Is yours full of dust? Pull it out of the dank airless cupboard you stuffed it in and look at the sides and back. There are vents designed to pull in air and cool the system. A hot computer crashes often. Dust holds heat, slows airflow, and gets caught in the works. Dust is especially bad for your computer, and there is often a lot of it because the fans suck it in. A noisy computer that seems to always have the fan running might simply be very dirty.

First, unplug your computer. Then ground yourself. Ideally, you should vacuum dust away regularly by holding the vacuum nozzle a couple of inches away from the computer vents. If you have not done this often (you would hardly be the first), unplug the computer and pop off the case. (This might involve unscrewing a few screws. If it is not immediately obvious how to get the lid off, consult the computer's manual for guidance.) I have seen many computers stuffed with dust. You want to gently vacuum away the dust without touching any of the delicate components. Even a small touch from a hand with a static charge can cause damage, so be careful. If the shelf the computer is stored on is completely airless or if the tower sits on a floor where it easily gathers dust, maybe you should revisit its location.

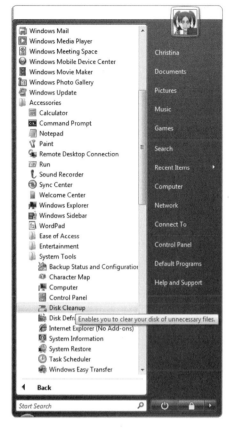

System Tools in Windows Vista

Maybe Some Physical Enhancements Would Help

If your computer still feels inadequate, it may be in need of some physical enhancements. With new computer prices dropping so low, this may not seem like the best way to spend your money—and sometimes it isn't—but it really depends on your computer. It's possible that, for now, an upgrade will save you (and the planet) the trouble of getting rid of your old system. Desktops are easier to upgrade, but even a laptop can accept a few enhancements. But be warned, this is a challenging undertaking; you might want to call the Geek Squad or some other technical service person to do the actual upgrades for you.

If you are simply tired of looking at (or don't have room for) a big ugly desktop, you can get an entirely new look with a flat-panel monitor and a new mouse and keyboard. (Just stash the tower under the desk.) If you've run out of hard drive space, adding an external hard drive to stash large files you don't need every day is very simple. Adding these new devices is as easy as buying new shoes. Pick out something you like and plug it in.

If your computer can't handle everything you want to do at once, adding more memory might be the way to go. If your computer can't handle your home videos or the new game you want to play, you might be able to get away with buying a new video card rather than a new computer. It is sometimes possible to replace your computer's processor, though that is not the sort of surgery I suggest you try at home without the help of a professional.

Upgrading memory is surprisingly quick and easy. The first step is figuring out what your computer needs and what it will accept. Your computer will have a certain number of "slots" available that you can install memory into. Memory comes on sticks that are also often called *DIMMs (dual in-line memory modules)* or *SIMMs (single in-line memory modules)*. Let's say your computer has two memory slots and 512MB of memory. Is that memory on one 512MB memory stick or two 256MB memory sticks? If your computer has one 512MB stick, you can add a second 512MB stick to double its memory for under $50. If it has two 256MB sticks, you have to throw those away and buy two 512MB sticks, making an upgrade more expensive, but still cheaper than a new computer. Once you figure this out, decide if it's worth it and order the right kind of memory stick. The sticks snap in like LEGO pieces. But what's the right kind?

The best part is that you don't have to figure any of this out if your computer is connected to the Internet. On the computer you want to upgrade, go to *http://www.powerleap.com/* and click **Upgrade Configurator**. Click **OK** at the warning, then click **Run**. A few minutes later, you will be looking at a complete description of the innards of your computer. This is so easy that it borders on fun. It will tell you how much memory you have and how many slots it fits into. It will even recommend the right kind of memory (with a guarantee that it will work in your computer). The Upgrade Configurator will even tell you if you can upgrade the graphics card or the processor. Order the parts you want and wait for them to arrive. When you receive the parts, you will have to pop open the computer and install them. This sounds scary, but the directions are incredibly thorough and simple. If the sight of computer guts makes you weak in the knees, call in a local geek to do the surgery for you.

Dear Geek Goddess,

I just got divorced. I was fine with it all until my computer crashed. When this happened in the past, my husband rushed in to save the day. I didn't even pay attention. Now I'm on my own. What do I do?

Alone in Atlanta

· · · · · · ·

Dear Alone,

Ah, the inevitable crash. Nothing works, you have a deadline, the baby is crying, and you have to pee. You don't need a guy for this, though. Hold down the CTRL, ALT, and DELETE keys at the same time. This will bring up the Windows task manager (in Vista, select **Task Manager** from the list that appears). It will tell you exactly which program is causing trouble in the Status description. Click the application that reads Not Responding, then click **End Task** to shut it down. Whew. Hopefully you didn't lose too much data. And now you realize the importance of saving often.

If your crash is so serious that the keyboard and mouse won't respond, you may have to turn the computer off. You may have to (Gasp!) use the power button (hold it down for five seconds if it doesn't seem to respond), or at your wits end (Yoinks!), unplug it. If it's a laptop, also pop out the battery. Now, count to ten, go pee, pet the dog, down a Scotch, or do whatever you need to do. If you enjoy prayer, this might be good time to pray. Now, turn the computer back on (put the battery back in the laptop first). What you have just done is called a cold boot. It has nothing to do with footwear—though I know a swift kick to something is tempting right now. This trick has been around since computers performed operations via punch cards, and it works well on cell phones, TVs, and other electronics too. All's well, right? (If not, you have problems, sister. Call tech support.) No need to wonder why. Everyone needs a little mystery in her life. Just be thankful. Now, back up your precious files. You might not be so lucky next time. (See "Disaster Preparation" on page 34.)

* NOTE: If the computer crash has not completely blown your calm, you'll want to jot down the error messages your computer displays at shut down and start up in case you end up on a call to tech support.

DISASTER PREPARATION

You know what to do if a hurricane, tornado, or earthquake strikes your home, right? But what if a power surge, juice-spilling toddler, or hard drive failure strikes your computer? Even if your computer is covered by a warranty, that won't get your family photos, research project, or financial information back from oblivion. Backing up your work—by placing a copy of it somewhere other than on your hard drive—is the digital equivalent of keeping flashlights and extra water in the house. Do it. Now!

There are several ways to back up your work: You can upload files to an online backup site (easy, requires broadband) such as *http://www.mozy.com/*, *http://www.idrive.com/*, *http://www.geeksquad.com/*, or a swarm of other sites that specialize in backing up your work. You could also burn a CD of your files every week (tiresome), or (my favorite) use an external hard drive, or *key drive*. You could go state-of-the-art geek and install a networked attached storage (NAS) device if you have a network and want a central storage repository for all the computers on it. (Tapes, Zip drives, and floppies are backup methods that have been superseded by these *much* easier solutions.)

Using an online backup service is an appealing solution. Your files will be stashed safely on a secure spot away from any mayhem that might occur in your life, and if your space needs are minimal, it's free. The online backup services want you to upgrade to the pay-for-storage option, though, so you will quickly outgrow the free option. Uploading all that data is time consuming the first time, and not an option if you don't have a broadband Internet connection.

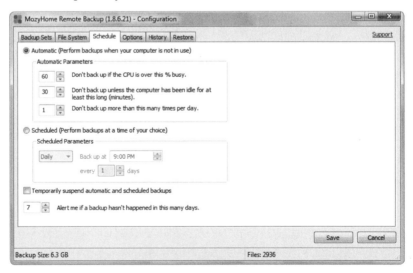

Mozy allows me to schedule backups automatically, when it's least irritating to me.

The first time I backed up using Mozy, it took two days to back up 1.8GB of data. But I was still able to use my computer while it was working. In fact, I didn't even notice that Mozy was running for two days. And, of course, it is only the initial upload that takes so long. After that, it only uploads changes to your designated folders, which is much faster. The best part is that this all happens automatically, every day if you like, so you don't have to remember to run it. Let me tell you, this is a weight off the mind. The free version didn't offer enough backup space for me, so I pay $4.95 a month for unlimited storage. I live in hurricane country, so now, if a hurricane takes out my house, I will be able to access my work, hobbies, photos, and music from the FEMA trailer I end up calling home.

I like external hard drives for backup, too. They will end up in Oz with the rest of my house in case of a tornado, but will be right here with me if my Internet connection goes down. External hard drives are easy to install, hold a huge amount of data, and aren't expensive. Some come with software to automate the backup process the way the online services do. (Just follow the directions that come with it.)

A lot of geeks these days run a second hard drive that automatically duplicates (or mirrors) everything they save to their hard drive. They are assured of always having another copy of everything right up to the last second before their computer crashes. A fairly geeky friend of mine keeps a mirror drive at a neighbor's house (he refreshes it weekly) the way some people do with an extra set of keys. I'm telling you this only so you will know what a mirror drive is and to demonstrate how strange you can get if you worry about this stuff too much. Some amount of paranoia is warranted because hardware failure, theft, or water damage will definitely occur at some point and you do not want to have to hire a forensics team to resuscitate your life's work. But even if all you do for now is copy important files to some kind of backup device and stuff it in the sock drawer, it's better than nothing.

You can find a USB external hard drive at Target, *http://www.amazon.com/*, an office supply store, or wherever you are buying your computer. They come in variety of sizes and shapes to appeal to any budget. I am particularly fond of the LaCie Brick and the LaCie Skwarim because they are so darn cute. What's not to like about an external hard drive that looks like a Lego piece? Or how about a

Dear Geek Goddess,

People keep referring to files, directories, and folders, and I don't really remember which is which. I feel like I'm at a party where I can't remember the hostess's name. But it seems too late to ask.

Socially Challenged in Syracuse

• • • • • •

Dear Socially,

No problem. Let me introduce you. A file *is a photo, document, spreadsheet, email, or other single thing created by a software program. A* folder *is collection of files gathered together with a name such as* My Photos, Work Files, *or* Letters and Faxes. *A* directory *is simply another, more accurate name for a folder. On a hard drive you have a* directory structure, *which is a fancy way of describing the organization of the folders (or directories). Double-click* **My Computer** *(or simply* **Computer** *in Vista) to see your files and directories.*

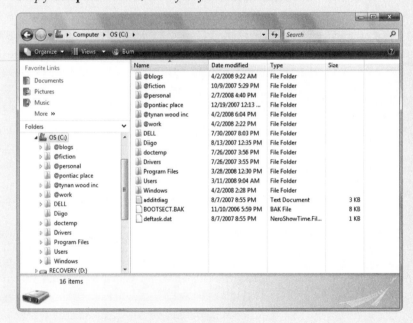

mobile version for your laptop that blends in with the cosmetics in your purse? Just plug them into the USB port (and into a power outlet for the big desktop model). Check them out at *http://www.lacie.com/*.

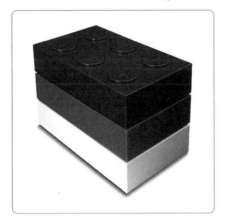

Photos courtesy of LaCie

Small external hard drives fit in your purse, and big ones stack charmingly on a desk. I have several external drives in various shapes and sizes not only because I believe in multiple backups, but also because I work on more than one computer. My husband and I share a laptop, so I drag all my work files from my desktop to a little cosmetic-compact sized Skwarim or a smaller keychain drive and drop it in my purse. I can then bring all my files along when I'm on vacation, gadding about on a day of errands, or waiting for my kids at the dentist's office. This is a form of casual backup, too. If my house is broken into while I'm out and all the electronics are stolen, all I've lost is some replaceable hardware, not my family photos or the project that's due tomorrow.

2 HOUSEBREAKING

I recently got a new puppy. First my family and I researched breeds and decided on the size and temperament that best suited our home and lifestyle. Then we set out on what we expected would be a lengthy search for the perfect dog. But on the first day, we fell in love. My daughter held the cute little bundle of young indeterminate canine in her arms and gazed at us with love in her eyes. The puppy, no fool, did exactly the same thing. Bravely we handed him back to the woman running the adoption center and said we would think about it. And then the inevitable begging and whimpering ensued from girl and pup. We were stoic for about 10 minutes, but the puppy had roughly the qualities we were looking for. His lineage was a mystery, but we were all in love. We paid, stocked up on puppy food and chew toys, and headed home with our new family member.

And then, of course, the work started. Once we got him home, we had to get him settled in, find him a place to sleep, and teach him not to chew our shoes or poop on the rug. He had to get accustomed to our ways and we to his. Computers aren't as cuddly and they don't chase the cat, but otherwise, getting a new computer is a lot like getting a new puppy. Getting your computer settled in, set up, and configured to your liking is where the work, and the fun, starts. Granted, like the puppy, computers bring with them a bit of extra mess, but with a little planning and a few tricks, you can easily deal with the hassles and get down to the business of enjoying your new friend.

A ROOM OF ONE'S OWN

If you're lucky enough to have a home office waiting for your new computer, let's hope you got the Great Dane of computers: big, powerful, and with the biggest monitor you could reasonably afford. Unrestrained by space or style, you have space for a desktop with enough power and upgradeability to keep up with whatever new technology comes along in the foreseeable future. If you have dedicated an entire room to your home office, you probably have a professional reason to justify overcompensating on speed, memory, and storage. (Otherwise, I'm guessing your office would serve another purpose.) "I have a very powerful tower on the floor of my office," says Jami Lin, (*http://www.jamilin.com/*) an interior designer, self-described nerd-in-training, and author of *Feng Shui Today* (Earth Design, Inc., 1995). "I'm all for anyone who has a home business to take

---

TRY THIS: *Spread Your Wings*

Did you spring for a big monitor? Aside from being easy on the eyes, having a lot of monitor space can change the way you work. A few mouse clicks will allow you to keep your calendar, email, and a draft of your novel open on your desktop all at once and to drag text from one to the other. In Windows XP, right-click the task bar (on the bottom of your screen) and choose **Tile Windows Vertically** (or horizontally if you prefer). In Vista, it works pretty much the same way: Right-click the task bar and choose **Show Windows Side by Side**. Choose **Show Windows Stacked** to see the last two files one on top of the other. Every file you have open will rise to the top and position itself on your desktop. (This is fun to watch.) You can minimize or close anything you don't want to see and rearrange what's left to whatever size and location you want simply by clicking and dragging from the bottom right corner of each window.

---

technology to its full potential. Just get the desktop and monitor in black. It will blend in better. And get a flat-screen monitor."

Outfitting your home office with a powerful machine and huge monitor doesn't mean your office has to scream "Geek!" any more than it means you have to wear bad shoes when you work in it. "Your home office is your sanctuary," says Jami. "Don't be afraid to decorate it in a way that encourages your creativity. Even though this is my office, I have fabrics draped on the wall that I call my French-whore draperies because they are dramatic and over the top."

I agree with Jami. In fact, I strongly believe that a woman needs a space to call her own. Virginia Woolf wrote an entire book on the subject—*A Room of One's Own*—and I'm sure she would have gone for the big-screen monitor if that had been available. Especially when women have a husband and kids, creating a space that is ours—even if we have to defend it like a snarling lioness—is a great way to improve sanity and decrease stress. What you create in your space is your business, of course, but having that space is a necessity that's right up there with food and fashionable footwear, as far as I'm concerned. But a room defined by the technology in it isn't very inspiring. I have a tower and a laptop in my home office—and a constant stream of ever-changing gadgetry—but my office is my refuge and one of the most appealing and inspiring rooms in my house.

TrY THIS: *Interior Decorating*

Did you move into your home without changing anything the builder or previous occupants left behind? I didn't think so. Redecorating your desktop is so much easier than painting or putting up curtains that there is no reason not to do it. Change it with your mood if you like. Right-click anywhere on the desktop. Choose **Properties**. You will get a handy box.

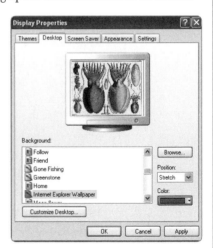

Click the **Desktop** tab (as shown in the image). This will let you choose a new background image. Simply scroll down the list and click an image name to see a preview of the image. Click **OK** when you find one you like, and you are done. Click **Browse...** in order to use a file of your own.

Even if you got a laptop so you can bring it along on business trips, a stationary office allows you the space to connect your laptop to a big monitor, a full-size mouse and keyboard, an uninterruptible power supply (UPS) to protect against power failures, a surge protector, an external hard drive to stash your data safely at home while you gallivant, and perhaps even a lava lamp that runs off the USB port. Perhaps you have a digital camera, a video camera, an MP3 player, and a printer all connected to your computer. Of course, each of these devices comes with its own power cord. You get the idea. A computer may not crap on the rug, but even when you have plenty of space for one, it will make a mess.

So before you hang your girly curtains, you'll probably want to hide all that mess. Jami hid her tower on the floor near her desk—as did I. Like I said, my office is important to me, so I have a matching desk, cabinets, and a desk chair that are comfortable and pretty. I arranged the entire thing to not only house but to conceal the technology as well. I hid my tower behind one of the cabinets. (Putting the tower inside a cabinet is also a possibility if it fits and allows airflow; you might want to drill a hole in the back to let the wires out if the cabinet is not designed to house a computer.) Then I ran the wires from the tower under my desk. A little careful furniture arranging is all it took to obscure those ugly wires, the tower, and the power strip they all plug into. My girlfriend Karen installed hooks along the bottom of her desktop and ran the wires through those so that the mess is really out of the way, even when she wants to vacuum under the desk. But I am always installing and testing gadgets for my work and am constantly plugging and unplugging wires, so I like to have access to the back of my computer. I simply use a lot of Velcro wire controllers to keep things tidy. And I have my tower on a rolling CPU cart so I can easily move it to reach the plugs in the back.

I recently installed a new surge protector, the Belkin Conceal, that sucks in all that wire and power cord mess—even the big power-bricks that many gadgets use—like a pair of tummy-control panties. It provides outlets, protects against power surges, and obscures the wires in a neat white case that blends in with the baseboards.

Wires, like dog hair, are a constant battle to clean up, which is why geeks get so excited about wireless technologies. Now that you are embracing your inner geek, you will probably find yourself craving wireless technologies too. You will find wireless peripherals, mice, keyboards, headsets, printers, and more, that promise to reduce the number of wires in your setup. But as of yet, you can't escape wires completely. I have a wireless mouse and keyboard, a wireless headset, and a wireless network that allows me to print from computers that aren't even in the same room with me. But even a wireless mouse needs to be recharged, so all wireless technologies need a place to plug in and juice up. Going wireless

Photo courtesy of Belkin

Like a pair of tummy-control panties, the Belkin Conceal hides your mess of wires out of sight. It also adds more outlets (even for bulky power-brick plugs) while protecting against surge. When closed, it clings to the wall and tries to blend in.

just creates a different mess of chargers and their cables. This mess is easier to stash in a drawer, though. I created a charging station in my office, which is simply a basket filled with Velcro-wrapped cords and a power strip, all hidden in a cabinet.

And, on Jami's advice, I got myself some call girl curtains, which improved not only the glare from the afternoon sun, but gave the room a sultry ambiance that I like.

If you plan to stash the tower some distance away from your desk, measure thoroughly to be sure the monitor cables that come with the system are long enough for what you have in mind. You want your monitor, keyboard, and mouse within reach of your fingers and eyes, but the only thing limiting where you put the tower is the cables that connect these devices to it—and access to power. If your mouse and keyboard cables don't reach all the way to the desktop, you can always go wireless and put the mouse to bed at night in its charging station near the tower. (The keyboard will probably use a disposable battery.) But the monitor will have to connect to the desktop via a monitor cable. You might also need to

Dear Geek Goddess,

My neighbor is constantly wearing a Bluetooth headset in his ear like some sort of futuristic man jewelry. I get that (even if I think he looks ridiculous). But what exactly is Bluetooth? I know it is what makes his headset wireless. But is it only for cell-phone headsets?

Fashionable in Fargo

• • • • • • •

Dear Fashionable,

Bluetooth is not just for cell-phone headsets, though that is where you see this wireless technology used most often. When you see wireless printed on the package of a product, it can mean a lot of things. Wireless Internet products will be labeled Wi-Fi, which is used to connect computers and other devices to the Internet and can have a range that covers your entire house. If the device is a mouse, headset, keyboard or other small peripheral, it is probably using infrared (IR) technology (like your TV remote control) or Bluetooth, which is another short-range wireless technology that has more capability than infrared. You may already use a Bluetooth headset to talk on your cell phone. Bluetooth holds much promise and there are all manner of predictions for it to take over all the devices in the home. Some day, perhaps Bluetooth will allow your fridge to talk to the oven and let your toilet alert your doctor (via cell phone) when it thinks you may be coming down with something (based on the evidence your toilet has access to—ick). Bluetooth has been around a few years, but all the pie-in-the-sky promises have not been realized yet, which is fine with me. The last thing I need to worry about is the toilet running up a cell phone bill. For now, Bluetooth is a handy technology for synching smartphones and transferring data to media players—as well as for looking silly while talking on the phone (though those headsets are convenient and getting more fashionable all the time).

get an extra-long cord for your printer if you want that near you rather than the tower. You can print wirelessly too, if you set up a wireless network, which is not nearly as hard as it sounds. (See Chapter 7 for more on wireless printing.)

Once you've neatly stashed all the messy wires out of the way and shoved the tower under the desk or into a cupboard, all that remains is that sexy flat-panel monitor on the desk. "A black flat-panel monitor is like a basic black dress," says Jami. "You can't go wrong." I rather like the way mine looks on my otherwise sparse desk. In fact, I consider it a design element. I set my computer preferences so that when I stop typing for more than ten minutes, the monitor begins a slide show of my favorite photographs. I'm not a dedicated photographer, though I sometimes get a good shot. My energy for photographs evaporates long before I get around to framing and hanging, so my monitor has become my preferred photo display method (though digital picture frames are also great—see Chapter 10) because it's so easy and, unlike the art on my wall, I can change the photos easily. Sometimes at a party, I find friends sitting at my desk enjoying the show.

A CORNER OF ONE'S OWN

Okay, so maybe you don't have a home office to call your own. That doesn't mean you can't define a private corner of your home for you and your new toy. Maybe there is a little-used corner of the kitchen or a breakfast nook that's rarely utilized. Perhaps you could claim a corner of the family room, formal dining room, or enclosed porch that otherwise gathers dust. There was a time when putting a computer in the living room was the equivalent of parking a bunch of cars on the lawn. Not anymore. Computers have been fully assimilated into our culture. I realize that you may be thinking that, as a geek, I might be the sort of person who would park a server in the kitchen and find nothing wrong with the way that looks. I assure you that that's not the case. My kitchen is very pretty—though there is a computer in it. In fact, I have six computers (and a lot of other technology) in my house, and I don't hide any of them in bedrooms, armoires, closets, or back rooms, but it all looks fine.

But since I'm a geek, not an interior decorator, I asked a not-so-geeky designer to back me up. "I find a computer to be a way of life," says Jami. "I don't think they are unattractive, so I don't have a problem putting them right out there in the living space. Refrigerators aren't that attractive either, but those are often the center of the kitchen, and somehow it works."

TRY THIS: *Customize the Start Menu*

Like most people, you probably have two or three programs you use all the time. You can easily arrange your Start Menu so that only the programs you like show up in the first layer you see. This might seem like a small thing, but it can save you a few seconds hundreds of times a day and limit your distractions. In Vista or XP, simply pull up the Program List from the Start Menu, right-click the name of a program you use often (Word, your email program, your browser), and choose **Pin to Start Menu**.

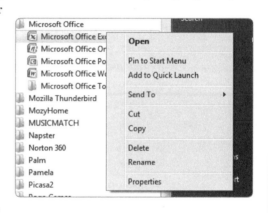

Of course, we aren't talking about the beige box look, circa 1985, either. Computers have come a long way aesthetically in the last five years. Sony and Apple started the trend, but now everyone is getting in the game, with slick colors, thin designs, and innovative form factors that have made the big beige box a thing of the past. Your options are myriad and improving all the time. Maybe you have a tiny pearl-white model that not only looks just right on the counter but also replaces what was previously a mess of cookbooks, notepads, and recipe boxes. Perhaps the computer in the family room is a sleek horizontal desktop that merges with the home theater equipment and brings gaming to the entertainment room. Or perhaps the craft table has a small flat-panel monitor in the corner and a tower on the shelf behind it. Even if you are adding only a diminutive communications center to the corner of the dining room, it can be pretty. In short, the computer you set out in plain sight is hopefully one you chose, at least in part, for its good looks.

Once you stop thinking of a computer as merely an office furnishing, you will start to find all sort of nooks and crannies or perhaps entire rooms that are little-used or at least not serving your needs as fully as they could be. "Ignore the intent of the room," says Nancy Llanas, who teaches interior design at The Art Institute of California in San Diego. "Even homes that were built 30 years ago have formal dining and living spaces. These days, those are being converted into home media and gaming areas."

Nancy suggests walking through your house over a period of a few days or a week and imagining where a computer might go. Observe who in your household uses the space and when. "I mentally move into a space before I move any furniture," says Nancy. "I imagine a few loads of laundry when placing a washer and dryer; I walk through the space imagining the movement I would make and the things I would bring with me, looking for obstacles and conveniences. With a computer, you need to imagine not only the tower, monitor, and keyboard but also the printer, cables, external hard drive, power supply, any other accessories you might want, as well as the chair, the desk, and the people who will use them."

If your computer is a machine that kids will use, for example, it should be prominently placed so that you can keep an eye on them while they prowl the Internet. When a group of kids is gathered in front of the computer, will they block a thoroughfare or get in your way? Or perhaps you are placing a computer for yourself. In that case, do you need to watch those kids while they play or do their homework? If so, find a spot that is central. If you need to get away from the kids so you can focus, you might need to encroach on your private space for the computer's landing pad. Will there be a lot of papers, a phone, a printer, a fax machine, files, along with the computer? Where will those go?

Take into consideration, too, where your phone, cable, and power outlets are located. Power is essential, and you'll need more than one outlet once you get the printer and other accessories installed. If adding an additional outlet to accommodate your computer setup isn't an option, consider a power strip. Don't fret too much, though, if you find it difficult to put the computer near a phone jack or cable outlet for a broadband Internet connection; that's easily fixed by adding a wireless network, which I'll cover in Chapter 7. Observe how bright

Dear Geek Goddess,

There is a geeky guy in my life who is always extolling the virtues of a "UPS" and telling me I really need a good one for my office computer. I love those brown uniforms the UPS guys wear, but I'm pretty sure he's talking about something else. Obviously I could ask him, but he's also always telling me he "really" likes my outfit and he is big and into weightlifting, so I try to keep these conversations short. Should I continue to ignore him or does he have a point?

Cornered in Connecticut

. . . .

Dear Cornered,

Hmm. He sounds like someone I once knew. A UPS is a big ugly box that you wouldn't want in the living room, but in a home office with a desktop computer (laptops have a battery backup already), you might want one because it protects you from losing your work when the power fails. If the power goes out, an alarm sounds, and the UPS keeps the computer running for 15 to 20 minutes or more— long enough for you to save your work and shut down properly. Even if you don't want the peace of mind of a UPS, I highly recommend a surge protector. Even small power surges can damage your computer—or even you. One of my friends (a computer columnist) was working away at his computer a few years back, oblivious to a storm raging outside, when lightning struck nearby and power surged through his electrical system. It fed him a hefty shock right through the keyboard he was typing on before he had any idea what was happening. He was hospitalized for quite a long time as a result. He now uses a high-end surge protector and turns his computer off and unplugs it during lightning storms.

the room is when you will be working in it. A room with lots of direct sunlight is pleasant for humans, unless they are trying to see a computer screen. Then it creates glare and causes headaches.

Also consider your work style and habits. For example, most sleep and sex experts say not to put a computer in the bedroom. A computer is even more of a detriment to sleep and sex than a TV, especially if it provides a constant reminder of work and the ever-present possibility that your mother-in-law will send an instant message at just the wrong moment. But Nancy, though she agrees with all that, put her computer in the bedroom anyway. "I have a very small house and I'm a social person," she explains. "If I put the computer in the living room, I'd always be chatting with my family or watching a game on TV with them. I'd never get anything done." To minimize the distraction from the computer in her bedroom, she is obsessive about turning it off and throwing a cover over it, as if it were a parakeet, to get it out of sight and mind when she isn't working. If you've got a laptop—even a very large one—you could simply turn it off and close it. I keep my big laptop constantly tucked into the Belkin PocketTop or the Laptop Hideaway, which zips up and keeps the computer and its power cord and mouse neatly tucked away. These accessories make it simple to move the laptop around the house, keep its mess contained, and make the computer look like something that belongs in a home.

Of course, you can buy an office armoire, drape a corner in curtains, modify an entertainment center, convert a closet, strategically place a bookshelf to create a room within a room, or find some other means of creating a private space for you and your computer, but be wary of anything that will be high-maintenance. "There are lots of furniture options that hide a computer and that have pull-out surfaces and cabinets for storage, just as there are for TV entertainment systems," offers Nancy. In fact, I am always tempted by them because they look so tidy in catalogs. "The thing is," says Nancy, "the only time a unit like this looks good is when no one is using it and the doors are shut. If you put the computer in a highly active area, you might find you are always looking at the messy interior and walking into the open doors."

A computer that's in sight will also get used more often. "If something becomes laborious or cumbersome to use, you won't use it," says Jami. "And it is much better to send an email, look up a recipe, or research something of interest than it is to sit vapidly in front of a television."

There is one exception here: Computers can be addictive. If you find yourself obsessively checking your email, preferring SPAM to a home-cooked meal, ignoring your spouse in favor of Mr. Big on the networking site Facebook (*http://www.facebook.com/*), or if you have taken to dusting a husband or kid who is parked perpetually in front of the monitor, it might not be such a bad strategy to move the thing out of your field of vision. If things get very bad in this regard, there are software tools that can help manage an obsession. Say you find yourself going broke from excessive online shopping or your marriage is suffering because your husband is addicted to porn sites; consider installing one of these tools to set time limits on Internet usage for yourselves. They are mostly billed as parental control software (and I cover them in Chapter 9), but lots of adults find that setting limits helps them as well.

You don't have to settle for the wallpaper that comes with Windows. You can use any photo or piece of art you like to create a personal look. From the desktop, right-click anywhere and choose **Properties** to bring up the Display Properties menu. (Note that this is where you change screen resolution too, if that ever comes up.) Click **Browse...** and select the photograph or scanned art that you have stored on your hard drive and click **OK**. Don't fret if you don't have any images of your own. You can download them from lots of places. I often get mine from the art book publisher Taschen (*http://www.taschen.com/*), *Garden Design* magazine (*http://www.gardendesign.com/wallpapers.jsp/*), *National Geographic* (*http://www.nationalgeographic.com/*), or deviantART (*http://www.deviantart.com/*). Whenever I happen upon a site with a wallpaper image I like, I download it to a folder on my computer called *Wallpaper* so I have plenty of images to choose from when the redecorating urge strikes.

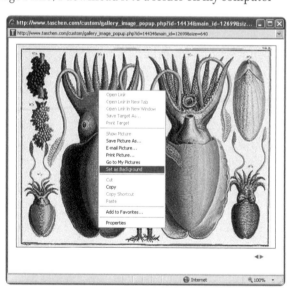

If you want to change your wallpaper quickly while you are at a website, right-click the picture you like and choose **Set as Background**.

PERILOUS POSITIONS

Don't make the mistake of letting a computer's appearance overshadow the physical comfort of the people who will use it—especially if anyone seems poised to become a frequent user. It's very easy to get so sucked into a game, project, or even feisty email conversation that you fail to notice you're hunched over your keyboard like Quasimodo, laughing maniacally, and doing yourself physical harm. I've watched people sit in front of computers—especially laptops—with their bodies twisted into all manner of unnatural poses. And I know several

Dear Geek Goddess,

I took a photograph of my daughter that I want to email, use as wallpaper on my computer, and upload to a photo-sharing site. But I keep getting an error message. Apparently, the image is too big. Is there anything I can do about this?

Shutterbug in Shreveport

. . . .

Dear Shutterbug,

Yes! No need to stage another photo shoot. This is easy.

In either Vista or XP, click the **Start** *button, look for* Accessories, *and then* Paint. *Once you have Paint open, use* **File ▸ Open** *to open your image. Then click* **Image** *in the menu bar and choose* **Resize/Skew***. Now take a guess at how much smaller you should make it. Fifty percent? Twenty-five percent? This depends on how big the image is to start with and the size you want it to be.*

women who have paid a devastating price for obsessive work habits and poor ergonomics. One friend had to give up her work as a graphic designer entirely, spent years learning a new career, and can't lift her own child. (I myself have damaged the sensitive nerves in my wrists so badly through years of repetitive computer work that I have had to completely abandon my dream of becoming a celebrity yogi.) Even little kids can damage their wrists and neck by using the computer while sitting on the floor or in a chair that's the wrong size, or by gazing at a monitor set at the wrong height.

While the table your computer rests on may be purely a design choice, your decision about where you place the keyboard and mouse, the height of the screen, and all considerations of ergonomics should determine the resting place for your own buttocks (aka butt, buns, bum, booty, ass, arse, or—my favorite—badonkadonk, all acceptable terms according to the democratic and fluid Internet encyclopedia Wikipedia). "Yes!" agrees Nancy. "The table needs only to be 29 inches high. Spend your money on a really good chair." A good chair is one that is comfortable and supports your back, yet is adjustable enough so you can lean back and relax. If there are armrests, they should be easy to adjust so they support your elbows without holding them too far from your body. Ideally your chair will adjust in many ways (especially height), but a dynamic back is important.

Here are the rules: The top of your monitor ❶ should be two or three inches above eye level, your arms should be close to your body, and elbows ❷ should be at a 90 degree angle. Forearms should be straight in front of you with wrists ❸ flat (not bent up or sideways). The monitor should be an arm's length away ❹ and you should be looking straight at it ❺ without turning your neck to the left or right. Your feet should rest flat ❻, though you may need a footrest to accomplish this. Even if you get this setup exactly perfect, though, never consider it a *fait accompli*. Be prepared to change it as you change, your work habits change, or you feel any twinges of pain or stiffness. And make frequent, short breaks a permanent part of your work habits.

If you are trying to arrange a laptop to fit these rules, you will quickly see why I think laptops are an ergonomic disaster area. When the screen and

Dear Geek Goddess,

My husband keeps telling me to minimize. I thought he was suggesting I start wearing those Spanks underwear for a while, but I think he may be talking about something computer related. Before I tell him where he can put his Spanks, tell me what you think.

Spreading Out in Spokane

. . . . . .

Dear Spreading Out,

I'm sure it's not you. This is a computer term. Almost every program that runs on any version of Windows has these three images in the top right corner of the screen.

The one on the left is used to "minimize" files or programs. It shrinks the file down and stashes it on the task bar at the bottom of the screen. (I often wish there was a minimize button for dirty laundry.) The one in the middle is a toggle. It either makes the file full-screen size or a mid-sized image that you can adjust. (To do this, hover your cursor over a corner of the file window until it changes to a double-ended arrow and then drag the corner until the window is the size you want.) The X on the right closes the file.

keyboard are permanently fixed together, it makes for great portability, but there is no way to make that arrangement comfortable for the human body.

"The three most common ergonomic mistakes people make," explains Dr. Alan Hedge, Director of the Human Factors and Ergonomics Laboratory and Co-Director of Design Concepts Laboratory at Cornell University, "is that when they set up a place to use a computer in their home, they don't think at all about how it will fit their body. The second is that they get so hypnotized by what they are doing that they don't take breaks. And the third is that, when they feel pain, they go out and unwittingly buy gear labeled as ergonomic without fully understanding what the products do or what their body needs and end up with products that are harmful." Setting up your workplace is like buying a pair of shoes, a backpack, or even a car. You have to make sure it fits you well and is comfortable to use for long periods of time. No one product or setup will fit every body or work habit.

Of course, if you plan to use your laptop only for quick stints, you may not care about any of this, just as you might wear a pair of fake-crocodile princess-heel pumps to a party but not for a day of hiking. If you do find yourself in front of the computer for hours—or even an hour—at a stretch with your neck twisted or hunched and your mouse arm reaching too far to the right or even above the keyboard, you will regret it just as you would regret wearing the wrong shoes. Hiking in a pair of painful shoes damages your feet; a bad ergonomic setup damages your hands, wrists, elbows, or neck. "This damage can take the early form of tendonitis that merely makes movement painful," says Hedge. "Or it can progress to nerve compression injury such as carpal tunnel syndrome, which is quite a disabling injury." Pay attention to those little aches and pains. They are telling you something. A tinge in the neck, a headache, a bit of pain in the hand, elbow, or wrist is an early warning sign. "The more you ignore aches and pains and carry on working," says Hedge, "the more harm you will do."

Neck and Eyes

Many newer monitors adjust in height, but if yours doesn't, you should find some way to raise it up. A monitor at the wrong height or placed so that it forces you to constantly twist your head will give you a pain in the neck and can also cause headaches and radiate pain to your hands and wrists. I typically find monitor stands to be ugly, expensive, or both. But there are some attractive (though still expensive) monitor arms that attach to your desk and the back of a flat-panel monitor. These are quite flexible and lift your monitor clean off the desk, making for a very tidy appearance and gaining back some work surface as well.

If you are the only one using the computer (so you don't have to adjust it for different heights) and you take a lot of breaks (so you don't seize up in one position), you can get away with something less expensive and low-tech. My monitor doesn't adjust and was about 5 inches too short, but I found a pretty painted box for $10 that matches my office and happened to be the perfect height. But I'd love to have the instant depth adjustment of the Humanscale monitor arm so I could pull it close to work on screen and push it away to work on my desk.

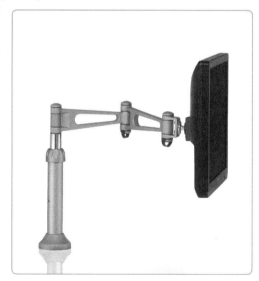

Photo courtesy of Humanscale

This Humanscale monitor arm lifts your flat-panel monitor up off the desk to make the monitor adjust easily and cleanly.

Arms and Wrists

One very common mistake people make with home computers is setting their keyboard (even an ergonomic one) or laptop on a desktop or tabletop, which is too high for typing. (Note both the angle and height of the keyboard in the illustration on page 52. Elbows should be at 90 degrees.) A keyboard tray such as the lovely (but expensive) ones by Humanscale (*http://www.humanscale.com/*) or a keyboard stand that can also serve a laptop stand or even as a tea table, such as the Herman Miller Scooter (*http://www.hermanmiller.com/*), is a good way to get the height, angle, and closeness to the body that you want for sustained typing.

There are lots of keyboard trays on the market, though, and if you are the only one who will work on the computer, you may not need all the adjustments that come with the higher-priced ones. The keyboard height and angle are most important, but once you get them set, an ergonomic keyboard can help too, if you do a lot of typing. I have used a Goldtouch (*http://www.keyovation.com/*) split keyboard for years and swear by it. It encourages me to type with my wrists in a neutral position by angling the keypad instead of making me angle my wrists to type on a flat keyboard. It has done wonders for the pain in my hands (and helped the participants of several studies as well).

Photo courtesy of Key Ovation

The Goldtouch Adjustable Keyboard from Key Ovation

I recently spied a new keyboard design from a small firm in Canada that has the mouse pad built into the keyboard—Jasper DesignWorks' freeBOARD (*http://www .jasperd.com/*).

This is a great idea. The basic design of the keyboard hasn't changed since the invention of the computer and it really

Photo courtesy of Jasper

The Jasper freeBOARD keyboard/mouse combo integrates the mouse pad and numeric keyboard into one slick unit, saving you from reaching to use the mouse—a common cause of wrist and shoulder pain.

isn't built for constant mouse use. For those of you who want a number pad in the place where the mouse pad is in this keyboard, it pops out on the side. Cute.

Laptops

Making a laptop ergonomically comfortable is a bigger challenge than making a desktop fit your physical needs. Something that raises the screen up so that you aren't hunched over to look down at it is essential if you plan to spend much time in front of it. But once you do that, you have to add an external keyboard and mouse and a keyboard tray or table so you can achieve the right height for typing. In the process, you lose many of the advantages that probably inspired you to opt for a laptop in the first place—clean lines and a small footprint.

Photo courtesy of HP
The HP Docking Station keeps all your peripherals at the ready for use with a laptop.

Some computer manufacturers sell docking stations for their laptops that make adding a mouse and keyboard or even a big monitor swift and easy.

Many accessory companies make desktop laptop holders that you slide your open laptop into; the holder grips the keyboard portion and positions the laptop at an angle, elevating the screen. Add an external keyboard and mouse to this setup, and you'll be able to lean back and get comfortable in your (ergonomic) chair.

I will admit that I have parked my laptop on a variety of cast-off materials in a pinch: a CRT monitor stand, a child's step stool, and—in true desperation—a couple of really big books. (Those looked pretty classy in an old-world-meets-new sort of way.) You can

Photo courtesy of Humanscale
Humanscale L2 laptop holder

find a better solution that fits your needs, budget, and decor. I can't emphasize enough to laptop users who are noodling around on their computers for hours at a stretch on a regular basis how seriously you need to take this advice. I don't know a single geek who has not learned this lesson the hard way and ended up spending a fortune on ibuprofen, medical attention, chiropractors, surgery, and complete lifestyle changes trying to repair a problem that could have been easily prevented.

OUT WITH THE OLD

In the past couple of years, computer manufacturers have started to listen to the voices of us women when it comes to building computers that not only possess the power, speed, and crisp displays that everyone wants, but that deliver in the style department as well. So your job of fitting a computer (or several of them for different purposes) into your home and making it fit your body comfortably is a lot easier today than it was a couple of years ago when a flat-panel monitor was an extreme luxury and the only ergonomic products on the market were targeted at corporations with gobs of money to drop in order to prevent disability claims. The future will get better in this regard as the computer and the Internet become more and more central to the home entertainment center. This is all great news, until you find yourself burdened with old technology you no longer want and don't know what to do with. And then you discover a dark side to all this innovation.

Like most things in life (except children), bringing something new into your home means last year's model has to go. If you're buying a new computer because the shine has gone off the old one, you will be faced with the chore of getting rid of something that's surprisingly difficult to dispose of. The end of life that all electronics face (much too quickly) has been plaguing corporations for years. Now it's our turn to deal with the same problem. Computers are full of nasty stuff—including cadmium, lead, and mercury—that leach toxins into the water supply or atmosphere if dumped in the landfill or burned. Since we have pretty stringent laws about disposal in the United States (compared to some parts of the world), much of our cast-off electronic equipment ends up in the landfills of poor countries, where it is burned or left to molder, and endangers the health of already impoverished people who didn't even benefit from those electronics in the first place. The Basel Action Network (*http://www.ban.org/*), a Seattle-based network of advocates focused on the trade in electronic waste, estimates that roughly "10.2 million obsolete computers with monitors are exported each year." Though no one is really certain of the exact numbers, the problem is huge and growing.

I find this export of electronic waste upsetting and I try to do whatever I can about it, which as a consumer means buying carefully and trying to find a new use for electronics that have outgrown their original purpose before I attempt to dispose of them. And when it is time to chuck electronics, I do so as responsibly as possible, even if that means I have to shell out a little money to make sure they are recycled instead of dumped. (Computers are difficult to recycle and it seems that even much of our supposedly recycled electronic waste simply ends up poisoning someone else's backyard, but I do what I can.) Even if you're okay with thoughtless planetary destruction, your local trash collector will probably refuse to take old computer equipment anyway.

© *Greenpeace/Hatvalne*
http://www.flickr.com/photos/
greenpeaceindia/
A boy winces at the smoke rising from the computer motherboards being melted over open fires in a recycling yard in Delhi.

I tend to upgrade computers when they become annoying to me but before they are completely useless. My kids, mother, and local schools all love this about me. Every time I upgrade, someone gets a hand-me-down. When my daughter was in preschool, for example, I got rid of my then-old-to-me computer by installing a handful of kid games as dated as the computer on it and setting it up in her classroom as a "play station" right next to the blocks and water table. (I asked the teachers and administrator first and, yes, the school was a non-profit and I took a tax deduction.) The next time I went in the classroom, the kids presented me with a giant thank you card and an adorable group hug. They were thrilled to get the computer and I felt like a hero. There are lots of people who might want your cast-offs and who will put them to good use. A teenage geek might want to pull out the memory and use it for his latest world-domination project. A lonely grandmother in your neighborhood might want to get on the Internet and need a hand doing it. The senior center might like an extra email station. The trick here is to move quickly. Don't shove the thing in a closet to deal with later. The older a computer is, the more challenging it becomes to find it a good home.

If you simply don't know anyone who wants your old gear, the National Cristina Foundation (*http://www.cristina.org/*) will find a needy home for a computer with a little life left in it (i.e., a computer that is less than five years old). Log on, answer a few questions about your computer, and this non-profit will find someone in its national network that needs just such a thing. Or list it at Freecycle (*http://www.freecycle.org/*) or craigslist (*http://www.craigslist.org/*).

If your computer is very old or hopelessly broken, recycling it may be your only option. (Though if you think it might just be old enough to be a museum piece, list it on craigslist just to see what happens. Maybe it has attained collector status.) You can search for a local computer recycler through the Basel Action Network (*http://www.ban.org/*). Or try the manufacturer. Many computer manufacturers are making an effort to help clean up this electronic mess—or at least prevent further mess. (In fact, planning for responsible end-of-life disposal is something I consider when I buy a computer. Can we all support new green technologies, please?)

Dell will take your old computer away for free if you're buying a new one (or for a small fee if you aren't). Go to *http://www.dell4me.com/recycling* to order a recycling kit. Hewlitt-Packard recently hauled away my old CRT monitor (and promised to recycle it responsibly) for a $17 shipping fee. I set it up at *http://www .hp.com/* (search for *trade in*) and they sent a shipper to pick it up at my door; all I had to do was slap a label on it, which seemed a fair arrangement. My monitor was too old to qualify for the company's trade-in program, which lets you sell back your old equipment in exchange for newer stuff, but I did get a coupon for $20 off at the company's online store, so I was pretty pleased. If you buy a new Macintosh, Apple will take back and recycle your old computer free of charge. Gateway will take back your old stuff in exchange for a discount on new purchases, and you can quickly find out what your gear is worth in a trade-in at *http://www .gateway.eztradein.com/gateway/*. The company also offers recycling services. Staples will recycle most electronic gear, too. Some of it (like printer cartridges) will even net you a small profit, though large items might cost you a bit for shipping. There are more of these programs launching every day, so check with your old computer's manufacturer or the company you plan to buy from. If they don't offer any recycling services, maybe you would rather buy from a company that cares about that toddler in the developing world who is breathing in our e-waste with his breakfast every day?

But What About My Files?

However you get rid of your computer, be sure to remove any personal data from it. Obviously, you should make copies of files you want to keep, but after you've done that, you want to make sure no one else can get stuff off the discarded machine, such as your credit card accounts, social security number, home address, pictures of you taken in a compromising position, or journals where you wrote down that embarrassing dream about your boss. You don't want to find that stuff on the Internet or in the clutches of an evil identity thief or blackmailer, do you?

If you delete all your files the way you normally do, you will have stopped only an inept or unmotivated data hunter. When you delete a file (even if you take out the trash or recycling), all you have done is tell the computer it can go ahead and use that disk space for something else. That gives your software permission to forget where it put the file, but the data itself is still there and can be retrieved by anyone with a little know-how and the right tools. You should run a disk shredder or sanitizer for real peace of mind. There are a lot of these programs available.

Data disposal is one area that really brings out the testosterone in guy geeks, who start using terms like nuclear strength, terms of engagement, and show of force when discussing it, which is why I usually ask my husband to delete my files for me. (I find that donning a pair of high heels to ask for this sort of help is very effective.) He gets all pumped up at the idea of data annihilation and flexes his geeky little muscles while the software does all the hard work of erasing the files by writing nonsense over them repeatedly. As far as I can tell, the process is about as manly as cleaning the garage, but incredibly, this gets the testosterone firing every time.

Even my editor flexed when I recommended the free disk shredder Eraser (*http://www.tolvanen.com/eraser/*). "I would recommend something that will eradicate the whole shebang and bomb that data back to the Stone Age," Tyler said. "Darik's Boot and Nuke (*http://dban.sourceforge.net/*) provides military-grade file destruction: It obliterates the data in a series of passes." Otherwise, he is a pretty mellow guy, but somehow, in this age of geeks, data erasing has become like

Greco-Roman wrestling was in the era of parchment rolls. Who knew? If you're really serious about destroying your data completely, give these programs a try.

I don't see disk erasing as bringing in tanks and trebuchets. It's more the digital equivalent of cutting up expired credit cards. But I'm happy to stand by while the guys thump their chests; one less thing I have to do. But be careful: Once everything is deleted with one of these programs, it's gone for good!

ASKING FOR HELP

Sometimes something does go terribly wrong with your computer. You foolishly open an email with a virus attached—Don't ever do that! Install virus protection now!—some mysterious piece of hardware fails, your toddler puts buttered toast in the CD drive, or maybe the thing just won't turn on one day. Needing technical support is a fact of life with computers.

TRY THIS: *Different Looks for Different Folks*

Do you let your kids or spouse use your computer? You can keep their dirty paws off your data by creating a separate login account for each of them. That way, when they use the computer, they will only see their own stuff. In Windows XP, choose **User Accounts** from the Control Panel. (In Vista, it's called *User Accounts and Family Safety*.) Then pick **Create New Account**. You can choose a *Limited* or *Computer Administrator* account type. (In Vista, they are called *Standard* and *Administrator* accounts.) Use the Limited (or Standard) account for the kids, and they won't be able to install software or make changes that might affect you.

If you are running Vista, you will be pleased with the parental controls that come with your computer. Not only can you create separate login accounts for the kids, but you can set all sorts of rules about when your little geek-in-training can log in and for how long and what he does once he's on. From the Control Panel, look for *User Accounts and Family Safety*. Choose **Add or Remove User Accounts** to set up a separate login for a family member. That will bring you to a menu of options. Choose **Create a New Account**, type a name (the kid's name is what you want here) into the text box, check **Standard User**, and click **Create Account.** The next menu allows you to make changes to that account, including stipulating time limits, website filtering, and even setting a rating for the PC games your kids are allowed to play on this computer.

But since a call to technical support can sometimes mean a long hold time, you want to make sure you actually *need* to call, call the right place, and be able to answer any questions you will be asked.

Who to Call

A lot of products go into creating your computing experience. The hardware manufacturer won't provide support for the software on your computer and vice versa. If your printer is causing the problem, you have to call whoever makes that. Or if it is another peripheral, such as an external CD drive, hard drive, or camera, that manufacturer takes the call. Sometimes this is obvious, sometimes not. If the computer won't start, makes a terrible noise, or gives you the same problem no matter what software you are running, it's probably a hardware problem. If the problem only happens when you run an email program or your new recipe manager (or immediately after you installed one), it's likely that piece of software is the culprit. You won't always get it right. Troubleshooting a technical problem—even for the most experienced technician—is informed guesswork. The more informed you are, the better your guess will be. I like to think of a tech support call as an educational experience. I find it easier to relax and go with the hassles if I don't expect myself to know everything at the outset. If I knew the answer, I wouldn't need tech support, right? So if you guess wrong on who to call, don't sweat it. It's all part of the process.

Before You Call

Put on your technician's hat and do your best imitation of the dweeby help desk guy from your last job, because we are going to do a little pre-call troubleshooting. Hey, maybe you can fix this thing yourself.

1. Do a cold boot. This is essentially just turning the computer off and back on again, but *cold boot* sounds so much more technical, doesn't it? This is the first step in every troubleshooting game.
2. Did you install a new piece of software or hardware before the problem started? Uninstall it. That is very likely the source of your problem, and removing it might be the cure. If that works, call the company that makes the product and get your money back. If it doesn't work, call the company or visit its website. They may know about the problem and have a ready fix.
3. Maybe your system is simply overheating. Heat causes computers to shut down, act erratically, make noise, and refuse to start. Internal heat can be caused by dust, lack of airflow, or simply by leaving the computer on constantly. Shut it down and let it cool off. While it's doing that, look it over for dust. If there is a lot of dust on the outside of a desktop, unplug it, make

sure you aren't giving off static electricity (get off the rug!) and open up the case and see how bad the inside looks. Bad? Gently vacuum away the dust without touching any of the delicate innards. Then turn it on and see if there is any improvement.

4.   Was there a terrible noise before your problem started? Does the computer start up but refuse to do anything beyond lighting up and spinning fans? Are you looking at a blank screen or some scary error message? This might be a hard drive failure. Bad news. Call your hardware manufacturer immediately. And let's hope you backed up your data.

5.   Does the computer do nothing? If no lights come on and nothing happens at all (and you are sure the computer is plugged in to a live outlet), you may have a failed power supply. This is easy to fix (though it will require a new part) and your data is probably fine. Call the manufacturer.

6.   If the computer is acting strange and you haven't installed any new software, but the problem only happens when you are using a particular software program, try reinstalling that program from the CD or file it came from. Software installation programs can usually figure out if something went haywire and can fix the problem themselves. If that doesn't work, call the software vendor or go to its website and contact tech support that way. They might know about the problem and have a fix you can download or have emailed to you.

7.   Make sure your Internet connection is working. A lot of software programs access the Internet frequently, and losing the connection can cause problems.

What to Have on Hand When You Call

If you have done everything your can think of (and tried the steps on my list above) and still have no clue what's going on, it's time to call for help. If you have an extended warranty, call the company that provides it and have on hand any account numbers you got, the computer's serial number, a credit card (just in case), a pen and paper, and any CDs that came with the computer. A desktop computer's serial number will be printed somewhere on the main box, and a laptop's will be printed on the underbelly. Look under the laptop battery if you can't find it anywhere else. If you don't have a warranty, don't worry. The computer manufacturer will usually provide technical support for the original components for a fee. It might even allow you to purchase a warranty right now to cover this problem and any future ones. Ask. Make sure you have time for this when you place the call. Troubleshooting computer problems can be time consuming.

3   GETTING IN TOUCH WITH YOUR SOFTWARE SIDE

I like software. I also like shoes, purses, and hats. I realize that for some people software is just a tool, but I prefer to think of it as an accessory. Like shoes, I think software is a topic on which men and women simply think differently.

Just as shoes are necessary to a wardrobe, software is necessary to a computer. But for most women, shoes are much more than necessity. They are an opportunity for self-expression as well as a mood enhancer. I don't meet too many (straight) men who enjoy shoes, though. For men, they are functional coverings for their feet. They buy a pair for a particular purpose, such as for work or for running. And when that pair wears out, they buy the same brand and style over and over again until someone (usually their spouse) points out that the 1980s are over.

For men, software is merely a tool—in this case, a tool for getting their computer to work right. When men talk about software, it's not unlike '50s-era guys talking about their Chevys. A woman listening to them wonders, "Why spend so much time enhancing something that works perfectly fine?" And then her mind wanders to more pressing topics like Brad Pitt in *Legends of the Fall* or the food in the fridge that has dinner potential.

Personally, I like searching for software almost as much as I like shopping for shoes. Sometimes I go on a hunt for something basic to make my work day easier. For example, I recently spent several hours trying out programs that turned my computer into a phone-recording device. Sometimes I go on a hunt for software to make socializing more fun. For example, I have spent several evenings trying out instant messaging software and other collaborative tools. I also have a closet full of software that I use for special tasks (in much the same way that I have a pair of shoes for gardening, date night, and the beach). I have software for listening to music, helping my kids with their homework, managing photographs, preparing my taxes, keeping track of my menstrual cycle, tracking my family's medical history, scheduling my life and my family's, and organizing projects and phone numbers. And I am currently on a hunt for the perfect video-editing software so that I can turn the raw footage on my video camera into hilarious videos that will make me famous on YouTube.

WHERE'S THE MALL?

First things first: Before you shop for shoes, you have to know where to shop. You probably have a favorite store where you buy your shoes, such as a boutique at the mall, a big department store, or one of those discount places. You can go to similar places to buy software, but the biggest selection and the best prices can be found on the Internet. The easiest way to get the stuff home is to download it, *if* you have a broadband Internet connection (high-speed Internet, available from your cable or phone company or an ISP; see Chapter 4 for more on this).

Big commercial software packages such as Microsoft Office and Intuit's QuickBooks and Quicken are still largely sold in the traditional shrink-wrapped box from the manufacturer's website, Amazon.com, or an office supply store in the real world. But you can also download trial versions from the manufacturer's company website that will let you take the program for a thorough spin before you pay for it; if you decide you want it, simply log in and pay up with a credit card. (You aren't likely to get the best price this way, but it's certainly easy.) But much of the software I use daily, I bought for almost nothing or got free on the Internet.

Dear Geek Goddess,

Whenever I download a bit of essential (or just frivolous) software from the Internet, I am always immediately faced with a choice. Okay, I know if I want white or red wine, or sweet or unsweet tea. But Save or Run? Do I honestly have to care about this? Just tell me what to do.

Decisive in Detroit

. . . .

Dear Decisive,

Well, it doesn't really matter which one you choose, but since you asked, I'll help you decide: If you choose Save, *you have to choose a place on your hard drive to stash the uninstalled code, remember this location and the name of the file, open My Computer (or Computer in Vista) and double-click the file to launch it (you might have to unzip it first, which is a matter of clicking one more time). If you choose* Run, *your computer will install the software right away without first downloading the code, which saves you a step. Either way, you get the software installed. But if your Internet connection kicks out during the installation when you chose* Run, *you might have to start over. You won't have a backup copy of the uninstalled code for the program. So it's probably a good idea to choose Save for any program bigger than a few MB, but otherwise, suit yourself. Whatever you choose, make your virus software give it a once over before you trust it.*

Entrepreneurial software programmers have been hawking their little creations online since before the Internet was popular, so by now there's a pretty evolved online marketplace for the cheap stuff. You can see what I mean by visiting Tucows (*http://www.tucows.com/*), Download.com (*http://www.download.com/*), or Fileworld (*http://www.pcworld.com/ic/fileworld/*). (Visit online shops such as Handango—*http://www.handango.com/*—if you are looking for tools for your smartphone, PDA, or other mobile device.)

Used to be, you could download a bit of software for free. If you liked it and you remembered to do so, you could send its creator a check. It was an honor system. More often nowadays, developers let you download a trial version (usually called *shareware*, but also known as *demoware* and *trialware*) that expires in 30 days or so. If you're still using it when the trial expires, it asks you to pay up. Alternately, the free trial might have some features disabled (which you can activate for a fee), or it might display ads until you pay for it.

Dear Geek Goddess,

I love to download little tools for my computer and Treo phone, but I told my son he has to stop downloading games because I'm sure he is crashing our family computer with them. He called me a hypocrite. While I'm proud of his sharp vocabulary, I'd like to tell him he's wrong. But before I embarrass myself, is he? Am I doing as much damage as he is?

Upper Hand in Eugene

· · · · · · · ·

Dear Upper Hand,

I don't know for sure which of you is causing the problem, but I'd bet it is your son. You can find terrific utilities, useful small applications, and even full-fledged office suites for free on the Internet, but you do need to watch your back. A lot of games, frivolous tools, screensavers, cute programs that add icons to email, and whatnot are a con. They sucker the gullible and innocent into downloading them and then install adware, spyware, or all manner of malicious infections for nefarious purposes such as bombarding you with ads . . . or worse. And a lot of these cons are targeted at kids because children are so gullible and innocent—plus they love games and don't have a lot of cash to buy reputable ones. Just be careful where you download from. Even if your best girlfriend recommends something or your kid assures you the game is fine, she may have been conned and hasn't realized it yet. Follow recommendations from computer magazines or stick to the shareware sites I've mentioned. If you give your son a couple of approved sites he can download from, such as Pogo.com (http://www.pogo.com/), GameSpot (http://www.gamespot.com/), Big Fish Games (http://www.bigfishgames .com/), and Yahoo! Games (http://games.yahoo.com/), he should be okay. If he can't follow this rule (likely if he's anything like my know-it-all geek tween), set up his account so he can't download games (see Chapter 9). Your computer will be a lot healthier. Also, run a program such as Norton 360, and let it scan your hard drive for problems frequently. And be sure to read that boring license agreement. Code fiends often slip egregious stuff in with the boring language to get you to agree to their evil plans for world domination. Learn more about this issue in Chapter 9.

Even cheaper, as in free, is *open source software*, which is built not by one entrepreneur, but by a group of noble programmers dedicated to their vision of a world where software is built for the people by the people. (See how cool geeks are?) The concept of free shoes might call to mind scenes from war movies where people steal boots off corpses, but in software, the stuff is shiny, new, and often terrific. The open source movement basically arose from that old adage, "Many hands make light work." Some person or company lets loose some basic code onto the Internet and invites programmers to work on it when they have some spare time to make improvements. The results of these community efforts are often outstanding, better than you would get when a team of paid but disgruntled workers, following orders from their dreaded Cube Leader, adds features to a commercial product.

And from the software shopper's point of view, it just doesn't get any better. You download it and if you like it, you use it. Sometimes the software is a bit goofy or not quite finished, but it doesn't cost you a dime. There may not be an official tech support department (the stuff is created by volunteers, after all), but there is usually free documentation online and a vibrant community of users who will happily help you solve problems.

Some of the more developed projects are surprisingly robust. I swear by Mozilla's open source Thunderbird email application and Firefox Internet browser (both available at *http://www.mozilla.com/*). I prefer these to commercial products like Microsoft Outlook and the ubiquitous but often troublesome Internet Explorer, and they cost me a whopping nada, zip, zero.

SOFTWARE WARDROBE FIT FOR A QUEEN

When shopping for software, wherever you choose to shop, your choices fall into categories, just like with shoes. Most of these categories come with businessy descriptions such as "productivity" and "communications" because software is still evolving from the business world into the human world. I prefer to think of software in the same categories in which I think of my wardrobe: essential, special occasion, and task-specific. Some I will care about and you won't and vice versa, in the way some people will never wear heels more than two inches high (my mother) and others wouldn't be caught dead in Birkenstocks (me). Just as with shoes, there is an infinite variety of choices. Some of it is so basic you use it every day for everything, some of it you use only for socializing or playing, and some of it gets a particular job done. Though my girlfriends and I can't begin to provide the skinny on all of it, we will share what gets us through every day.

Dear Geek Goddess,

When my sister-in-law emails me files, the filenames always have three letters at the end that mean nothing to me. Files on my own computer don't seem to have them, so I thought it was one of her crazy systems. I deleted the letters and gave the files names I liked. Oops. You are probably laughing at me because I obviously did something stupid. Now my computer can't open any of those files. It gave me a good excuse to not read her novel or look at 2,000 blurry vacation photos, but what did I do wrong?

Name Freak in New Jersey

. . . .

Dear Name Freak,

There was a time when naming files was an art. Companies issued rules so everyone understood how it worked. Then the concept of long files names hit the average computer (it was once only on Macintosh computers) and people forgot about the file extension, which is what those letters after the dot in your filename are called. These letters simply indicate what program created the file. That may not matter to you, but it matters to your computer, which can't open the file unless it knows what program to use. The files on your computer all have file extensions. They may simply be hidden. (To see them, choose **File ▶ Open**, then click **Views**, and select the **Details** option from the drop-down menu. Now you will see the complete filename, as well as the date it was last saved and other details.) If a file ends in doc, it is probably a Microsoft Word document, though many software programs can open these. If it ends in zip, the file has probably been compressed with a program like Winzip, ALZip, or Filzip. (Compressed files are ones that have been shrunken to reduce their size.) If the file ends in jpg, it's probably a photo or other graphic. (A lot of virus creators use the JPG extension to trick you into thinking the file is a picture—usually a funny or sexy one—so you will open it. In fact, any attached file can be a virus no matter the file extension, so don't open attachments unless you know who sent them and what they are.) New software applications are installed using files that have one of two extensions: msi and exe.

If you don't know what file format the letters are referring to, just double-click the filename (in your email attachment or Windows Explorer) and see if Windows can figure it out. Windows will automatically launch the right software program if it can determine the file type and if you have the right software installed to view the file.

LIKE THE IDEA OF FREE?

If you like to keep your money, you will love these popular open source software programs. Full featured, terrific, and—did I mention?—free.

Firefox (http://www.mozilla.com/)

Firefox is a terrific Internet browser. If you are unhappy with either Internet Explorer or Safari (for Macs), take this one for a spin. (Or you Mac users might want to check out Camino—*http://www.caminobrowser.org/*.) Check out the available add-ons to customize Firefox to your liking. (Just click the **Add-ons** tab at Mozilla's website to see what's available.)

Thunderbird (http://www.mozilla.com/thunderbird)

I love this email program from the Mozilla team. It downloads not only your email but also any of the blog or news feeds (RSS feeds) you subscribe to. It also has great spam filtering.

The GIMP (http://www.gimp.org/)

Want to crop people in and out of your photos, eliminate red eye, and perform all manner of photography tricks but can't bring yourself to shell out for Adobe Photoshop? Take five minutes to download and install this baby.

Pidgin (http://www.pidgin.im/)

Sick of all those ads plastered over AIM or Yahoo! Messenger? Tired of having three different chat programs open at once? Try Pidgin, which allows you to connect to all major chat networks, including IRC, AIM, Yahoo! Messenger, ICQ, and more.

Audacity (http://audacity.sourceforge.net/)

Got a teenager hankering for a high-end sound editing system for his garage band? Earn his undying respect to your geek mastery by pointing him to this open source solution and save yourself a fortune while you're at it.

Blender (http://www.blender.org/)

Always wanted to create your own 3D movie but don't want to go work at Pixar to do it? This 3D graphics editing tool is your zero-commitment first step.

OpenOffice.org (http://www.openoffice.org/)

How about a complete office suite for absolutely nothing? How sweet is that?

Sunbird (http://www.mozilla.com/)

Just want a basic calendar that will automatically download from one or more online calendars and keep track of a to-do list? The makers of Firefox and Thunderbird have got one.

Still want more? You greedy girl! Well, it's out there and new stuff is appearing all the time. Check out SourceForge.net (*http://www.sourceforge.net/*) for leads.

Dear Geek Goddess,

I'm loving this idea of free software, but is there a downside? Out here in the 3D world, when I go on a "get new stuff" spree-free or not-my (admittedly tiny) home is quickly overrun with crap, and I can no longer find a place to sit. Is there a similar downside in the digital realm?

Spare Living in San Francisco

• • • • • •

Dear Spare Living,

Trialware is a great deal (as long as you don't accidentally get something malicious). You get to thoroughly try out a program and determine if it's something you will actually use before you drop a dime. But yes, if you go crazy, you will litter your hard drive and system tray with stuff you never use. Fortunately, it's as easy to get rid of this stuff as it was to acquire it. From the Control panel (click the **Start** button, then choose **Computer** to get here), choose **Add or Remove programs**, scroll through the list till you see the software in question, click it, and choose **Uninstall**.

This doesn't delete the original installation file (that's still in the folder you downloaded it to), but it removes the installed software and any triggers that pester you for money.

Basic Black

The office suite (sometimes called a *productivity* suite) is your comfort flat. You will wear it every day to work; it's presentable, comfortable, and extremely functional, but not really what you'd call sexy. The tools in an office suite usually include a word processor, spreadsheet application, email client, and a slideshow or presentation tool. In Microsoft Office, these tools are better known as Word, Excel, Outlook, and PowerPoint, respectively.

Just like your everyday shoes, you want this suite to fit you properly, go with all your stuff, and reflect your lifestyle and budget. While the standard suite is from Microsoft, don't let all the Microsoft devotion out there persuade you that you don't have options. You do. It's your money, your work, and your computer. Buy what you want and what you can afford. If you are buying a new computer, you might feel pressed to buy your software suite at the same time. (That's how salespeople make the big bucks, after all.) It's true that getting a suite pre-bundled with the computer is convenient and will probably save you some money over a shrink-wrapped version of same. But you can buy that same office suite at retail chains like Best Buy and Office Depot or at warehouse clubs like Costco and Sam's Club. There are cheaper and even free suites that you can download from the comfort of your broadband-enabled living room that you might want to check out first. So there is really no pressure to buy everything all at once.

If you want the most popular office suite ever to walk the face of the earth installed on your computer and you can afford it, there is no shame in that. I and most of my geek girlfriends use some version of Microsoft Office, and we love it. "Everything I do is there in Microsoft Office," says Jamye Chambers of Dell, which sells many computers preloaded with Microsoft products. "There is usually some kind of template for whatever project I'm working on. It makes it so easy to get stuff done; you don't have to reinvent the wheel."

"My clients use Microsoft Office, and I can exchange documents easily with them," explains grant writer Karen Henke. "I also use styles for all my word processing documents and love that." *Styles* are preset fonts for headlines and body text and the like so that the software knows what you like and you don't have to fiddle with this stuff every time you write.

I too love Microsoft Office. I'm a writer and Microsoft Word is like my favorite paintbrush. I rely on some of the other tools in the suite as well. I have used it for so many years that the initial cost doesn't seem so bad anymore. But that doesn't change the fact that the Microsoft Office suite is expensive (anywhere from $150 to $600, depending on the suite you choose and where you buy it). And money is money.

Dear Geek Goddess,

I feel like I spend the first 20 minutes of every work day setting up my word processor, email application, and other software so that they look and work just how I like them to. I'm sure this is silly. This is a computer. It should be doing my bidding, right? So help me get it right once and for all.

Time Waster in Toledo

. . . .

Dear Time Waster,

Any time you find yourself repeating the same task over and over to the point of irritation, there is always a way to make a computer do that work for you. That's why they were invented in the first place. Often, it's a chore to figure out how to teach your computer to do your work, but not in this case. Most software programs allow you to easily tweak them so that they remember the way you like to work. For example, maybe you want Microsoft Word to always open in the Reading Layout or your Calendar program always to open in the day-at-a-time view. This is usually handled in a menu choice called Options, *which can be found in various places in software programs; look under the Tools, Edit, or File menu. Once you find the spot, you can customize to your heart's content. For example,*

SOME ALTERNATIVES TO MICROSOFT OFFICE

Microsoft Works is the suite Microsoft targets to home users, and it is much cheaper ($40). It includes a word processor and spreadsheet program that will let you share files with Office users, a calendar and contact manager, a project manager, and some other not-quite-hot-off-the-presses software that you might outgrow if you turn into a geek. It's enough to get by, if you're not going to use heavy-duty features.

Some computer manufacturers save a little cash by selling computers with WordPerfect (another word processing app) or the WordPerfect Office suite instead of Microsoft products. The home version of the WordPerfect suite includes a word processor, photo album, video editor, Norton Internet Security, a spreadsheet program, a personal finance program, and lots of templates and other tools. At about $150 to $300, depending on features, it is cheaper than Microsoft Office, but if you've used Office at work and gotten comfortable with it, it might be aggravating to learn something new at home. It is compatible with Microsoft Word, however, so you will still be able to share files with people who

in Microsoft Word, choose **Tools**, *then* **Options** *(in Word 2007, choose the* **Office** *button, located in the very top-left of the screen, then* **Word Options**) *and you will get a handy menu:*

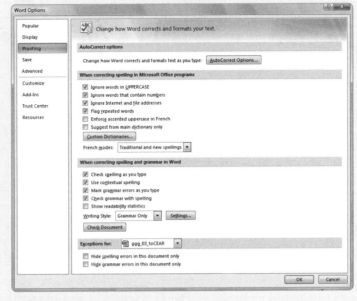

The options menu in Word 2007

Click a tab at the top of the menu to pick the category you want to customize. Then select checkboxes for options that appeal to you and deselect those that don't. If something disappoints, it's easy to change it back, so feel free to play around here.

use Word. However, you'll have to save your files in Word format before you do so, which adds a tiny extra step when you are saving a file.

But honestly, if you aren't going for the dominant player in order to save money, why not keep *all* your money and go with OpenOffice.org (*http://www .openoffice.org/*)? This open source suite has a word processor, spreadsheet application, presentation program, and drawing program. Heck, if you hate it (you won't), you can always pay money for something later. Even if you are already accustomed to Microsoft Word, you won't feel much pain switching to Open-Office.org's Writer. Just download it, install it, and get it to work. OpenOffice.org doesn't have the number of templates that the commercial programs have, so you won't have the many ready-made solutions that Jayme is fond of. But it does have some nice features, is compatible with Word, and it's really hard to complain about the price. It supports styles, tracks changes, and has many other advanced features found in Microsoft Word. It will also open Microsoft documents. For most people, OpenOffice.org has more than enough power to satisfy. It will even create PDFs (portable document format files) from your documents, which is a new feature in Microsoft Office 2007. So if you want to create contracts or forms and email them to people in an unalterable format, you don't have to pay up for Adobe's PDF creator service or the latest version of Microsoft Office.

"I am currently using Office 2003," explains Tracy DuBay, who teaches education technology through Western Michigan University's online education program. "But I use OpenOffice.org frequently because I suggest it to my students who are on a budget and need to find viable alternatives to cost-prohibitive Microsoft products." There is a version of OpenOffice.org for Mac users, too. It's called NeoOffice (*http://www.neoffice.org/*).

If you have a speedy Internet connection, you might also want to take a look at the free tools Google lets you use online. Google Apps includes a word processor, spreadsheet, and calendar program that are easy to use and are always there as long as you have network access—even when you are using someone else's computer. More than that, Google Docs will let you selectively share your work with others, making it perfect for collaboration. Better still, it can leverage the power of the Internet so you can set up spreadsheets that, more than merely adding up numbers, actually find the best price for things on the Internet or the current stock price. How cool is that? Also, it's free! Just go to *http://docs.google.com/* to sign up. Google isn't the only company offering what used to be desktop software programs for free on the Internet either. This is the wave of the future, so keep your eye out for more tools being delivered this way. Meanwhile, you might also want to try the complete online office suite (spreadsheet, presentation, contact management, calendar, and more) delivered by Zoho (*http://www.zoho.com/*). There are others as well.

My husband and I used Google spreadsheets to set a budget and shopping list for our Christmas shopping, even though we both have Microsoft Office on our office computers. But this way we could work on it together, even when we weren't in the same building, or update it for the other to see. (This in itself is worth trying out. The first time you watch someone else's changes appear on your document when no one else is home is a bit *Blair Witch Project* freaky—or at least *I Dream of Jeannie*.) After we marveled over that, we managed to stay within our Christmas budget for the first time since the kids were born. Ah, the beauty of communicating in black, white, and red.

But you don't have to commit blindly to one office suite any more than you have to buy a pair of shoes without trying them on. You can try almost any software before you pay for it. Just go to the publisher's website and download a trial version. Heck, download them all if you have the time, space on your hard drive (delete the ones you don't like), and a high-speed Internet connection.

DATABASES AND SPREADSHEETS

These may not seem like the most thrilling of toys, but you'll be surprised at how much you enjoy organizing information to make it more useable and efficient. Getting your information out of address books, index card boxes, file folders, and binders isn't exactly a Saturday night out in Vegas. It's more like organizing your closet: It's not that much fun to do, but is pleasant for how it makes every day afterwards go a bit more smoothly. "I could never live without my spreadsheets," gushes Melissa Lavengood about Microsoft Excel. "I know that makes me sound really boring. But I don't care."

A spreadsheet is handy for organizing and presenting information in grids, especially when math is required, such as for budgets and expense reports. It organizes your information into cells that are arranged in rows and columns. If you change the number in a cell or add another cell in a column where you need those numbers totaled, for example, the program automatically recalculates the total.

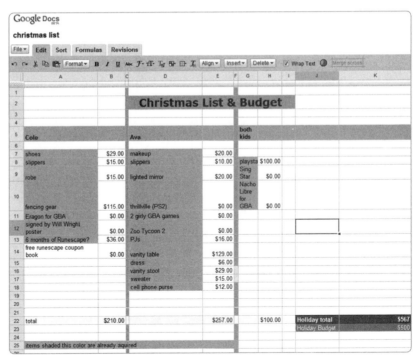

A spreadsheet is a great way to keep track of a budget. In this Christmas budget, just change the price—or add an item—and the total and money remaining changes automatically.

A database is better for keeping track of large amounts of related information when you don't want to see all your data on the same page, but you do want to be able to search it easily and see small portions of it at once. A database can store names, phone numbers, addresses, and other relevant information in a *record*. Then, if you do a search of one *field* in the record—say, the phone number—it brings up every piece of information about the person associated with that phone number. So, if you run a shoe store, you won't have to remember what you talked about the last time a particular client called or what size shoe she wears. Just use her phone number to look her up in your database. (There are some contact management databases that will do this automatically from a caller ID–enabled phone connected to your computer.) You can use databases for keeping track of just about anything: recipes, your record albums or art collection, students in a school, your 200 close personal friends and all their shoe sizes, or the names of all the ex-husbands of the women in your book club . . . whatever you need.

In addition to Access (Microsoft Office) and Base (OpenOffice.org), you might consider FileMaker Pro (*http://www.filemaker.com/*), which is powerful and easy to use. There's a Mac version too. It's my favorite.

It's not exactly fodder for cocktail party conversation, but I use both spreadsheets and databases pretty liberally. I use Excel to figure out the overhead on a piece of property I own so I am sure to charge enough rent to cover my expenses, to create timelines for a work of fiction I'm writing, and to do all sorts of calculations I'm too lazy to do myself. I use FileMaker Pro to design all manner of databases for my business and personal lives, including sources I spoke to for this book you're reading, fictional characters I plan to use someday, and recipes and how they turned out.

Bring Order to Every Day

The calendar is possibly the most basic organization tool after paper and pencil. I know a lot of women are as devoted to their paper Filofax as they are to carrying a purse, but I love managing my contacts and calendar digitally. I don't have to erase or scribble out an address every time my sister moves or changes boyfriends or phone numbers (or both). I can cut and paste a person's details into email when someone asks me for an address, and I can click *print* to get a stack of addressed Christmas card envelopes. I like to put appointments that repeat (such as yoga class or my kid's piano lesson) on my calendar once and get a reminder 20 minutes before the event without giving it another thought. In short, I don't have the patience to maintain a paper calendar, and I require heavy-duty organization. The software tools that handle address book, calendar, and to-do list are often called *personal information managers* (*PIMs*).

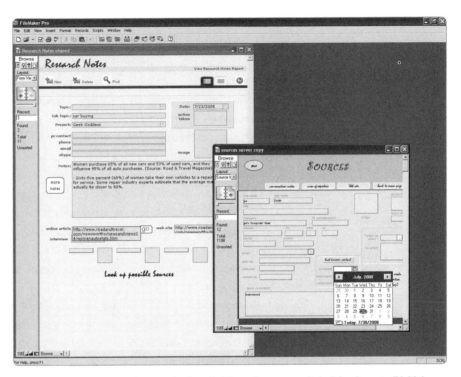

A database is a great way to keep track of people. Shown here are two linked databases in FileMaker Pro. One keeps track of information, interviews, and online resources. It links to the other one (do this by clicking Look up Possible Sources), which keeps track of people and their contact information. A software program that bills itself as an address book is basically a database. But a full-fledged database program lets you design your own way of keeping track of information as I have done here. FileMaker Pro comes with templates to get you started. I simply altered one of those.

Mac users get iCal as part of OS X, but we PC users will have to grin and claim we prefer to have options. I was once a devotee of the IBM Lotus Organizer (*http://www-306.ibm.com/software/lotus/products/organizer/*) for keeping track of people, websites, and time management. I have also used Palm Desktop (*http://www.palm.com/us/software/desktop/*), which comes with a Palm handheld organizer, so you can enter things on your computer as well as on the handheld version. There are others available. Microsoft Outlook (*http://www.microsoft.com/outlook/*) is popular, but I don't care for it. There are also several good shareware ones, such as EsssentialPIM (*http://www.essentialpim.com/*), and expensive ones targeted at sales professionals, such as ACT! (*http://www.act.com/*).

If you are always trying to track down a husband, teen, or friend to talk scheduling, an online calendar might be the thing to bring you all back from the brink. I dismissed these for a long time because I thought I couldn't be bothered with having access to my calendar only when I had access to the Internet, but I was wrong about that. I have lately become a devotee of Google Calendar. My husband has one, my kids each have one, my kids' school has one, and even the dog has one. I can see everyone's schedules overlaid on mine or get rid of the noise and focus on my own day by simply ticking a box. I put appointments on my kids' or husband's calendars without even consulting them. (That's fun.) And they can see if I'm busy without pestering me and put events on my calendar when they see I'm free at the time they need me (if I give them permission; digitally, that is).

Even better is the invitation feature. If I'm planning a party, I first schedule it on my own calendar. To invite people to the event, I just enter their email addresses and the calendar sends them an invite. My invitees get an email with a link to my party page on the Internet where they can RSVP, announce what they plan to bring, offer rides, or whatever else is appropriate. I decide if others can see the guest list or invite other people. And no one has to call me unless they actually want to talk to me.

Perhaps my favorite part of the Google Calendar, though, is its ability to accept appointments through text messages. When I run into someone at the supermarket who invites me over for drinks, I get out my cell phone and text message the details to my calendar. First I had to register my cell phone number with my Google Calendar (click **Manage Calendars** from your main calendar page; then choose the **Mobile Setup** tab and follow the directions). Then I stored the Google Calendar's SMS messaging address, GVENT (or 48368), in my cell phone's address book. Now that I have it set up, all I have to do is send a text message with basic details, such as "Jan 21 Ava's birthday party 6pm." Google Calendar somehow figures out what I mean and puts it on the calendar on the right date and at the right time. And whenever I set up an event on my Google Calendar, I choose how I want to be reminded. It can send event reminders to my cell phone or email, or pop up a reminder on my computer screen—or whichever combination of those options I like.

I like Google, but there are other online calendar services too which offer much of the same function. 30 Boxes (*http://www.30boxes.com/*) lets you add your blog and MySpace profile to your calendar page. MyHomePoint (*http://www .myhomepoint.com/*) will keep every family member organized and let you assign chores to each of them, as well as keep track of phone numbers, addresses, and your home inventory. 37signals (*http://www.37signals.com/*) publishes some great online tools for organizing and collaborating, including a calendar and personal organizer called Backpack.

Most online calendar services will export your calendar (in the iCal format) so that you can have it fed into a piece of software on your computer or even another online calendar. I use EssentialPIM (the basic version is free) to keep a to-do list and contacts. I feed it the web address of my online calendar so I am always on track, even when I'm offline. I use the Windows Calendar on my Vista computer. It also checks my Google Calendar for new appointments as often as I tell it to. Sunbird (*http://www.mozilla.com/*) is another free calendar, with no contact management, that reads your online calendar. On my Palm PDA, I can sync my Google Calendar without even touching a computer using a little tool I downloaded from GooSync (*http://www.goosync.com/*). Or from my cell phone, I can access my calendar and other services as well. (Set this up at *http://www.mobile.google.com/*.) Or I can just let my calendar prod me with a text message. Even if someone else puts an event on my calendar, it shows up on whatever computer I'm using soon after they do so. So you see, I have access to my calendar even when I don't have access to the Internet—or even to my computer. All I really need is my cell phone to keep it all together. I find this very liberating.

ORGANIZATION IS THE ROAD TO ENLIGHTENMENT

Sometimes, when I feel as if my life is getting away from me or I'm not getting any closer to my dreams, a calendar and a to-do list aren't enough. Rather than hire a life coach to help me work toward my goals, keep me on track, and remind me to schedule things I value into every day, I use a digital one. I've tried several of these. There are some that focus on specific tasks, mostly getting in shape, such as The Athlete's Diary (*http://www.stevenscreek.com/palm/tad.html*) or reaching weight goals, such as Diet and Exercise Assistant (*http://www.keyoe.com/*). I have been known to use that last one to track my calorie intake and exercise when I want help losing a few pounds. It has a database of foods and calorie counts, so all I have to do is type *donut* to see why I'm starting to look like Homer Simpson.

But for overall life management, I prefer Life Balance by Llamagraphics, Inc. (*http://www.llamagraphics.com/*). It is essentially a project manager and calendar that encourages you to think of more esoteric endeavors such as "spend time with my family" or "pursue spiritual enlightenment" as just as important as your dentist appointments and work deadlines. It adds them to your to-do list in small increments. It also helps you keep track of more mundane stuff. Once you have it all set up, with your aspirations broken down into manageable chunks, you tick off tasks in your to-do list as you complete them. At the end of the month (or whenever you chose), a pie chart shows how well your actions match your priorities. It can be enlightening and lead to real life change.

COMPUTER SECURITY

I know computer security might be a bit dull. But it's like putting socks on under your shoes: It's essential if you don't want to hurt your feet and ruin the shoes. You do need this stuff—immediately. Don't connect to the Internet without it unless you are connecting to download a security suite. Security software falls into, oh, let's say, three basic categories: antivirus, firewall, and spyware protection. But you can get a suite that covers it all.

I have used several antivirus programs, including Norton Internet Security (*http://www.symantec.com/*) and McAfee Internet Security Suite (*http://www .mcafee.com/*), as well as ZoneAlarm's offerings (*http://www.zonelabs.com/*) and a couple of others. Don't let a shortage of cash lead you to making unsafe choices here. There is good, free protection available. AVG (*http://www.grisoft.com/*) offers a free version, and ClamAV (*http://www.clamav.net/*) is an open source solution. In fact, tools that cost money aren't necessarily better. Bill Pollock, publisher of No Starch Press, which not only publishes this book but also publishes books with titles like *The TCP/IP Guide* and *Hacking: The Art of Exploitation* (so we are talking true geek here—but in the best possible way, of course), says, "AVG is probably as good if not better than commercial choices, and it's less intrusive." Jamye prefers McAfee. Me? Well, I would never go out without protection, but I can't claim to actually *like* any of them. I usually just go with whatever free trial came with my computer or is the latest fashion, and I am universally disloyal. (Yes, fashion choices involving security software do sometimes happen in my life, I'm sorry to admit.) I always obediently update the virus protections whenever the software tells me to, even if it's the last thing I want to do, because getting a virus is much worse than whatever small irritation this may feel like at the time.

"The minute you purchase a computer and before you connect to the Internet," Jayme warns, "make sure you have a great piece of security software." Jayme made the mistake of not making this a priority when she bought one of her computers and lived to regret it. "It was bad," she says. "It opened up my PC to every awful thing out there. What a mess that was." And that's a point well taken. Once one piece of spyware or virus is on your computer, your computer is often even more vulnerable to other viruses as a result, which is why you want to run regular scans of your computer and practice safe browsing by never going out there without a full computer body condom.

The topic of security is a big one, and I treat it more fully in Chapter 9.

INSTANT MESSAGING

A lot of adults think instant messaging (IM) is for kids. Well, call me (and most of my geek girlfriends) a kid then, because I love it. I stay in touch with friends all over the world in quick, frequent conversations that happen in real time but

a QUICK 411 on security software

Here is a quick definition of the tools you should expect in your security software. Whether you get them in a suite or separately, don't miss any of these essentials.

A *firewall* creates a barrier between your computer and the Internet, preventing programs from accessing the Internet if you don't want them to and keeping intruders out. A firewall can prevent viruses from spreading, and prevents malicious code from opening a secret backdoor (secret from you that is) on your computer that lets in bad guys. Windows machines come with a firewall built in, as do Macs. So if you get a shiny new firewall with your security suite, be sure and turn off the Windows firewall. Having more than one firewall will create conflicts and problems and will not improve your security.

Antivirus software scans emails you send and receive and periodically scans all the files on your computer for viruses. It won't let you open files with viruses and can nuke any infections that do manage to get in.

Spyware protection is like a good watchdog that follows you around the Internet barking at any code that tries to track what you are doing, collect information about you, or change your computer configuration. You sometimes have to tell it "down boy" when it gets overzealous because sometimes these activities are okay with you, but it's nice to have someone watching your back.

are typed using MSN Messenger (*http://www.msn.com/*), Yahoo! Messenger (*http://www.yahoo.com/*), Skype (*http://www.skype.com/*), AOL Instant Messenger (*http://www.aol.com/*), or Google Talk (*http://www.google.com/talk/*). It is somewhere between an email and a phone call in that you read and write the discussion and you can pause and do something else (like an email) but the other person is on the line with you (like a phone call). In fact, some of my girlfriends and I stay in touch almost exclusively via instant messaging. "It's more personal than email," agrees Tracy, who I stay in touch with almost entirely via Skype. You can read all about the many features and uses you can put this wide new world of Internet communication to in Chapter 6. For now, I will just introduce you to the software tools.

There are several software tools to choose from—Yahoo!, MSN, Google, Skype, and AOL each offer one—that can get you instant messaging right now on your Internet-connected computer. (Mac users already have one. It's called *iChat*.) They are universally free, simple to use, and a lot of fun. But they are easiest to operate when all parties are using the same tool. So the best way to get started is to ask your friends what they use, and then sign on with the service they have (or choose one yourself and get a friend to join you). If you survey your friends and everyone you want to instant message uses different services, try out Pidgin (*http://www.pidgin.im/*) or Trillian (*http://www.ceruleanstudios.com/*). Mac users will want to check out Adium (*http://www.adiumx.com/*). These programs serve as a universal translator between instant message tools so you will be able to chat with everyone using a single piece of software. I even use Pidgin to chat with my iChat-using girlfriends.

Money Matters

When it comes to accessories, the most important (after shoes) is your purse. And what's the original purpose of the purse? Stashing your money. So let's talk about software that keeps track of your money. I'm not naturally very good with money, and neither is my husband. So for us, money management software was a godsend. It changed the way we relate to our money in ways you can't imagine until you try it for yourself. When I first started using the popular personal finance program Quicken from Intuit around 1993, I was working full-time and renting a house. I could not visualize how I would ever be able afford a house in the San Francisco area or how I would even be able pay for childcare. (My kids weren't born yet, but I was plotting to have them.) My husband and I both had decent jobs, but we were barely making ends meet. Then I got a writing assignment that required me to install Quicken to track every dime I spent.

In a few months, I knew why I was broke. And the raise I needed was only part of it. All those impromptu café stops, a shoe-shopping habit, drinks after work, vacations, sushi dinners, and a thousand small expenses that, when totaled up, were as much to blame for our strapped state as the insane housing market we lived in (and our writer's wages). Until I saw how much of our money was slipping away, displayed in a neat and irrefutable pie chart, I never would have believed it. That sort of clarity is hard to achieve with a pencil and ledger. I hate to sound like one of those "before and after" ads, but I am still a writer (and so is my husband) and while I no longer have a daily triple latte habit, we do own a big house and a rental property and have two kids (both of whom required childcare). Knowledge is power.

Several of my girlfriends also swear by Intuit's financial management software for staying within a budget, keeping track of all things financial, and even running a small business. "I use Quicken for home and QuickBooks for my office," says Karen Henke. "I like getting my checkbook to balance. I like seeing the reports. I've been using it since 1995, and I can do a net worth chart and see my worth change over time. It's very empowering."

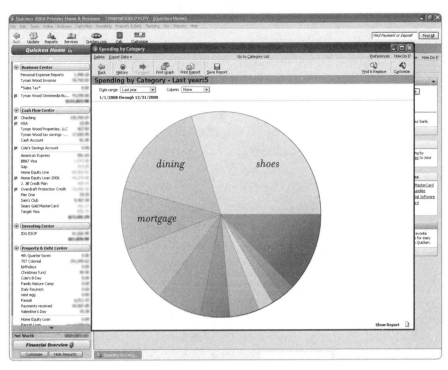

Seeing your spending in a pie chart can be an eye-opening experience and help you to evaluate your goals and compare them to where your money actually goes. Ten years ago, the biggest slice of my pie was going to restaurants and splurging on shoes. Today, that slice pays for my house.

You don't have to enter every transaction religiously into these programs or turn yourself into a receipt-collecting slave, either. Set Quicken up to communicate with your bank, credit card company, and investment accounts, and it automatically downloads and categorizes your spending and earnings. It'll take you almost no time to see exactly where your money goes. "Quicken helped me see when the amount I spent on clothing doubled one year because I had moved from a home office to a downtown San Francisco office and passed Banana Republic and other shops on my way to and from work," says Karen. Though I am a long-time devoted Quicken user, Microsoft makes a competitor to Quicken called *Microsoft Money* that gets good reviews too.

Even the dreaded tax experience can become a moment of empowerment through software. I was once helpless when it came to taxes, begging advice from the accountant at work and paying someone to fill out tax forms for me. But shortly after my "Fiscal Empowerment through Quicken" experience, I decided to buy Intuit's tax product TurboTax and see if I could become similarly competent on tax day. (H&R Block also sells a tax product, called *TaxCut*, at *http://www.taxcut.com/*.) Like a very patient accountant (who happened to live inside my computer), the software asked me questions, told me exactly where to plug in numbers, and did the math for me. Then it double-checked my work, printed the forms, and gave me instructions on where to mail them. It was fantastically easy. And it saved me money. Not only did it save me the accountant's fee but doing the taxes myself helped me to become a savvy taxpayer, which has influenced how I spend my money and structure my business. Every year I do my taxes with whatever product (online at Intuit's website, using Intuit's full-blown Home and Business tax program, or at my bank's website) is appropriate for me, I get a little smarter. I doubt I would ever have become the sort of person who looks up tax code before renting office space if it weren't for the handholding I got from this software. If your tax situation is so crystal clear and simple that this sort of empowerment is unnecessary, you can still save money and the hassle of meeting with an accountant by doing your taxes yourself. It's very easy.

DRESSING FOR THE JOB AT HAND

Each one of my girlfriends has some piece of software that she swears by because it helps her accomplish something that she loves to do, just as everyone has a favorite pair of shoes (sexy stilettos, comfortable mules, weathered cowboy boots, running shoes, or even just a pair of flip flops) that she wears when she is doing what she loves. Melissa swears by Microsoft Visio, a technical drawing program, because she works in the construction field, where visualizing how something will look is essential. But she also uses it at home for hobbies and home improvement projects. "I've been using it for years," she says. "We're currently using it to plan the addition to our house. We figured out that the room we had in mind isn't big enough to fit the wet bar and home theater we want, not to mention the office and half bath, too. I don't know of anything else I could use to map out my office's network infrastructure, make org charts, create architectural plans, and make a potty training reward chart for my two-year-old."

I am a fan of the menstrual calendar Woman Calendar (*http://www.beiks.com/woman/*). I used to count days to figure out when to expect my "friend," but no more. A glance at this calendar shows me when in the next six months I should "expect company." It will also predict fertility and calculate when a baby is due. But I mostly just use it so I know when not to schedule a sexy swimsuit vacation. There are a lot of these products. A search at Tucows (*http://www.tucows.com/*) will turn up several similar products, many of which are free, including Cycle Calculator (*http://www.soundtells.com/cyclecalc/*) and Advanced Woman Calendar (*http://www.softorbits.com/awc/*).

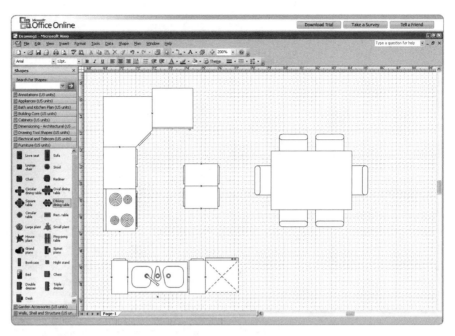

Microsoft Visio (in Microsoft Office 2007) will help you visualize anything from a kitchen design to potty training goals. Simply drag shapes onto the grid and move them around until they fit.

Melissa loves Google Earth, which puts satellite images of the globe, with detail right down to house numbers, at your fingertips. "It is just the coolest thing," she says. "The first thing everyone does is search for her own address. I've spent a whole lot of time 'traveling' the world checking out different places."

Tracy's hobby is photography. "Life can be told via photos," she says. "I take my camera everywhere. I try to capture the moment. But I cannot live without Photoshop—I live and breathe by it," she says. "If, for example, someone's eyes are closed in the best group photo I've taken, I can grab him from another photo, resize him, and drop him in." Adobe Photoshop is a photo-editing tool used by professionals, but Adobe (*http://www.adobe.com/*) also publishes a lightweight version called Adobe Photoshop Elements intended for home users. Even that's pretty expensive though, so you will might want to try out the open source (and free!) equivalent to Photoshop, the GIMP (*http://www.gimp.org/*). It is available for Macs too. Pixel (*http://www.kanzelsberger.com/*) is another image editor (it's not free, though it is inexpensive—under $40) that claims to replace Photoshop and is available for both Mac and Windows. If all you want is something with more features than the Paint tool that comes with Windows, but that's just as easy to use, I rather like the free Paint.NET program (*http://www.getpaint.net/*). It was originally intended as a replacement for the Windows Paint tool but, in the way of open source software, has evolved into something much better and now lets you do some fairly advanced image editing without being very complicated.

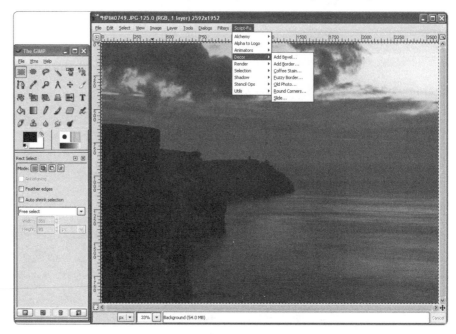

The free open source program the GIMP allows you to edit photos, add effects, cut out mistakes, and otherwise "Photoshop" your images without spending a dime for software.

Karen is more casual about her photography hobby. She uses a free tool from Google called Picasa to keep track of the photographs she's taken and do some basic editing, like cropping, red-eye removal, and tinting. "Picasa is fantastic," she says. "It's free and finally organizes all my pictures so that I can see them and scroll through them quickly."

GAMES

I will also admit to being something of a convert to gaming. And I'm apparently not the only woman who is. The online gaming site Pogo (*http://www.pogo.com/*) claims that 15.8 million users a month hit the site and play for an average of 39 minutes a day. These aren't all geek teens by any stretch either, since 55 percent of these users are women aged 18 to 49. A lot of women I know find that 10 minutes of cards or another simple game helps them cope with stress and gives them a little brain vacation in the middle of the day that helps them focus. More involved games are often too time consuming for busy women, but these less involved (casual) games are better than a trip to the candy bowl when a break is in order.

I personally get bored quickly with games that require me to shoot, whack, explode, or chase things with no real goal beyond getting to the next level. But I have disappeared for days—ignoring children, editors, and personal hygiene— playing games that test or instruct my knowledge of history to create a world apart from my own. These games are like a really engrossing book, only without the plot and with much better graphics. I love Sid Meier's Civilization (*http://www .civ3.com/*), Sid Meier's Pirates (*http://www.2kgames.com/pirates/*), CivCity Rome (*http://www.2kgames.com/civcityrome/*), and most of the SimCity games (*http:// www.simcity.ea.com/*). These are mostly world-building games where you start out with a few people in the wilderness and create a civilization or city.

The games I tend to like fall into the game category called *sandbox* games, so named because, like in a sandbox, you start with the raw materials and poke around until you have created your own world. The ones I have little patience for—but teenage boys seem to love—are called *first-person shooters*. You see how sometimes simply knowing the name of a thing explains why you don't like it? These are the games where you are a character with a gun and it is your mission to shoot everything in sight. If you think you are the sort of parent who doesn't allow their kid to play games, these are the ones you really mean. But they are a small percentage of what is available in the vast world of games.

The smaller games women tend to like because they are a bit of fun without so much time demand are often termed *casual* games. You can get them at Pogo. com (*http://www.pogo.com/*), MSN Games (*http://www.msn.games.com/*), and other similar sites. These games tend to be puzzles, card games, or word games.

My son loves *mission-based adventure* games, where there is some killing of other characters, but the main goal is to solve a mystery (or in the vernacular of these games, a *quest*). There are lots of these, and I find them mostly harmless. I don't get too excited about playing them myself, but it's sort of fun to watch my son play, since the games are often beautiful and he is very skilled. Many of these games have an online component to them, which makes them *multiplayer* games. This makes the whole deal intensely interesting to kids and is something parents need to stay abreast of because it brings kids into contact with millions of strangers. It's a very compelling form of entertainment and has lots of benefits. Sometimes the game exists entirely in an online virtual world. Some of these last include Second Life (for adults and teens), World of Warcraft (violent), Club Penguin (cute and harmless; for smaller kids) and RuneScape (Dungeons and Dragons for the digital set; harmless enough, though there is some killing and it is very addictive). But there are so many of them that I can't begin to list them all. I will say that you should thoroughly check out the virtual world your kid wants to play in before you okay it, but don't be a stick-in-the-mud and ban games altogether. And be on the lookout for addiction because, as I said, this is a very compelling form of entertainment.

A lot of parents fight with their kids over games, and I have been known to do that too. But mostly I prefer to join them. There is nothing like engaging in a heated discussion over military strategies in history or the technology of Rome with my middle-school kid to convince me that computer games are far from a waste of time. And one study I saw found that surgeons who grew up playing computer games thrashed their nongaming colleagues in their ability to do modern (laser) surgeries. Even doctors with better education and more experience couldn't keep up with the gamers. And if you have ever tried to stay alive in a 3D game, it's pretty obvious why. It takes real skill. Though my son and I are in a constant battle over how much time he should spend playing, I have to admit that he has learned to type fast, spell (he doesn't want embarrassing mistakes among his virtual friends), and make friends with people all over the world through this virtual world. It's a better way to waste time than TV (which no longer interests him) ever was. And lately he has decided to learn coding so he can make his own games. I'm not the kind of parent to discourage a kid from learning a skill with a starting salary that exceeds what I currently earn.

The world of software is huge and constantly changing, so I'm sure I have left out a lot of it. But you can't explain everything there is to know about shoes in one sitting either. We go to the store, pick up a pair we like, turn them over, examine the heel, ponder the style, and come to our own conclusions. Software isn't that much different, except you can do it without leaving the house or spending any money (at least not until later).

4 HOOK IT UP

Around my house, we use email and instant messaging more than we use the telephone. In fact, we don't even have a home phone or much in the way of cable TV. We (even the kids) rely almost entirely on the Internet for our communication and entertainment. This isn't a bizarre social experiment. We didn't wake up one day and decide we would rely entirely on the Internet just to prove we could. It simply evolved this way. The telemarketing calls that constantly disturbed dinner via our landline (and the phone bill for that line) were annoying. The people we really want to talk to use email, instant messaging, or our cell phones to reach us. So we canceled our landline. We almost never watch TV because we prefer watching programs on the Internet and ordering movies through Netflix (*http://www.netflix.com/*). So we whittled our cable service down to a spare and economical basic package. We have yet to miss any of it. In fact, we are happier now, and we believe the kids are smarter.

We use the Internet for everything. It's our workplace, shopping mall, gabfest, hangout, post office, telephone, library, news outlet, and entertainment center. We don't send photographs in the mail; we post online photo albums. We don't mail holiday letters full of tired jokes and a boiled-down version of our lives; we write a blog (an online journal) all year round that our friends and relatives can read to see what we're up to. We don't stick notes on the fridge; we use an online calendar with email reminders to keep everyone's schedule in a central location. We don't run out to the post office to ship packages; we print postage and shipping labels using the Internet. Our Internet connection is vital to our existence. On those occasions when we lose power—we do live in hurricane country—we panic first over the loss of our broadband connection. Only after we recover from that shock do we worry about the food in the freezer and the water supply.

GETTING HOOKED

The first step in my family's long road to complete dependence on technology was hooking our computers up to the Internet. This process isn't as much fun as shopping from the comfort of your couch, but it is a necessary step to getting there.

In fact, connecting a computer to the Internet is such a mundane chore that when I asked my girlfriends to talk to me about it for this chapter, they all, coincidentally, had other things to do. "Sorry, I'm just too busy cleaning my closet," Melissa said. "Um, sure," said Karen. "I'd absolutely love to talk about that, but unfortunately just now I have to go . . . um . . . to a meeting." Tracy was happy to hear from me until she heard the topic. Then suddenly the kids were crying and there was a flood in the bathroom. So you'll have to get the scoop from me.

Like most dull-but-necessary decisions, connecting your house to the Internet is best done after careful research (rather than in response to direct-mail flyers or CDs stuffed in magazines). The choice involves some boring technical decisions, and it is tempting—my girlfriends and I are certainly tempted—to ask your husband, brother-in-law, or the geeky guy who works down the hall (the one who's always talking about World of Warcraft) to set up the Internet on your computer in exchange for a home-cooked meal or some baked goods. If you have one of these types handy, and he is competent and desperate to demonstrate his technical prowess in the hope of making you swoon, we understand the temptation to let him do it. But wouldn't you rather feel powerful

Dear Geek Goddess,

I know you won't laugh at me for asking this so here goes. Even though my husband is a supergeek and I use the Internet daily, my six-year-old son asked me what the Internet is, and I realized that I don't really know the answer. I showed it to him, but he wanted to know where it was and what it was made of, even who owns it. I distracted him with cookies and wished he'd asked my husband so I could listen in on the answer. That was weeks ago, and now it's bothering me. What exactly is the Internet?

Wondering in Wilmington

. . . .

Dear Wondering,

Smart boy you've got there. I find it surprising that so few people ask this question. A few short years ago there was no Internet, but these days it has become as necessary as the telephone. It may be hard to believe for anyone who relies on the Internet today for everything from communicating to buying shoes, but not all that long ago, in 1992, I got into an argument with an editor at a computer magazine over whether the Internet was something the average consumer would ever use. At that time it was debatable. We have come a long way since the seed for the Internet was planted in 1959 in a little-heard-of government agency called Advanced Research Projects Agency (ARPA). That seed—a response to a national feeling of technical wimpiness caused by Sputnik—has evolved into a loosely connected network of computers around the world, not wholly owned by any individual or agency. You shouldn't be embarrassed to ask the question, "What is the Internet?" Not surprisingly, the best place to find a detailed answer to the question is on the Internet itself. Start at Wikipedia (http://wikipedia.org/) and think while you are browsing that democratic information source not only about how the Internet has changed how we access information, but also how it has changed the very way information is created. My own son recently asked me why it costs money to host a website if no one owns the Internet. He's 11 years old, so I suspect your son will soon move on to this question. To save time later, I'll tell you that it's because people own the servers that connect to the Internet and when they host your website, they are renting you space on those servers and employing geeky know-it-alls to keep it all running.

and independent than feign interest in this guy's virtual life? And if you do it yourself, you can wear pajamas. I don't think there is any shame in getting a little help. I like it when men open doors for me, even though I'm capable of getting through the door on my own. Most times though, I just walk through without any assistance, and you can probably accomplish this little chore on your own as well.

Connecting to the Internet is no harder than ordering cell phone service or making sure your house has electricity and water, once you understand the terminology and choices. And what you get is so much more fun than any of those other basic utilities. A phone might make it possible to call your old boyfriend from college after you've had a couple of drinks, but the Internet makes it possible to run a search on him so you can find out what he's really up to now (as opposed to what he would tell you) without embarrassing yourself. Heck, you can even run a background check on that "friend" your daughter is bringing home for Thanksgiving.

Guys in Work Belts

The first step in hooking up your computer to the Internet is selecting an Internet Service Provider (ISP). You probably only get to pick from one electric company, but there are many ISPs to choose from. If you have a reasonably new computer, it very likely came with a built-in modem for connecting to the Internet through standard phone lines; this is called *dial-up* service. Start by connecting your computer to a phone jack. Unplug your phone, find your computer's phone jack—on the back of your desktop tower or the side of your laptop—and plug the phone line in there.

If the computer is new, it no doubt came with an offer for free Internet service. Look on the desktop for an icon that says something like, *Connect to the Internet for Free*. This can entitle you to as many as six months of free dial-up service. These sorts of offers also come in the form of CDs and arrive in the mail uninvited, can be found bound in with magazines, and are probably the free prize in Cracker Jack boxes at this point.

There is no harm in signing up and taking that trial for a spin while you weigh your long-term options. It is easier to research the prices and services of different ISPs if you already have an Internet connection. Just be sure to note when the free trial is over and cancel it (unless you decide you like it), or the ISP will start billing you and keep right on billing you, whether you use the service or not. I have heard a lot of complaints over the years from people who had the darnedest time canceling free trials, so keep an eye on your credit card statements to be sure your cancellation was correctly processed before you tick this off your to-do list. A lot of people stop right here, continuing with the pre-bundled ISP and accepting the email address handed to them during the

anatomy of a web address

Even if you don't think about it every day, you probably understand your phone number. The area code indicates the region you live in, the three-digit exchange narrows it down to a neighborhood, and the four digits at the end are specific to your phone. Internet addresses, also known as URLs (uniform resource locators), have their own lingo, though the geography they point to is virtual. Let's break down one of my favorite web addresses so you can understand a URL as well as your phone number: *http://www.zappos.com/*.

* *http://* is the *protocol*; *lingua computera* for *set of computer instructions*. Here, the protocol tells the computer that we are dealing with hypertext transfer protocol (HTTP).

* *www* stands for *World Wide Web* and indicates that this site is included in the network of sites that use the hyptertext system invented and named by Tim Berners Lee in 1989. This network constitutes most of the useable Internet. He describes it rather well: "The Web is an abstract (imaginary) space of information. On the Net, you find computers—on the Web, you find documents, sounds, videos, . . . information. On the Net, the connections are cables between computers; on the Web, connections are hypertext links." There is no reason you need to understand the Web in order to use it with style, but knowing stuff is cool.

* *zappos* is the domain, or host. This bit is somewhat like the unique four digits in your phone number. There is only one domain by this name, so any computer can find this spot. You can leave out the *http* and *www*, but as long as you type this part correctly and include the next bit (the *.com* or *.org*), most browsers will find the site just fine.

* *.com* is the most common *top level domain* (*TLD*), the name for this bit after the dot. This particular TLD stands for *company*. There are others, of course. There is *.org*, *.net*, *.info*, *.name*, and many others. There are many that indicate countries; for example, *.ie* for Ireland and *.jp* for Japan.

  Anything that comes after the TLD indicates a specific page on a website. If you follow a link that has a lot of stuff following the TLD and it leads nowhere, delete everything after the TLD and it will take you to the site's home page, which often works.

trial. (Or they move right to signing up for broadband and going with the email address that comes with that.) But you have the benefit of the collective experience of my girlfriends and me, and we strongly suggest you save yourself the inevitable hassles this passive strategy will cause you later. We've all taken the lazy route and lived to regret it. Consider your options before signing up.

Beyond your phone company, cable company, Earthlink (*http://www.earthlink.net/*), America Online (*http://www.aol.com/*) and the cheap offerings, such as NetZero (*http://www.netzero.com/*) and Juno (*http://www.juno.com/*), there are a host of small, regional ISPs that offer dial-up services. These small companies might give you good personal service, or they might be a few minutes from bankruptcy. How do you tell which is which? Check out the reviews of ISPs at CNET (*http://www.cnet.com/*), DSL Reports (*http://www.dslreports.com*), *PC World* (*http://www.pcworld.com/*), *Consumer Reports* (*http://www.consumerreports.org/*), and specialized websites such as ISP Rank (*http://www.isprank.com/*). Also, since this stuff varies by region, ask your friends and family which service they use and if they are happy with the technical support and the features they get. And listen to your intuition.

The first thing you will discover is that the big choice isn't between ISPs. It is between dial-up (through the standard phone line) or broadband (much faster service, typically via cable or digital subscriber lines, called DSL).

Broadband vs. Dial-Up

If you've used dial-up service, you've probably noticed how slow the connection is when you load a web page with lots of pictures or download an email with an attachment. Using broadband allows for a much better online experience. A 2008 Pew Internet study found that 55 percent of all adult Americans now have a high-speed Internet connection at home. That's a huge jump from previous years but still leaves you with plenty of company if you decide to stick with dial-up. Though I don't consider "everyone else is doing it" a good reason to limit your experiences in life. "The only thing I would say, if I weren't so busy cleaning the closet," agrees Melissa, "is that I would never use dial-up again. Once you go broadband, there's no going back."

Broadband is infinitely superior, but like all good things, it's also more expensive. You can probably get away with spending around $10 a month or less for dial-up service. A broadband connection will cost around $25 a month, and a really fast broadband connection could go as high as $70. It all depends on where you live and what's available. You can usually save a little money if you get your cable TV, cell phone, landline phone, and broadband from the same company in a product bundle. The service providers like having you on the hook for everything, so they'll probably cut you a break.

With broadband, you'll realize the full potential of the Internet and understand why some people spend hours and hours online. In fact, a tricked-out computer with a dial-up connection is less fun than a cheap computer with broadband. Your Internet connection is a better place to put your money than fancy hardware. You might find you like online games—a lot of women do—or enjoy watching silly homemade videos at the wildly popular site YouTube (*http://www.youtube.com/*). Maybe you keep hearing about funny skits airing on Comedy Central but you always miss them on TV; with broadband, you can catch up with your favorite TV shows online. Maybe you like to gab on the phone with far-flung friends. You might discover that the world of Internet phones (and webcams) not only saves you a fortune in long-distance calls and mobile minutes but is also more fun. (See Chapter 6 for more on this.) Maybe you'll decide you don't need a newspaper delivered and don't want to deal with the hassle of recycling it when you can get the headlines you want fed daily to your email inbox or home page.

If you stick with dial-up you will save money, no question about it. But you will barely scratch the surface of the Internet because you will be crawling around at the pace of a sloth in pursuit of plants. Looking up the answer to questions that pop into your head (or out of the mouths of your children) will mean waiting to connect, inching slowly toward your search engine, waiting an eternity for the results of your search, and slipping into a coma as the inevitable ads load. Your kids will have demolished the living room in the meantime. By the time you find your answer, you will have forgotten the question. I'm not even kidding about this.

But only you know what you can afford. If you choose to stick with dial-up, all you have to do now is a quick price comparison to see if you got the best deal. If you stick with the provider who gave you the free trial, don't start handing out your email address till you read "Your Digital Calling Card" on page 104.

Broadband

If you decide to spring for broadband, good for you! You do have a bit more research to conduct now, but it'll be worth it. First, it's worth knowing that it is called *broadband* because the pipes (geekspeak for wires) that send information back and forth between your computer and your ISP's big servers are physically fatter (wider) than the ones that transmit traditional telephone data. In other words, *broad*band has more band*width*.

Broadband comes to your house in one of three possible ways: cable, DSL, or satellite. Those first two are most widely used, while satellite is only worth considering if you live in a remote or rural area where the first two aren't available. Satellite is expensive because it requires a dish. It also requires a dial-up connection, because a satellite dish can only receive information, not send it.

Internet TOOL BOX

Whatever service provider you choose, connecting to the Internet will require a few simple tools.

Modem

Whether you use dial-up, DSL from your phone company, high-speed cable Internet from your cable company, or any high-speed Internet from one of the big ISPs that offer it (such as Earthlink), you will need a modem. The modem communicates the digital information you create on your computer (or want to view on your computer) into a format that can be transported. It sends this translated data in little digital *packets*, which is why you always hear that word in discussions of networks. Each type

Photo courtesy of D-Link Systems, Inc.

of service requires a different type of modem. Fortunately, you don't have to worry because DSL and high-speed cable companies will provide (and service) the right one for the type of service you order. If you stick with dial-up service, your computer already has a built-in modem, unless you got it at an antique auction. Look for a phone jack somewhere and connect your computer to the wall jack with a bit of standard phone cord.

Ethernet cable

This bit of cable is necessary to connect your computer to a broadband modem. It looks like a beefy phone cable (because that's sort of what it is) and is readily available in computer stores and mass market retailers. Your service provider will probably hook you up with one when the technicians come set up your service. If you travel, stuff an extra one in your computer bag so you don't have to rent one from your hotel.

Router

If you want a wireless network, you will also need a router, which transports data from the modem to your computers via a wireless signal. Networks that use cables (called *LANs* for *local area networks*) also require a router, but you don't want one of those. Really. Even if your geeky brother-in-law says you do. You don't. Wireless is the way to go. See Chapter 7.

You know what cable is because you know about cable TV and you haven't been living in a cave. Just place your order and your cable company will dash eagerly out to your house bearing a cable modem, which connects you to the Internet using the same wires that are already delivering cable TV to your living room. Even if you aren't a cable subscriber, the wires are probably there already. If you do get cable TV, this might be a cost-effective choice as part of a bundle offer. Before you sign up, however, check with the phone company to see what kind of deals it will make with you. Phone and cable companies are in stiff competition for your monthly bill, and they are desperately trying to outmatch each other's deals. Cable connections tend to be a bit speedier than DSL but there are lots of offers (usually with a term limit) for DSL service that almost rival dial-up in terms of price.

Your phone company can deliver broadband over its fancy, new, upgraded DSL (digital subscriber line) phone lines. The phone companies have been busy rewiring the country for years, so that they can easily sell you broadband the very instant you decide you need it. On your phone company's website, there will be a place to enter your home phone number in order to find out what service is available in your area and what it will cost. You will most likely be offered a special deal to bundle DSL with your phone service and, sometimes, TV.

Earthlink, AOL, and other Internet companies also want to sell you broadband service. They just lease DSL or cable wires from the phone and cable companies, so the delivery method will be the same as if you got it directly through your phone company or cable provider. But do some price shopping. And ask around about service, technical support, and that sort of thing. You may already know how bad the service is from your cable or phone company, but an Internet company may be a complete unknown. Don't blindly believe claims of "award-winning service." Call them or send an email. Ask some inane questions to see if they are helpful.

DSL and cable are comparable services, and you can shop according to price and their competing claims about speed. Each will probably offer "light" and "power" versions. Your need for speed will depend on what you plan to do on the Internet. Unless you are launching a mega-corporation with a web presence, or enjoy downloading movies (which is not always illegal; check out Amazon Unbox or Netflix's Watch Instantly feature before you insist this isn't for you), the basic service is probably fast enough. In fact, even if you do want to download movies, the basic service will serve; it will simply be slower. You don't need to go all out if you're not sure. Let your budget dictate. You can always upgrade later.

Dear Geek Goddess,

My cable company claims that its "Super Size Me" service is much faster than the basic package. It's also more expensive. Is this a con?

Suspicious in Schenectady

· · · · · · · ·

Dear Suspicious,

Internet service providers make all manner of speed claims regarding their lightning-fast service. All of these claims are confusing. For example, my cable company claims its standard high-speed Internet is 100 times faster than dial-up and that its turbocharged service is a "lightning-fast" 8Mbps. But there is no way to compare those two numbers. (Though I happen to know most standard cable service delivers download speeds of about 1.5Mbps, so the turbocharged service should be considerably faster.) So I called to ask. And a nice but not-so-helpful representative told me that the standard service gets 384Kbps and the turbocharged gets 512Kbps. Two more numbers I can't compare to each other or the original two! If I wasn't a geek, I'd be pulling my hair out by now.

Part of the problem is that the ISPs are dodging the question. They don't want to quote speed numbers because they can't guarantee them and know that you can

Wired Nomadic Tribes

There is one other method of getting connected to the Internet that doesn't involve your house at all. You could become an Internet nomad, and rely entirely on Internet cafés and other public Internet "hotspots" that you find around your town or in your travels. (Obviously this would require a laptop.) These hotspots use wireless, or Wi-Fi (short for *wireless fidelity*). But unless you live in a city like Philadelphia with free municipal Wi-Fi for anyone to use, or you live on a college campus, where wireless Internet is pretty much a given these days, or you are like Tom Hanks' character from the movie *The Terminal* and live in an airport with Wi-Fi, you'll have to leave your home to take advantage of this option. This is probably something you will want to consider when you are traveling. It can be easier than talking a relative you visit frequently into getting broadband. All you need is a Wi-Fi card in your laptop, which most new laptops come with. Some restaurants, hotels, fast-food stops, and cafés charge for Wi-Fi, and some offer it for free. Some cities are covered by subscription services like Boingo (*http://www.boingo.com/*) or T-Mobile.

Many libraries and other public places also offer free Wi-Fi. (At the very least, your library will likely have a computer with a broadband connection if you want to get a taste for speed before you decide if you need it.) You can search for free hotspots in your area at *http://www.wififreespot.com/*. This solution, in combination with dial-up and perhaps a cellular data plan (a high-speed connection to the cellular network that allows you to surf the Internet and send email using your cell phone as a modem) is one that's used by road warrior types who spend their lives traveling for work or fun. But that doesn't mean you have to be on the road to take advantage of it. You could use it to get out of a noisy house, for the occasional trip, or just to see if you like broadband enough to ante up for it at home.

Dear Geek Goddess,

I just got my first laptop and want to head out to a local café to join the world of hip and beautiful public web surfers. Anything I need to know before I go? I don't want to be the only dork in a roomful of geeks.

Mobile in Mobile

. . . . . .

Dear Mobile,

There is nothing wrong with asking one of the beautiful people for help. It would be frustrating to settle neatly into a café that sports a sign in the window offering free wireless Internet only to stare helplessly at a browser that is claiming not to be connected to the Internet—especially when the solution requires only a second of tweaking. Remember where the system tray is in Windows? (Bottom right hand corner; you will find an assortment of little icons.) Look there for an icon that looks like this:

Right-click it. You will get a menu that looks like this in Windows XP:

| Change Windows Firewall settings |
| Open Network Connections |
| Repair |
| **View Available Wireless Networks** |

or like this in Windows Vista:

| Connect to a network |
| Turn on activity animation |
| Turn off notification of new networks |
| Diagnose and repair |
| Network and Sharing Center |

Click **View Available Wireless Networks** *in XP or* **Connect to a Network** *in Vista, and you will be treated to a list of every wireless network within range of your computer. Often there are more networks available than simply the one offered by the café you are in.*

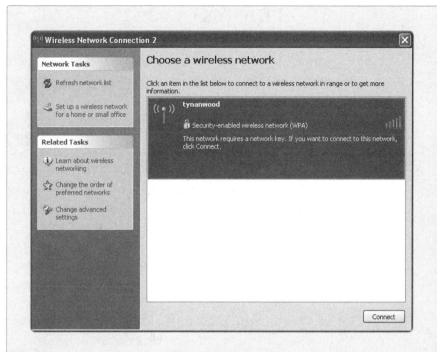

You can connect to any network that is not security enabled (the secured ones sport a little lock) simply by clicking it and clicking Connect. But choosing one that is not offered as a free network is something of a guerilla activity. Perhaps the people who live next to the café have a Wi-Fi network and don't really intend to share it. Connecting to their network instead of the café's is a bit rude, though there is no real harm done to them as long as you aren't a hacker. But if you are in an airport or other very public place and you see a long list of free networks available in addition to the one offered by the airport, be careful. Hackers often set up unsecured wireless networks like this to lure people to log on and type their passwords. It is possible for them to access information sent over an unsecured wireless network. So before you take up the habit of wardriving (which inexplicably has become common vernacular for this activity), you might want to think twice about your own safety.

YOUR DIGITAL CALLING CARD

My girlfriends and I (those that would talk to me about this, anyway) strongly advise you to come up with a strategy before you start handing out the email address you got from your ISP. In addition to the Internet connection itself, your ISP will probably give you a bunch of extra goodies, such as online storage space, one or more email addresses, and perhaps some software. (You could take these into consideration when you are comparison shopping, but except for the low-cost dial-up services, whatever they give you is likely to be more than you need.) Usually the email address your ISP gives you has the name of that ISP in it. And a lot of people assume it has to be that way—that their email address and Internet service are somehow inseparable, the way phones and phone numbers are. That is not so. (That's not even true of phone numbers anymore, actually.)

ISPs don't give out email addresses just to be nice. They do it to remain competitive and make their service attractive. Mainly, they know people are not very loyal to ISPs but they *are* very loyal to email addresses.

"I admit it!" agrees Annette Goodfriend, an artist, firefighter, and one of my geeky girlfriends. "I stay with my ISP, even though I have better options, because changing my email address is a hassle. It's not a huge hassle. But it's enough of one that I haven't done it. I even signed up again with the same ISP when I moved because I couldn't be bothered to change my email address along with my phone number and mailing address. Yuck."

That email address is a hook. It keeps you tethered to your ISP no matter how many times the urge to pursue a better deal calls to you. It's not hard to announce a new email address, but it's one more chore to deal with in your already busy life. Keep your ISP and your email address separate, and you will always be free to move fluidly from ISP to ISP, home to home, state to state, even country to country without ever having the hassle of telling the world you have a new email address.

There is another reason for choosing your email address carefully: vanity. In the modern world, your email address is like those calling cards women are always leaving for each other in Henry James novels. While your phone number is a meaningless series of random digits and reveals only your geographic location, an email address is made up of words and, therefore, it creates an image in the mind of people who know you through it.

The email address you sport says something about you—accurate or not. For one thing, the domain name in your email address directs anyone who looks at it to a website. The domain is the part that comes after the @ sign. So if your ISP is Bell South, that company's domain name is *bellsouth.net* and your email address will be *yourname@bellsouth.net*.

Dear Geek Goddess,

Every email program I've used has this thing in the address field called BCC. I get what CC is, because people used to put it on letters in an office I once worked in when someone was copied on that letter. But what the heck is BCC?

Protocol Challenged in Paducah

. . . . . .

Dear Protocol Challenged,

BCC also hails from office lingo. To CC someone on a letter simply means to carbon copy them. (Carbon? How quaint.) To BCC, then, means to blind carbon copy them. A blind copy is one where the recipient can see the email but not the address list of everyone else who got a copy of it. Use it when you want to protect the privacy of your recipients (like when you want to send everyone that chain letter) or if you don't want them to know you sent the same "personal" note to 200 people.

If you type *www.* and the email address's domain into the address line of any web browser, it will take you to that carrier's website. This can be relatively meaningless, or it can reveal a great deal about you. For example, if I send you an email from *christina@geekgirlfriends.com*, you could type *www.geekgirlfriends .com* into any browser and learn all about my book, my girlfriends, and how we use technology. Maybe you could even sign up for my email newsletters and meet other women who are getting hip to technology.

Liberated Email

You can get a free email address—not associated with your ISP—from many different online services. Try it. It costs nothing. Go to *http://www.yahoo.com/*, *http://www.hotmail.com/*, *http://www.aol.com/*, or *http://www.gmail.com/*. There are lots of others. Some of these even make it easy to access your email from your mobile phone. But you will be stuck with that Hotmail or Yahoo! domain name. Your email address will be something like *notyourname@hotmail.com*. If, for some reason, you want to use your ISP's email service but also want to give your friends an email address that will follow you if you leave this ISP, you can set up your email hosting account to forward your email from your liberated address to your address at your ISP. That way you can use any tools or features you like at your ISP or have as many email addresses as you like—one each for work, school, home, your secret spy identity—and check them all from the same email address provided by your ISP.

✳ note: *You may have problems getting an address that is your exact name or a popular nickname because someone else got there first, but whatever you end up picking, this address is portable: It can go with you no matter where you move or how often you switch service providers.*

When pressed to choose from the very limited list of names available at free email sites, people often choose things they later regret. I know someone, rather a serious and shy person, who in a moment of desperation chose *cutechick* because she glanced at her rubber ducky when her 90th choice was already being used by someone else on one of these free domains. You can only imagine the sort of attention *that* generated in online gatherings. You will use your email address a lot and might grow weary of the cute, hip, cryptic, or simply number-heavy ID you felt forced into when everything else you wanted was taken.

Custom Email

Free email accounts liberate you from your ISP, but there is no reason you can't buy a domain name and get an email address that is completely of your choosing (such as *christina@geekgirlfriends.com*). If you feel up to it, you can build a website to go with your domain, but you don't have to. You can just have the email address. It won't cost much; in fact, it will probably cost less than business cards. This way you can pick any email address you want. So if your name is Jane Somethingorother, you could have *Jane@somethingorother.com*. Now that's easy to remember. And as long as you renew your registration and hosting of the domain name annually, you will never have to change your email address.

Here's how you do it. First, go to *http://www.register.com/* and see if your last name is available. If that name is *Smith* or anything very common, I'll save you the trouble—it's taken. If you are desperate to own your last name but someone else got there first, you can visit *http://www.whois.com/*, find out who owns it and offer to buy it. Undoubtedly, the owner will want to charge you much more than it would cost to get creative and come up with something novel that's not registered yet. Maybe you want to use your company name, a nickname everyone knows, or a hobby.

Sometimes people use their first and last names together as the domain, making the email address *me@firstnamelastname.com*. If that's available, register it. You don't have to do it at Register.com. Lots of places register domains; it's very competitive and can cost only a few dollars if you shop around. Once you register the name, you own it. But you still have to *host* it, which means you have to find it a place to live on the Internet.

This isn't hard or expensive. At Register.com, Yahoo!, Network Solutions (*http://www.networksolutions.com/*), Namecheap (*http://www.namecheap.com/*), and a bunch of others, you can do the registering and the hosting all in one fell swoop for a couple of dollars a month. For example, at *http://www.homestead.com/*, you can follow the onscreen menus to register the name you want for your domain, host it, and get your email set up for one small monthly fee. Then you can use online tools to pick a template and build your website if you like. (If creating yourself a presence on the Web is on your to-do list, see Chapter 11.)

Lock Your Doors

Now that you are hooked up to the Internet, you are free to shop, learn, talk on the phone for free, and do lots of other fun things. You are also free to catch viruses, let in Trojan horses, and accidentally acquire spyware and malware of all kinds. Broadband comes with a lot of responsibility. You also might fall for scams that try to get you to type your social security number, bank account information, and other sensitive information into websites that are not what they claim to be.

So right after you get connected, update your computer. (If you are using Windows, go to *http://www.update.microsoft.com/*.) Then, once your computer is entirely up to date, locate the free trial on your computer for Internet security, or install a free anti-virus product like ClamAV or AVG Free. Then read Chapter 8 and Chapter 9 (if you have kids) so that you recognize the dangers to you and your family. Using anti-virus programs and being able to spot a virtual crook are costs of living in the modern world, like locking your car, not talking to strangers, practicing safe sex, and holding onto your purse in train stations. Just do it. And do it now.

Dressed for Company

For many people, email is the social draw that made them break down and get a home computer in the first place. It's hard to function in life without an email address, and it is certainly hard to stay in touch with friends or get party invitations without one. There are two ways to use email, and one of them requires that you have email software installed on your computer. The other way is to use an online email service like Gmail, Yahoo!, Hotmail, or a host of others which you access through your browser and which store nothing locally on your machine.

You don't have to acquire or install any software to use email, but you can. Outlook is part of Microsoft Office and does a lot more than allow you to access your email; it also has a calendar, an address book, and a to-do list. Because of this, many people find it overkill if all you want to do is exchange messages. For a little while, I succumbed to peer pressure and committed my contacts, calendar, and email to Outlook, despite my reservations. Fortunately, it is very easy to export files out of Outlook (and for that reason, it may be worth having around) because within six months, I turned tail and ran, too frightened to look back. Outlook's temperamental fits, like freezing up randomly, made me crave paper or even a stone tablet. In my opinion, Outlook is not one of Microsoft's best efforts, despite its horde of devotees. Outlook Express, on the other hand, comes free with Windows and isn't a bad program.

Mac users seem to like the email program that comes with Mac OS X, Mail 2. I like the open source program Mozilla Thunderbird (also available for the Mac) for its delightful junk mail filtering and ability to pull feeds from news sites and blogs right into my email.

Mastering Your Missives

Next, you will need to configure your email software. There will be directions on your ISP's website for configuring whatever email software you use, and there is no way you can set it up without checking there first. Configuration involves entering server names and settings that are specific to your ISP. If you are trying out your ISP's technical support to see if you want to stay with them, calling to have them walk you through email setup is a good test. (Also see "Try This: Set Up an Email Account" on page 112 for help understanding what all this means.)

When you are traveling or jetting about in cafés, you will probably want to use the web mail feature that comes with your email address rather than your email software.

Web mail is your best option if you want to check your email on a friend's computer or on a public machine at an Internet café. Web mail simply allows you to read your email inside a web browser, while it is still sitting on your email provider's server and not downloaded to your own computer. If you use your ISP's email, go to its website and follow the links to its web mail area. Keep in mind, however, that you will need your password to log in, so make an effort to remember it. Then, once you're back home on your own machine and you check your mail, all those messages you read on the road and left in your inbox will download as usual.

Dear Geek Goddess,

I get that I should use my web mail when I'm out and about because of some problem with my ISP's outgoing mail server, but I don't like it. I am traveling around Europe and want to write my emails when I have the chance and then log in quickly when I have access to the Internet to send and receive them. (Do you know what they charge in those Internet cafés in rural Ireland?) Isn't there a better way?

Surfing in Sligo

. . . . . .

Dear Surfing,

Well, now who's going all geek on me? But you are right about two things. Those Internet cafés in rural Ireland are too expensive, and there is another solution. It's a bit geeky but here goes: You need an SMTP (outgoing mail) server that doesn't belong to your ISP. And fortunately third-party outgoing mail servers are out there, and some are even free (though some charge and even offer extra features). If you have a Hotmail, Yahoo!, or Gmail account (they are free and easy to get if you don't), find their instructions for setting up your email as a POP account, and use the outgoing SMTP server they provide. The specifics vary by your email software and email address, but here is an example using Mozilla Thunderbird and Gmail. (To find a particular outgoing mail server, google it. Searching for hotmail outgoing smtp server should get you some specific instructions.)

In Mozilla Thunderbird, choose **Tools/Account Settings**. You will get the window shown here.

Replace that server name with the one that Gmail provides (smtp.gmail.com) and save your changes. Now you should be able to send and receive your emails from any network you connect to in Ireland, at the café in San Francisco, or at home.

Even if you always bring your adorable laptop with you when you hit the cafés for Wi-Fi, and it is already rigged to download your email, you will still want to use the web mail feature there.

Here's why. You waited in line for ten minutes for your double decaf mocha in a San Francisco café and are finally settled at a perfect corner table ready to write emails and do a little people watching. You dressed stylishly for this little outing because your laptop is cute, you are hip, and this whole Wi-Fi surfing thing is cool. But when you try to send those pressing communiqués, you get an error message: "Outgoing SMTP server not found" or something equally cryptic.

You weren't having this problem at home. (This doesn't always happen since it depends on your ISP.) So what's wrong? What's wrong is fairly simple to fix, but it requires information available only from the café's ISP. And you'll have to remember how to change the server settings in your email software. You can get back in line and ask the barista the name of the outgoing mail server and pray you remember what to do when you get it. But rather than waste time and let your coffee get cold, surf gracefully over to the web mail page for your email account. You'll be able to read and send your email without any pesky server problems, and you won't have to remember to change your server settings back when you're online at home again.

GO TO TOWN

You will need software—called a browser—to browse the Internet. Fortunately, you already have it. If you have a Windows XP PC, it comes with Internet Explorer (IE). If you don't like that one, you can download the free open source browser Firefox from *http://www.mozilla.com/*. (On your Mac, look for Safari.) Simply start your browser as you would any piece of software, and you are surfing. If you know the name of the website you want to go to, type it into the address bar at the top of the screen. If someone emails you a web address (this is called a URL, or uniform resource locator), just click it, and your browser will automatically launch and take you to the site.

Once online, most people head straight for *http://www.google.com/*, the mother of all search engines. Even if you've never gone online, you've probably heard of Google. From this one web page, you can search for anything under the sun. Try it. Type your own name. This is called *googling*. If you want to eliminate some of the irrelevant pages, put quote marks around the name you are googling. Google your kids, friends, husband, boss, ex-boyfriend. But be prepared. You might happen upon your daughter's personal blog and find out more than you wanted to know. Google will even act as your online dictionary. Just type *define:* followed by the word you want to define. Google has many fun (and free) functions and features; there are even entire books about it. Other popular search engines include MSN, Yahoo!, and AltaVista.

Beyond the search engines, everyone has her favorite website. Search for your hobbies, TV shows you like, products you are thinking about buying, or anything you have questions about or are curious about. Also read Chapter 5 on shopping to find out where my girlfriends and I like to browse when we are trawling the Internet. If you crave virtual companionship, read Chapter 11 on cybercommunities.

If you always start your Internet surfing from the same place, make that your home page. (See "Try This: Set Up a Home Page" on page 115 for how to do this.) The *home page* is simply the web page that loads automatically when you launch your browser.

The Information Feed

As you are trawling around on the Web, you may discover a particular news or magazine site, blog, or even shopping site that you'd like to remember to check back on frequently. As you acquire more of these, you will quickly realize that setting your favorites as a home page (or using the Favorites menu choice in your browser) is an awkward solution. Indeed, there is a better way: Customize the Internet for your own needs. In short, you can create a portal, or start page, to the Internet that includes all your favorite sites, tools, gizmos, and whatnot on one (or several) pages that launch automatically when you log in.

There are many ways you can set up a start page. Your computer may have come with one already set up, or maybe your ISP set one up when it first connected you to the Internet. But don't accept the out-of-the-box solution. You can set one up yourself at MSN, Yahoo!, Google, and other places and customize it to *your* needs, not your computer manufacturer's or your ISP's. Setting up a start page is free. My favorite is iGoogle, so I'll explain how to set up a start page using it as an example.

Just launch your browser and go to *http://www.igoogle.com/*. You will see a window like this:

You can click **Get Started** and browse through the many fun gadgets, news sources, and other tools Google has gathered together so that you can customize a page in a few minutes.

While setting up an email account in Microsoft Office Outlook, Mozilla Thunderbird, or whatever email program you use is not very hard, it often sends people scurrying for cover and calling tech support at their ISP. Feel free to call, but if you want to be able to do it yourself (or if the hold times are really long), I can help.

The questions each piece of software asks are essentially the same, though the menus it takes you through vary. I will demonstrate how to set up an email account in Microsoft Outlook Express, because every Windows XP computer has this program. (If you are using Windows Vista, the email software that comes with is called *Windows Mail*; the directions are the same.)

Assuming you have an email account that supports POP email (the kind you can download to email software on your computer) and you have already downloaded, installed, and have your email software open, here is how you get your email address and this software to work together:

Choose **Tools ▸ Accounts ▸ Add** and then choose **Email Account** to tell the software you want it to connect to your new email account. You will get the window shown at the right.

Type your name where I have put *Jane Doe.* Click **Next** and you will get the next window.

Type your email address where I have typed *me@janedoe.com.* Click **Next** again.

Okay, here is the part that scares everyone. You will be asked for your incoming and outgoing mail servers. This may

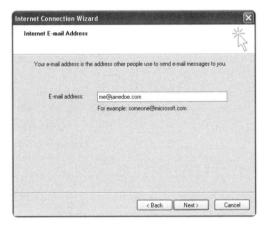

sound like geek gibberish, but don't worry. We'll find them.

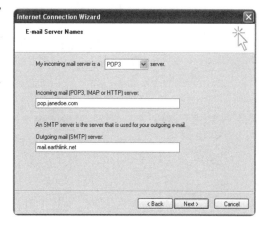

Make sure *POP3* is selected in that top choice. For the second one, you will need your incoming mail server. This is made available to you by your email provider, which might be your ISP but isn't necessarily. If you replace the part before the @ in your email address with *pop*, that usually works. So *me@janedoe.com* becomes *pop.janedoe.com*.

The outgoing mail server (SMTP) is usually provided to you by your ISP (though you can get one from some email providers). If you have no idea what yours is (and why would you?), look in the materials your ISP sent you when you signed up, or call them. You can also find the information by searching their website. If your ISP is Earthlink, go to that website and search for *outgoing mail server* (the Earthlink outgoing server was, last I checked, *mail.earthlink .net*). If this search fails, look for directions on setting up your email account. Once you have the server name, carefully type it in the text box. Click **Next** and you will get the window shown here.

Give this email account a name in that first selection. It doesn't matter what it is; no one will see it but you. Then type your password in that field and, if you feel comfortable that no one will use this computer to download and read your email, check the box asking the software to remember this password. Now, click **Next**, then click **Finish**, and you are all done.

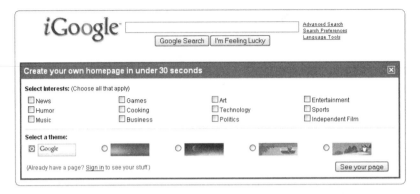

But you don't have to stop at the prepackaged choices. Click **Add Stuff** and you will get pages of fun toys that look like this:

When you are done adding stuff, click **Back to homepage** to see how it all looks. If you have set Google as your browser's home page, all of this will load

TRY THIS: *Set Up a Home Page*

If you have spent any time on the Internet, you probably have a few places you always go: a favorite news site, store, online calendar, search engine, and so on. It takes only a few minutes to change the page that automatically loads when you launch your browser to one or several of your favorites. This is called the *home page*. You can set anything as your home page: *The New York Times*, Salon, your favorite blog, CNN.

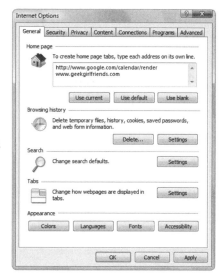

To set your favorite website as your home page in Internet Explorer (you can also do this in Mozilla Firefox), choose **Tools** and then **Internet Options**. You will get the window shown here.

Simply type the complete web address of the site or sites you want to load automatically whenever you launch your browser and click **OK**. The next time you launch your browser or click the home icon these sites will load.

automatically when you start your browser. If you really go to town on the gadgets, though, it will slow down your startup time. Creating a customized home page this way stores a small file (called a *cookie*) on your computer so that the next time you launch your browser from this computer, it is able to remember what your home page should look like.

If you'd like a personalized home page that includes all the gizmos you use, your email, calendar, a list of your favorite web pages, and anything else you like, you can create an account with Google. This way, all your settings will be associated with your login and will move smoothly from computer to computer with you. If you already have a Gmail (Google email), GoogleTalk (chat), or Google calendar account, simply log in with that. Click **Sign In** on the iGoogle page and either log in or create a new account. Not only can you add content, you can customize the whole thing with a theme that changes color with the time of day in your time zone.

There is something comforting about logging into the Internet from a café in a town on the coast of Ireland that you have never been to and finding your email, goofy theme, and calendar waiting for you, all customized to the local time.

The next thing you might want to do is subscribe to some feeds to customize the content of your home page even more. Feeds, also called *RSS (really simple syndication)* feeds, are sort of the digital equivalent to subscribing to a magazine instead of buying it at the newsstand. Instead of going looking for the news, jokes, or blogs you like, they come to you. You can have them delivered directly to the home page you just created (as well as to some email programs), or you can subscribe to a feed reader such as Rojo, NewsGator, Bloglines, or Netvibes that allows you to gather all your feeds into one place. Many people seem to get scared at the idea of RSS feeds and react as if I am trying to make them wrestle an alligator. I don't understand that. Feeds are very easy to subscribe to and make it easy to keep your finger on the pulse of whatever interests you.

When you find a website you like, look for the icon that matches the service you use. If you want to add feeds to your Google home page, look for an icon that looks like this:

If you use Yahoo!, look for the My Yahoo! icon.

If you find the right chicklet (that's what these icons are called), click it (you might have to log in) and the job is done. If you don't find the perfect little icon for your particular service, no worries. Look for this one: (this is something of a universal chicklet) or the words *RSS feed*, and click there. If you are taken to a blank web page, you might  think you have failed, but you are actually doing very well! Simply copy the URL from the address line of your browser and head back to your RSS reader. Paste that URL wherever your feed reader is asking you for a feed. There will be detailed instructions on how to do this at whatever reader you choose. In Google, click the **Add Stuff** link from your home page and look for the *Add feed or gadget* link in the iGoogle customization page, as shown at the right.

You will get this:

Paste the URL you copied from the website you are subscribing to into the address line there. Click **Add**, and you will see a message telling you that you have added the feed. Though the menus and directions may vary slightly from reader to reader, it always works essentially this way. And now you can browse headlines from all the sources you like (and add more whenever you want to) in a matter of seconds from one central source. Just imagine how clever and informed you will be.

Should Kids Drive?

If you have kids who want to use the Internet too, be careful. You will need a strategy for making sure they don't step into a mire of porn, perverts, and scams. There is no single technical solution here, just as there is no technological solution to preventing teen pregnancy or car accidents. But do keep a couple of things in mind. First, do not deny kids Internet access because you are afraid. The Internet is an amazing resource, and their future depends on becoming familiar with it. But you should not trust that your kids, even if they know more about technology than you do, can handle it alone.

People tend to leave a trail on the Internet. It isn't always the one they intend to leave (if you've ever streaked naked through a college campus and later discovered your photo online, you know what I mean), but it makes tracking down that college buddy, ex-boyfriend, or lost relative a fun game of detective. Sometimes simply typing the person's name will turn up a wealth of information. If the person's work causes them to be mentioned in publications that get published online or if they work someplace with a Web presence, you might find everything from a current location to a recent photo and work summary. Sometimes individuals have an entry on Wikipedia, so if you are looking for someone who may have a public following, check there.

If your subject writes a blog or has a website, a Web search won't always find it. Search engines such a Google, Ask.com, and Yahoo! use a complicated formula when they show a match. (There is an entire industry dedicated to search engine optimization.) So failing to turn up the site you're looking for this way doesn't mean it doesn't exist. Try also using Google's Blog Search. From the Google home page, you can click *Images* for a search of images or *Video* for a search of videos. Clicking *More* brings up additional options.

Choose **Blog Search** and type the name you are looking for. That will limit the search to blogs and turn up entirely different results than a general search.

If your Google search fails, try ZabaSearch (*http://www.zabasearch .com/*) or Zoominfo (*http://www.zoominfo.com/*), which specialize in locating people in the real world. Also check WhitePages (*http://www.whitepages .com/*), where you can search by name for a phone number and address, look for an address using only a phone number, and do lots of stuff the paper version can't do. One of these will usually turn up an address, phone number, workplace, or other helpful information, even if all you know is a name and state.

If you want more details before you pick up the phone, try searching the social networking sites. There are lots of these, but the major ones are

MySpace (*http://www.myspace.com/*), Facebook (*http://www.facebook.com/*), LinkedIn (*http://www.linkedin.com/*), Classmates (*http://www.classmates .com/*), Friendster (*http://www.friendster.com/*), and Twitter (*http://www .twitter.com/*). Each will have a search tool to allow you to search members by name, though you may have to register to send a message. PeekYou (*http:// www.peekyou.com/*) and Spock (*http://www.spock.com/*) search for people with a Web presence and gather their blog, MySpace, LinkedIn, and other social network pages, as well as anything else they post online about themselves into a neat package you can browse for a snapshot view of your subject's online life. This way, you might easily find a recent photo, life summary, daily journal, list of friends, and more personal details than you ever wanted to know.

If you are doing some checking on a potential tenant, employee, or spouse or trying to track down someone who wronged you or owes you money, you might want to dig a little deeper and spend a little cash. "If someone owes you money, you have a lot more leeway when it comes to the documents you can access on them," Ryon Gambill, president of Marauder Corporation, a collection agency, and publisher of the software program Bill Collector in a Box (*http://www.billcollectorinabox.com/*). "The kind of people I look for don't have a MySpace page," he says. Gambill starts with a credit report, which offers a lot of information. However, you probably can't get one unless the person owes you money. In that case, Gambill suggest starting at Ancestor Hunt (*http://www.ancestorhunt.com/*), where you can find out if the person is in prison, dead, and a host of other things. Or try Pacer (*http://pacer.psc.uscourts.gov/*), which has court records for many states so you will be able to find criminal proceedings and suits and other interesting stuff. Gambill also suggests checking to see if your person owns property by running a search at NETRonline (*http://www.netronline.com/*), where you can search for deeds, vital records, and tax data. If you don't mind spending some money to find this person, try Intelius (*http://www.intelius.com/*), which can turn up a complete address history, criminal and civil suits against the person, phone numbers, and much more. Though these searches can set you back as much as $50, there are times when that is worth it. "My husband and I used Intelius's FCRA background checks as part of our nanny-hiring process when we returned to work after our daughter's birth," explains Joni. "We felt secure knowing that we were using all the information available to make one of our first decisions about the safety of our new addition to the family."

You know more about the world than they do, and the Internet is a virtual world, huge and populated by millions of strangers. You are the parent, and parenting is what they need here. Your strategy for keeping them safe online should depend on a lot of factors, just as your strategy for letting them go to the mall alone does. First, you should know what they are doing. And second, they should know some basic safety rules. That they never give out personal information is foremost. But they are kids and they forget and fall for persuasive arguments, so always revert to the first rule. If your kids are under 10, start them at *http://www.yahooligans.com/*, which is a search engine that won't show sites inappropriate for children. It might be too restrictive for a teen who legitimately needs to access some areas that this site blocks. There is more on this in Chapter 9.

Big City Streets

The Internet is a big place, and no one can tell you everything there is to know about it. But my girlfriends and I suggest you enjoy yourself. Click things. Don't worry too much. Just be careful and aware, as you would in a city, and stay out of the bad parts of town. Go shopping. Explore. Go to museums. (I like the webcams at the Monterey Bay Aquarium, *http://www.montereybayaquarium.com/*.)

You'll run into all kinds of people online. Most of them are nice, interesting, out enjoying the world just like you are. But some of them are running a scam, peddling porn, or are out to steal your virtual wallet. You probably know how much of a target you are. If you can handle going into a public space, you can handle this. As long as you remember that, though you may be wearing pajamas on the couch, you are also out in public. Be careful, keep an eye on your wallet, never go anywhere with anyone you don't know, learn from your mistakes, and have a good time. Remember that anything you say online may be recorded for your children to read. So be nice! But just as when you are in New York, if you find yourself in a great store with shoes to die for, in the words of Betty Rubble and Wilma Flintstone, "Charge it!"

5

where the stores never close

I recall fondly those days of idle youth when shopping was an activity I enjoyed with my girlfriends. Annette (a firefighter and an artist) and I liked to make an event out of it. We'd meet for a cup of coffee and a pastry, catch up on the latest date or boyfriend problem, and plan our attack on the closest shopping district. There were never practical concerns in these outings. We called it foraging. We liked small boutiques and places with personality. Often, we never bought a thing. These were social outings, and the acquisition of goods was icing on the cake.

I suspect women have been bonding this way in the marketplace for eons. But for my girlfriends and me, and perhaps for our entire culture, things have changed: a few weddings, a handful of divorces, children, careers with serious time demands, long-distance relocations. Time is in short supply and foraging is time consuming. We rarely do it. I miss those outings, and Internet shopping is no replacement for them. But while Internet shopping isn't conducive to girl talk or people watching, it is—from the acquisition-of-goods angle—an improvement on the old way.

For one thing, you don't have to leave the house, which means you can shop for spices from the kitchen (*http://www.spicehouse.com/*), buy used books while looking at what's already on your bookshelves (*http://www.powells.com/*), or toss through your Imelda-like shoe collection to make sure you don't already have that pair of black pumps before you click "buy" (*http://www.zappos.com/*). You can even have things you use regularly, such as coffee, prescriptions, and cosmetics, delivered to your door automatically. This is not only convenient but can even offer an education in a new cuisine. Maybe you can turn your husband's penchant for greasy diners into a culinary hobby by signing him up for The Bacon of the Month Club (*http://www.gratefulpalate.com/*).

The point I'm making is that you are no longer limited to the services that are available locally, and if you know where to look, the bargains are outstanding. The Internet makes ducking out for retail therapy something you can do in tiny increments. Check out the sale at Old Navy (*http://www.oldnavy.com/*) while doing the laundry; browse the furniture at Target (*http://www.target.com/*) while helping the kids with homework; buy a new purse from eBags (*http://www.ebags.com/*) while cleaning out your closet; replenish your sock and underwear drawers without enduring the mall at Bare Necessities (*http://www.barenecessities.com/*), HerRoom (*http://www.herroom.com/*), or Sock Dreams (*http://www.sockdreams.com/*); or explore the workout wear at Athleta (*http://www.athleta.com/*) or Title Nine (*http://www.titlenine.com/*) while doing crunches. I have solved my husband's inability to buy me jewelry by collecting handmade and vintage stuff that I like in my Favorites section at Etsy (*http://www.etsy.com/*), the online marketplace for all things handmade, and giving him my login information. And I have gotten through many a dull work assignment with small doses of The Sundance Catalog (*http://www.sundancecatalog.com/*), J. Jill (*http://www.jjill.com/*), and UncommonGoods (*http://www.uncommongoods.com/*) to keep me at my desk. "One more draft and I'll check out the online sale at Gap," I tell myself. And somehow I get through it, though sometimes with a new garment on its way.

But just as often, I don't buy anything. "A lot of times," agrees Karen Henke, a grant writer, "I fill up my cart but leave without buying anything." That's common enough that Internet merchants have a name for it: *cart abandonment*. They think there is something they can do to minimize it, but I think that only shows how little they know about women. We don't abandon carts because the checkout is cumbersome—though it often is. We have been shopping like this since we carried straw baskets and rode on donkeys. We are foraging. We pick things up, carry them, think about them, and often decide we don't need them or can get a better price elsewhere. This is so easy to do online that I often use it as a tool for keeping spending in check. I drop things in shopping carts all over the Internet until I find the best price or decide there is not a price that appeals to me.

But, according to April Lane Benson, author of *I Shop, Therefore I Am: Compulsive Buying and the Search for Self* (Jason Aronson Publishers, 2000), this convenience also makes Internet shopping a serious danger for the six percent of women for whom shopping is a compulsion. "Some people don't go to stores because they are reclusive or depressed," she explains. "But Internet shopping fills some need—boredom or loneliness—and the mouse-click is even more removed from spending than the swipe of a credit card at the checkout." This can add up to a serious hazard for compulsive shoppers, so if this is you, skip this chapter.

At the very least, April recommends you ask yourself the following six questions before you buy anything:

* Where am I?
* How do I feel?
* Do I need this?
* What if I wait?
* How will I pay?
* Where will it fit?

Also, there are some dangers to shopping on the Internet. They range from scams to illegitimate websites designed to capture credit card information to legitimate-seeming sites that sell you something small and then tack on a charge to your credit card every month hoping you won't notice. I love to shop online, and I've been doing it for years with no ill effects, but my husband never tires of lecturing me on the dangers. His concern for me is sort of cute, but to keep him quiet for a few minutes, I asked him to write down his lecture for you. Check out "How Safe Is That Website?" on page 142 to get a dose of the sort of lecture I deal with daily.

CLOTHING AND ACCESSORIES

Women often tell me they don't like Internet shopping because they can't try things on. My girlfriends and I could not disagree more. "I love shopping for clothes online," says Annette. "You get to see how the outfit looks on a body. Okay, granted, it's always an emaciated unrealistic model's body, but I can usually extrapolate and tell what it'll look like on my overweight, aging body."

Some merchants use technology to help you extrapolate. "I like the virtual tools," says Melissa. "What's the first thing you do with a pair of shoes in the shoe store? You pick it up turn it over and look at it from all sides. And Zappos has this great online tool that does exactly that with the shoes virtually."

Melissa also likes the My Virtual Model tool at Lands' End (*http://www .landsend.com/*). "You can personalize the image with your body dimensions to be able to see what the clothes will look like—or at least get a much closer approximation than those ultra-thin catalog models who look fabulous in everything," she explains. Enter your actual measurements and My Virtual Model shows you a computer drawing of someone who matches them. Then you can choose clothes and see how they look on her and which size fits her best.

I find that shopping for clothes on the Internet requires a Zen-like acceptance of the return process. (Read "Easy Returns" on page 138 to help with this.) I think returning items through the mail is easier than driving to the mall, but it does take a little getting used to. Once you accept the inevitable return, you will find yourself willing to buy in two possible sizes or explore styles the way you do when you take the time to go to a department store. My daughter is moody and contrary in shoe stores, for example. So, when she needs shoes, I order a selection of items she might like, sometimes in two sizes each, from the massive online shoe store Zappos. Then I set up a pretend shoe store in the dining room. That way her choices are limited to the things I think are school-appropriate, and she can try them on when she is in the mood instead of when I have time to haul her to the store.

Once she makes her choice, I put the rejects back in the box, slap on a return label and leave it for the mailman to pick up. "I love Zappos," agrees Annette. "Free shipping both ways, what's not to like?"

The pretend in-home store works just as well for me too. I like to try things on in my own bedroom, with the right pair of shoes and jewelry, before I decide if they are keepers. Sometimes, especially with dress-up items or lingerie, I like to have a glass of wine and get a second opinion from someone I trust. Items that fail these tests go back. I sometimes lose money on the shipping charges—sometimes both ways, sometimes only one way—for a fashion that looked great on that skinny model but will never work on me. But driving to the mall, parking, using up my precious time, and having a cup of coffee while I'm there isn't free either. I think Internet shopping is cheaper, even with the shipping charges, because it eliminates the impulse purchases, like the earrings I didn't need and the skirt that was too cheap to resist but will still have the tags on it in two years.

But one of the best things (and most dangerous, according to April) about online shopping is being able to shop the sales at your favorite merchants without actually going to the store. Merchants are more than willing to send emails to let you know when things go on sale. "I love Anthropologie stores," explains Annette. "The clothes are way overpriced, but they are cute and they fit. And if you go to their online sales (*http://www.anthropologie.com/*), things are only somewhat overpriced." Just go to the website of a merchant you like and sign up for email sale alerts.

Don't limit yourself to the stuff my girlfriends and I like, though. The world of Internet shopping is as vast as the world itself. If there is something in particular you want, it is out there. For example, I was recently in the market for a very specific garment: a hat that was stylish, warm, and waterproof for a trip to Ireland. I did a Google search for *hat waterproof stylish* and quickly landed on the site of San Francisco Hat Company (*http://www.sfhat.com/*), where I found the perfect black velvet crusher hat lined with Gortex. I bought it, and it arrived five days later. I spent a grand total of 15 minutes on this, most of it while talking on the phone.

DESIGNER GOODS

Annette loves clothing, shoes, and purses created in small quantities by interesting boutique designers, but she has neither the money for such things nor the time to hang around tiny boutiques shopping for them. Still, she manages to wear the styles she likes by shopping online. Her favorite bargain stop is the massive auction site eBay (*http://www.ebay.com/*). The idea behind eBay is that you look for the item you want, place a bid on it, and hope the bidding doesn't go out of your reach but instead nets you the item you want for a fraction of its value, just like in a real auction. But of course, like anything good, crooks and scam artists use this site too. (See "Watch Your Back on eBay and craigslist" on page 140.) It's also easy to get so caught up in the action that you end up paying too much.

Still, if you are careful and you can control yourself, eBay is a lot of fun. There is no shopping experience quite as exhilarating as bidding on something, watching the time run out on the auction, and winning a terrific deal on something you need and could never have otherwise located. Next to this, putting something in a shopping cart is downright lackluster. And if you really get hooked, there is nothing stopping you from getting on the selling end of the auction. I regularly turn the junk around my house into cash. It's much easier than a yard sale, I make more money, and my mailman does all the hauling away.

Annette's eBay conquests are legendary. "My husband Seth saw a pair of Mecca shoes in London that he loved, but they were $180," she says of one particularly successful auction. He tried them on in the store, and Annette made a note of his size and the style of the shoe. Back home, she entered the details of the shoe into eBay's search engine so that it alerted her any time a pair was listed.

***

Dear Geek Goddess,

I love shopping on eBay, but I recently got carried away and—not to be outdone—paid a lot more for a purse than I could really afford. Is there a way to set a maximum amount before I get too caught up in the action to stop myself?

Competitive in Chattanooga

· · · · · · ·

Dear Competitive,

Yes, excitement is a real hazard on eBay, which is great if you are selling stuff but not so good if you are blowing all your mad money on something you don't need just because you don't like to lose. It is easy to get so excited by the thrill of the bid that you keep upping your maximum until that great deal isn't so great. So I suggest that you do your research, know what the item is worth, how likely there is to be another just like it, decide how much you want to pay for it, and walk away. You can use the automatic bidding process (or proxy bidding) for this. When you bid for an item in an auction, you enter the maximum amount you are willing to pay. eBay automatically bids for you in small increments to beat other bidders but will not exceed your max. Don't look again until the bidding is over.

It took a little patience, but ultimately she got Seth his shoes for $1.99 plus $7.00 in shipping. Annette herself had long coveted an An Ren coat, but at $200 to $400, the designer's styles were out of reach. On eBay though, she managed to buy two of them for less than she would have paid for a jacket at the Gap. Her list goes on: "Olivia Rose Tal (*http://www.oliviarosetal*

.com/) shoes are so sweet, but they retail for $185 or more—mine cost $35; Fluevog (*http://www.fluevog.com/*) shoes retail for $160—mine cost $55."

Of course, you can also find big-name designers online if your tastes run more to Prada and Gucci, but here you have to be careful. When the price on designer goods is too good to be true, it's usually because it's counterfeit. "I love to buy purses on eBay," agrees Sara Gates, a technology consultant and former vice president of identity management at Sun Microsystems. "I won't buy designer goods because they are usually fakes. But I have gotten some great vintage stuff at terrific prices." Annette avoids counterfeits by avoiding big-name designers in favor of obscure boutique designs.

But counterfeiting high-end labels is big business, and any time you find famous labels selling outside the designer-authorized retail channels, it is safe to assume you will not receive a Kate Spade purse but a cheap knock-off of one. This is not limited only to eBay. Do a Google search on a designer you like, and it will very likely turn up sites that specialize in knock-offs. Sometimes you can easily tell that's what the site is selling; for example, if the site's address is *http://www.anyknockoff.com/*.

But sometimes you can tell only from the price or, when the goods arrive, from the sub-par workmanship, lack of label, or misspelled label. If you find the Kate Spade purse you want for a price you can afford on eBay, contact the seller before you bid. Maybe you have discovered a clothes horse cleaning out her closet. Check her seller rating for reports of counterfeits, and make sure she isn't selling 1,500 of the same purse (a sure sign she didn't originally buy it for herself). You can find deals on designer goods elsewhere online, though the prices are rarely as rock-bottom as the fake stuff. If there are particular designers you

The fine print at this site states clearly that the designer bags are merely "inspired" by the designer. Not all knock off sites are so scrupulous.

like, google their names to see if they offer bargains on their websites, check to see if there is a sale at a department store such as Saks Fifth Avenue (*http://www .saksfifthavenue.com/*) or Nieman Marcus (*http://www.neimanmarcus.com/*), go to the online designer discount store Bluefly (*http://www.bluefly.com/*), or check the deals at Overstock.com (*http://www.overstock.com/*). Sometimes items that are simply unusual, though not made by a big-name designer, are also found on eBay. "When my Italian friends came to visit," Annette says, "their teenage daughter Francesca saw a California license plate purse she desperately wanted in a shop in Monterey. But it was $150, so she couldn't have it." Annette, in the habit of trawling eBay, wondered if she could do better. "Sure enough, I got one like it on eBay for $17. It was a little worn," says Annette. "But the design is nicer." Francesca was thrilled.

Shopping the Internet doesn't mean you have to buy from a big retailer or a yard sale, though. The smallest specialty merchant or designer can go global by opening an Internet shop. So it's possible for you to buy directly from the little shop you saw on your recent vacation, from that hip boutique you heard about in New York City, or from a specialty merchant you've never heard of in Tokyo simply by prowling the Internet. Just google the store, brand, or type of item and see what you find. Maybe you will find yourself a regular customer of a store you have never set foot inside.

Dressing your cell phone in cute accessories may still be a trend with limited appeal in the United States, but in Asia, it's big. By shopping the Internet, you can join in without suffering jet lag.

ELECTRONICS

When it comes to buying electronics, I don't know how I would manage without the Internet. Recently, I was in the market for a camcorder. Since I wanted it for a vacation that was already breaking the bank, I was on a tight budget. I had a few criteria: The camera had to be small enough to drop in my purse, easy to use, and able to produce high quality footage I could edit later.

I started at the online home electronics retailer Crutchfield (*http://www.crutchfield.com/*) because the expert reviews there provide an excellent education in features and products. The site sells stereo, home theater, camera, car audio equipment, and other electronics. The people here really know their stuff and publish reviews and buyer's guides. While there, I noted the price, including shipping, of the cameras they recommended that had the features I wanted. (A spreadsheet is a good tool for keeping track of this sort of information.)

Next, I went to Amazon.com (*http://www.amazon.com/*) to note the prices and read the customer reviews. A lot of smaller merchants sell through Amazon.com so it is a great way to get the lay of the land in terms of what sort of discounting pricing is available. Just remember that people can have lots of reasons for writing reviews; not all of them will be objective.

By now I had honed in on the model I wanted and was on a quest for the best price. I shopped at some smaller camera stores online, such as Ritz Camera (*http://www.ritzcamera.com/*). I also shopped at the websites for merchants like Target (*http://www.target.com/*) and Best Buy (*http://www.bestbuy.com/*) to see what they had in stock and their current prices. I also did a quick search of the shopping search engines—BizRate.com, Yahoo! Shopping, PriceGrabber.com, Slickdeals.net, and NexTag.com—to make sure I wasn't overlooking someplace reputable with great bargains. (Not everyone listed on these sites is necessarily reputable, so I do check up on anyone new to me that I find here.) I also checked Overstock.com to make sure they weren't selling my camera for less. (You can find great bargains at this site on everything from socks to diamonds to computers—but not usually on cutting-edge electronics; still, it's always worth a look.)

I did take a drive to some local retailers to put my hands on the camera I'd chosen to be sure I liked it. I spent about two hours on this project in total (not including the time I spent convincing my husband that we needed this camera in the first place). I ended up buying the exact camera I wanted for $275 at Amazon.com with free shipping. The same camera was nearly $400 at a local electronics store and "on sale" for $350 at Target. I follow this shopping strategy whenever I buy small electronics, stereo equipment, or home entertainment goods that have a price tag big enough to warrant the time required.

FOR THE HOME

It might seem as if you are limited to your local merchants when it comes to buying large items for the home simply because of shipping costs. But the Internet can be a real money saver in this department too. I have bought everything online, from bedding (*http://www.companystore.com/*) to leather couches (*http:// www.samsclub.com/*) to blinds (*http://www.target.com/*) to bar stools (*http://www .overstock.com/*). Of course, you can shop online sales at Pottery Barn (*http://www .potterybarn.com/*), Ikea (*http://www.ikea.com/*), Design Within Reach (*http://www .dwr.com/*), West Elm (*http://www.westelm.com/*), and other mail-order furniture stores. But the Internet can also help you locate items that are geographically close to you but hard to find.

For example, sometimes a local seller has a Web presence that can not only make it possible for you to locate an item with a minimum of trouble, but also save you from driving for hours to poke through inventory. "We found salvaged hardwood random plank flooring for less than $1 a square foot because a salvage place (*http://www.driftwoodsalvage.com/*) posts its inventory online," says Annette. She found the place through a Google search. The seller itself was about an hour's drive for her and required she pick the goods up with her own truck, but since she knew they had exactly what she wanted at a price she liked before she set off, it was worth the effort.

Sometimes, though, the thing you seek is right down the street going to waste in someone else's house, and its owner is willing to let it go cheap—if you only knew about it. The Internet excels at locating this otherwise difficult-to-find item. The online version of your local paper's classified section is always worth a look, but craigslist (*http://www.craigslist.org/*) is even better. Craigslist is a vast classified ad site for the world. (The listings are organized by region.) "I buy so much stuff through craigslist," says Annette. "It's also a great way to locate weekend yard sales nearby."

Like anyplace on the Internet where you deal with individuals (as opposed to merchants such as Home Depot or Sears), you have to beware of scams. Craigslist has become one of the most popular places on the Internet because of the deals to be had, and you can often find someone nearby selling or renting just what you need. (This is a great way to find an apartment or vacation rental too.) "I bought my gorgeous O'Keefe & Merritt 1953 chrome-top stove on craigslist for $250," says Annette. "The sellers loved it, but they measured wrong when they remodeled their kitchen and it wouldn't fit. Their loss, my gain. I also bought our fire-clay kitchen sink there for $500 less than retail because another poor guy had measured wrong."

It's also possible that someone may consider the item you are looking for junk and be willing let you have it for free just to keep it from going in the landfill. Check out The Freecycle Network (*http://www.freecycle.org/*) to see if there is a network in your area.

Sometimes you can find a difficult-to-find item or one you simply can't get locally by going straight to the maker. When I remodeled my kitchen, I bought a Whitehaus faucet I loved without realizing that it was a fragile princess that no plumber in my area would carry parts for. So instead of throwing it away when it broke down (twice in five years) and every plumber in town had taken one look at it and said, "Nope, can't help you," I went to the manufacturer's website (*http://www.whitehauscollection.com/*) and ordered replacement parts myself.

Sometimes the things you seek from the manufacturer are not so much the goods themselves as the tools for choosing the goods. "I love the Behr ColorSmart system (*http://www.behr.com/*) for the Behr paints available at Home Depot," says Melissa. "It lets you test paint colors in a room setting in just a few clicks. It is much easier than buying seven sample quarts only to find out that none of them look right together."

You can buy everything from flatware (*http://www.surlatable.com/*) to a self-contained home office (*http://www.cedarsheds.com/*) to a greenhouse (*http://www.charliesgreenhouses.com/*) if you are willing to spend a little time and energy tracking them down online. I vastly prefer wandering around websites to driving in traffic, and I frequently shop around online when I need something specific to make sure a retailer carries what I'm looking for before I get in my car. It can often help me decide which part of town I'm headed to and eliminates fruitless stops.

AUTOMATIC DELIVERY

When I was considering moving away from the San Francisco Bay Area, the first thing I did was make sure I wouldn't have to give up the coffee that made—and still makes, thanks to the wonders of the Internet—each day possible. My favorite brand, Peet's Coffee, has a limited regional reach in terms of physical locations, but it does have a website (*http://www.peets.com/*).

And the company offers automatic delivery through the site. Getting my caffeine fix in my new home is actually easier than it was in the Bay Area because all I have to do is open that heady-scented box when it arrives. This type of auto-refill service is handy for prescriptions and other personal items that get easily lost or used up, such as lotions and vitamins (*http://www.drugstore.com/*), contact lenses (*http://www.lens.com/, http://www.1800contacts.com/, http://www.visiondirect.com/*, and others), reading glasses (*http://www.readingglasses.com/*), and prescription eyeglasses (*http://www.eyeglassestogo.com/*, among others).

If you have a favorite cosmetic brand, it is likely to have a website that makes replenishing that must-have red lipstick either automatic or a matter of a few clicks. MAC Cosmetics (*http://www.maccosmetics.com/*) sells online and offers makeup tips from the pros. Origins (*http://www.origins.com/*) frequently offers online-only deals and invitations to in-store spa days. Or try the beauty super-stores Sephora (*http://www.sephora.com/*), Beauty.com (*http://www.beauty.com/*), or ULTA (*http://www.ulta.com/*).

Many of these items are difficult to choose online, so the Internet is handy only for refills or staying informed of product announcements and sales. "I'd be in total shopping heaven if someone invented a scratch-and-sniff monitor," says Melissa. "You just can't buy scented lotions, candles, and that sort of thing without going to the retail store to smell them first. Can you imagine trusting someone's marketing description for something like perfume? Of course, once you know that you love Origins Orange and Cardamom hand lotion, reorders are much easier online."

Before I discovered the automatic delivery options for stamps at the US Postal Service (*http://www.usps.com/*), I was forever finding myself out of stamps when I wanted to send a birthday card or mail a check. I also go online to restock checks (*http://www.checksinthemail.com/*), business cards, and personalized stationery. I have been getting business cards printed at iPrint (*http://www.iprint .com/*) for years. Not only does it save time and make reorders a matter of a few mouse clicks, but I get to design them myself. More recently I've become enamored with the adorable personal cards at MOO (*http://www.moo.com/*).

Automatic delivery is also a great way to let an expert guide you through a product category you want to explore such as wine, cheese, or gardening. Sign up for one of the wine clubs at Wine.com (*http://www.wine.com/*) and take your palate on a world tour. Sign up for one of the cheese programs at Dean and Deluca (*http://www.deananddeluca.com/*) and enjoy an expert-chosen, home-delivered cheese experience. Go to the plant experts at White Flower Farm (*http://www .whiteflowerfarm.com/*) and have a different houseplant mailed to you each month, or simply browse for bulbs or plants and have them shipped to you, with instructions, when it's the right time to plant them. Or have your movies delivered automatically from a wish list you set up at Blockbuster (*http://www.blockbuster .com/*) GreenCine (*http://www.greencine.com/*), or Netflix (*http://www.netflix.com/*). Netflix carries everything you'd ever want to see, including complete seasons of your favorite TV shows, classics, and hard-to-find films. If you have a gaming maniac in the house, maybe a subscription to GameFly (*http://www.gamefly.com/*) will keep him happy without breaking into his college fund.

CARS AND AUTOMOTIVE

The Internet has completely transformed the way people buy cars. There was a time when negotiating a price on a new car meant looking at the sticker price and trying to talk the salesman down a few hundred dollars. Then websites such as Edmunds (*http://www.edmunds.com/*), which provides a bounty of information on new and used cars, started publishing invoice prices (the price the dealer pays for the car). Customers learned how grossly inflated the sticker price was and the jig, briefly, was up.

Of course, the invoice price is no longer as important as it once was because car dealers are a slippery lot. But that's why you *must* go online before you shop for a car. It is a simple matter of finding the lowest price people are paying in your area for the same car you want before you head to the dealer to haggle. In fact, you can even complete the order online in many cases. Check out CarsDirect (*http://www.carsdirect.com/*) or the website of the car manufacturer. It's always a good idea to drop by Consumer Reports (*http://www.consumerreports.org/*) and check out the reviews before you make a major purchase like this. You can get access to all the online reviews by signing up for one month of an online membership for $5.95.

If you are shopping for a used car, don't forget about that old standby, the classified ad, and its digital equivalent. "I found my 2002 Mini Cooper by placing a 'wanted' ad in the for sale/car section on craigslist," says Annette. "I got a call two days later, and got a screaming deal on the exact car I wanted!"

But don't limit your automotive shopping to the car itself. I dread shopping in auto parts stores, typically a bastion of condescending men sporting an early-this-century chauvinism and a brain size inversely proportional to that of their beer belly. Even my husband hates auto parts stores for this reason. I recently lost the gas cap on my Honda and endured two of them, neither of which had the part, before a light bulb went off over my head and I went home to my Internet connection. Five minutes and one Google search for *auto parts* later, I found the part at Auto Parts Warehouse (*http://www.autopartswarehouse.com/*) for less than half the price my mechanic had quoted. It arrived two days later.

REAL ESTATE

When it comes to buying and selling real estate, you can rely on the Internet for information. It was consumers who forced this industry online with our persistent habit of logging on to shop home prices and mortgage rates. My friend Jennifer, a realtor, would be the first to admit that she would remain a Luddite to

this day if it weren't for the fact that she would never sell a house if she didn't have a presence online. As it is, you can log on to quickly check the cost of housing in an area you are considering, glance at pictures, and take a video walk-through of a dozen houses before you ever get in your car to look at homes. Check out Realtor.com (*http://www.realtor.com/*), Zillow (*http://www.zillow.com/*), HomeGain (*http://www.homegain.com/*), or the websites of local real estate agencies. This can save hours or even days of driving around looking at neighborhoods or houses that are not what you seek. You can also get a quick idea about considering a city or neighborhood in your plans.

Once you have narrowed your search to a particular area, you can quickly go beyond house prices to discover other factors that might be important to your choice. Find information on school districts (*http://www.greatschools.com/*), get neighborhood data (*http://www.neighborhoodscout.com/*), and other pertinent deals. And before you call a realtor, find out if you can afford your dreams by shopping for mortgage rates (*http://www.eloan.com/*), calculating what a particular mortgage will cost you before you get your hopes too high on a property that's out of reach, and even get a preapproval letter from a lender that will allow you to go right up to the "making an offer" stage of the process.

If you seek to rent rather than buy, the Internet can help you here too. Try Rent.com (*http://www.rent.com/*) or For Rent (*http://www.forrent.com/*). But don't forget about craigslist. I recently discovered that I could do a better job at renting a condo I own than the realtor I'd hired, who had been working in the business for over a decade. I simply posted my property on Look And Rent (*http://www.lookandrent.com/*), a local site dedicated to rentals, and craigslist. I fired my realtor and now pocket her commission each month because she failed to go digital.

BOOKS

Everyone knows about the massive online retailer Amazon.com, which started out selling books and now sells just about everything. But I also like to shop at Powell's Books (*http://www.powells.com/*) because it sells used books right alongside the new ones and offers some of the best book reviews around.

Of course, there is also Barnes and Noble (*http://www.bn.com/*) if you like superstores. If the book you seek is not only used but rare, try Alibris (*http://www.alibris.com/*). It specializes in the rare and hard-to-find book. I highly recommend also finding the website for your local library, because it very likely has an online catalog. I once found it too much trouble to scour the library for a particular book only to find it unavailable, my time wasted, and faced with purchasing the book after all that. But the Internet has changed that spendthrift attitude by making it so easy for me to check the library's online catalog and put a hold on or request the book I'm after. It takes very little time and saves me a fortune.

You can also download books immediately from Amazon.com, eBooks (*http://www.ebooks.com/*), and many other sites if you are willing to read them on your computer or another device (check out the Sony Reader or the Amazon Kindle for a more pleasant reading experience; more on this in the Chapter 10). Though you don't save nearly as much money by doing this as you'd think, it does make it possible to travel with dozens of books rather than only the one that will fit in your luggage.

easy returns

I recently ran into a friend in the UPS store. She was struggling through the door with several shopping bags, an armload of big boxes, and her address book. I held the door for her . . . and held my tongue. Watching her struggle with the packaging, the awkward assistance she was getting from the guy in the store, and the stress this was all causing her made me want to offer her a tutorial in Internet shipping, but I sensed this was not the time. So I merely waved at her as I dropped off my neatly packaged and labeled box and went out for coffee. I ship something somewhere almost daily, and I rarely leave the house to do it. On this occasion, I had a box with a prepaid shipping label under my arm because it was a nice day and I was looking for an excuse to get out.

It doesn't matter which shipper you prefer; a computer with an Internet connection, a printer, and a credit card are all you need to get those packages to their destination with minimum effort. The first step is to open an online account with your favorite shipper—or all available shippers if you want to be sure you always pay the least and get the best service for your shipping priorities. Go to UPS (*http://www.ups.com/*), the US Post Office (*http://www.usps.com/*), DHL (*http://www.dhl.com/*), or FedEx (*http://www .fedex.com/*), and sign up by typing a few details.

If you want to ship parcel post or media mail through the USPS, you might want to consider a Stamps.com account (*http://www.stamps.com/*), which is the only one of these shipping sites that has a monthly fee. Each shipper will ask you for a credit card number, but it won't charge you until you ship. Once you set up your accounts, order a few supplies. (These are usually free.) At the very least you will want some airbill envelopes (those clear plastic envelopes with sticky backs you can stick to boxes or envelopes) or some labels. I like the shipping labels, but it's up to you and your printer as to which you prefer. Using the airbill means you can use standard printer paper for labels.

Once your supplies arrive, you are ready to ship. First, choose the shipper that meets your needs and offers the best prices for that particular package, destination, and speed of delivery. You can go to each site and get an estimate or ask RedRoller (*http://www.redroller.com/*) or iShip (*http://www.iship.com/*) to give estimates for a few shippers at once. Once you have chosen the right shipper, enter the address you want to send it to, the weight of the package (you can guess, but the cost estimates are only as accurate as your weight estimate), and its dimensions.

Now seal up your package. (I save the packing materials that come with things I order, but shredded newspaper and air-popped popcorn make nice light packing material too.) Print out your label, slap it on the box, and use the shipper's website to schedule a pickup. (Or if you prefer, bring it to a nearby drop box.)

The process is basically the same at all the shippers, though the costs, the color of the couriers' uniforms, the prices, and speed of delivery vary by package.

THE PRIVACY OF YOUR OWN STORE

Online shopping is not only efficient, it is private. And there are times when private shopping is nice. I'm too old to be squeamish about buying personal items such as feminine hygiene products, pregnancy tests, or condoms at the drugstore, but for those who are embarrassed by this, the Internet provides an easy solution. Visit sites like Drugstore.com or CVS (*http://www.cvs.com/*). Just be careful of online pharmacies that sell without a prescription (there is a lot of fraud and counterfeiting on the Internet when it comes to pharmaceuticals). Despite my blasé attitude toward most personal items, there are goods I'd prefer to peruse in private. My girlfriends all agree (in a just-don't-use-my-name sort of way).

We are all women here, but I'll use a euphemism anyway. Let's face it, shopping for "intimate tools" is, in most cities, somewhat out of the question, especially if you have children in tow. If you live in San Francisco, New York, or Los Angeles, you might feel comfortable in the Good Vibrations or Babeland stores, but in most places this sort of store is likely in a nasty setting near a freeway or adjacent to a strip joint. And if its geography doesn't put you off the idea, the guy behind the counter will. (Not that I know for sure, of course.) I am certain this is why this type of item has become a popular gift at showers. That way we can always claim we didn't actually want the item ourselves; we were just buying a joke gift.

"I bought a gift for someone at Goodvibes.com once," says Karen. "But only because I didn't have time to go to the store." Exactly. Who has time? Melissa says, "I have never shopped there myself, but I hear that Babeland.com is worth a visit." I don't personally shop at any of these sites either, but in researching this book I did notice that some of the . . . er . . . toys have cute names, like Tex, Woody, and Randy. I wouldn't have been relaxed enough to chuckle over this sort of detail in a retail environment.

WATCH YOUR BACK ON EBAY AND CRAIGSLIST

Whenever you buy from or sell to anonymous individuals, you open yourself up to the risk of dealing with a bad hat. That doesn't mean you will necessarily get robbed. I buy and sell goods on eBay and craigslist all the time and so does just about everyone I know, but none of us have had a terrible experience. "Well, I bought some rugs once that weren't quite what I expected," confesses Annette. "The ad said they were wool, but they are synthetic. I kept them, though, because shipping them back would have been expensive, and they are actually pretty cute. In fact, I'm pretty happy with them."

Our joint experience does not match that of the general population though. According to the Internet Crime Complaint Center (*http://www.ic3.gov/*), Internet auction fraud was by far the most reported offense in 2006, comprising 44.9 percent of referred crime complaints. And a July 2007 *Consumer Reports* report found that "half of eBay buyers surveyed by the Consumer Reports National Research Center said they'd encountered deceptions. Some sellers took their money and ran, failed to disclose key details about merchandise, or overstated its condition." The reason my friends and I get away with shopping at these online flea markets without getting fleeced goes beyond luck. We are careful. We all follow some ground rules, and we went to school on how to spot a scam before it hits us. Do the same, and you'll likely be fine.

Here is a plan for coming out ahead.

Watch your wallet.

Never, ever, wire money to anyone you met online, be it at an auction site, through an email, on craigslist, or anywhere else. You will never see it, or the goods, again. Don't make exceptions. Always use the eBay-approved transaction methods, such as PayPal, or the eBay-approved escrow services. There are a lot of scams involving shady escrow services. Or the seller might send you an email after an auction has closed offering a deal if you transact outside of eBay. Don't. If you are selling, don't take checks or money orders. You are safest with PayPal, using an approved escrow service, or accepting a credit card.

Know as much as possible about the seller.

On eBay, check the seller's feedback. Read the comments and look for a rating of 99 percent positive. And check if an eBay auctioneer has changed identities to ditch a bad reputation. (New sellers will have an icon indicating as such.) When dealing with craigslist merchants, deal locally whenever possible, speak to the seller on the phone, and if possible, go look at the goods. Ignore (or steer clear of anyone making) claims of craigslist buyer protection. There is no such thing.

Learn as much as possible about the goods.

Call the seller or send an email and ask for more pictures. Be sure to ask detailed questions about the product's condition. And check the return policy and shipping rates. A great deal might not be so great if you've agreed to pay $50 to ship it.

Don't bite the bait.

eBay won't ever send you an email asking you to follow a link and enter sensitive information. (Neither will your bank.) Any such request, no matter how convincing, is probably a phishing scheme. These are meant to lure you to a dummy website, where you enter your account information and password, and then . . . someone has your account info and password and you get nothing but a sucker label. These schemes don't only seem to originate at eBay or craigslist. They can appear to be from a bank, credit card company, or anywhere. If you aren't sure an email is legitimate, launch your browser, type the site's URL, and ask. Phishing schemes are rampant. Don't get caught.

HOW SAFE IS THAT WEBSITE?

As promised, here is the lecture my husband loves to deliver when he sees me shopping online.

You're about to give your credit card number to a website you've never heard of before? Are you nuts? An illegitimate site could take your money and not send you the product you bought. It may be selling knockoffs, gray-market goods, or counterfeit items instead of the real deal. It might be a phisher site designed to steal your identity. Or you may have a perfectly delightful transaction, only to discover mystery charges on your bill months later.

Admittedly, the vast majority of commerce sites are perfectly legit. But don't trust just anyone. Here's how to tell the good guys from the bad.

Does the web page use encryption?

Encryption scrambles your credit card number so that it can't be intercepted between your computer and the site. If you're using a credit card, the address of the page where you enter your number should start with *https:* and your browser should display a tiny padlock icon. (In Internet Explorer, this icon appears next to the web address; in Firefox, it's in the bottom-right corner of the browser window.) When you roll your mouse over the icon or click it, your browser should display information that the site has been authenticated by a verification authority like VeriSign or Thawte. Steer clear of stores that don't use encryption or whose verification certificates don't display this info.

Who are you buying from?

Most legitimate commerce sites provide their street address and (hopefully) a phone number on the site. Call the number and ask a few pertinent questions. If the site offers no contact information besides an email address, use a domain lookup service like WHOIS (*http://www.whois.net/*) to find out who registered the site's domain. If the registration information is marked private, if the site is registered overseas, or if it just looks funky, like the phone number is 123-456-7890, do not pass go and do not give them your $200 (or whatever).

What's their rep?

Some legit ecommerce sites are still a bad idea because of shady business practices, like making it nearly impossible to get a refund. (For example, if you're shopping at an electronics site based in New York City that's offering incredible deals on digital cameras, be very wary.) Fortunately, the Internet makes stores with bad reputations easy to spot. Start by googling the site's name (try also adding *problem*, *complaint*, or *scam* to the search), and visit sites like ResellerRatings (*http://www.resellerratings.com/*) and Epinions (*http://www.epinions.com/*), which offer consumer reviews of commerce sites.

–Dan Tynan, author of *Computer Privacy Annoyances* (O'Reilly Media, 2005): not a goddess, just a geek.

6 HELLO, OPERATOR

When Tracy DuBay's family relocated from the Netherlands to California, her husband made the move to his new job in advance—solo—so that their children could finish out their school year in Wassenaar.

That left Tracy and her husband Bill carrying on a relationship across the Atlantic for three months. And the kids missed their dad. Fortunately, Tracy and Bill both use Voice over Internet Protocol (VoIP). *VoIP* is a terrible acronym for a great technology. It's basically a telephone on steroids that runs over the Internet. Tracy and her husband spoke almost every day during the period of their separation, despite the distance, time difference, and what would have been, using other phone systems, prohibitive overseas charges.

✳ note: *This technology is marketed under many different names: Internet telephony, digital voice, and phone service for broadband, among others. Forget the marketing; They're all pretty much the same.*

"The kids and I were talking with Bill one morning," says Tracy. "I was cooking breakfast while the boys chatted with their dad through the laptop speakers and microphone. It was such a great connection," says Tracy. "I told Bill it seemed like he was here in the room with us. He said, 'Yes! But I don't have a cup of coffee.'" He could hear her sipping hers. So six-year-old Grant stood up, went to the kitchen cabinet, pulled out a coffee cup and put it in front of the monitor announcing, "There you go, Dad!" The intimacy of the digital connection helped to keep the family together.

But it was the low cost of the calls that allowed them to simply spend time together over the phone. Tracy and Bill used Skype, a free Internet phone, to connect. Because the calls were made between two Skype members, they were completely free—no monthly fees, no per-minute charges, nada. You see, there are definite advantages to being a geek and keeping up with the latest technology. Internet phones allowed them to forget fiscal concerns and simply call when the mood took one of them to discuss small matters, enjoy a meal together, or simply check in when one or the other had time. Intrigued?

FREE PHONE SERVICE

The Internet is taking over territory that has long remained stagnant under the control of phone companies. Yep, these are the Wild West days of Internet phones. There are deals to be had for anyone willing to sort through the options. While not all Internet phone calls are as scot-free as the ones Tracy and Bill made between California and the Netherlands, most are a good deal cheaper than the Ma Bell variety.

✳ note: *All of the Internet telephony options in this chapter require a broadband connection. If you are looking for financial justification for going broadband, this could be it.*

Internet phones also come with a lot more features than landlines. Some show you the time zone of the person you're calling, let you share documents or photos, or see each other over a live video feed. Some let you instant message at the same time as, or instead of, gabbing aloud. Some let you send text messages to cell phones. Most let you take your phone, and your phone number, with you when you travel, whether it's to Paris for a month, to Mom's house for the weekend, or to a café (with wireless Internet) for the afternoon. Some let you check your voicemail on the Internet or email your voicemails to you so can hear them when you are at work. And for one low price, some package together voicemail, call forwarding, extra phone lines, and other features that the phone companies like to charge big bucks for. To sweeten the deal even more, most of the Internet phone companies allow you to bring your existing phone number with you when you switch to their service.

The reason there is such variety of Internet phone services is that they are brought to you from a wide array of companies: cable companies, Internet service providers, and standalone Internet phone companies. Each one is trying to outdo the other—and the traditional phone company—by providing you with the best combination of services and tools for the lowest price. Also, the stuff is just so darn new that the companies that provide them seem to be able to offer new features and lower pricing to their arsenal every time you blink. Yes, phone companies, this is what competition looks like—better toys for the customer at low prices.

I think this is great. Every day, I'm tempted to switch phone providers so I can pay less money for more services. The problem is that all this stuff is as confusing as a roadmap at the end of a New Year's Eve party. Many people, including women as well as seriously geeky men with tape on their glasses and everything, back away from conversations at the first mention of the word *VoIP*. Even those who try to grasp the basic terminology tend to go blurry at the mess of pricing schemes and companies they've never heard of. Those rare few who remain undaunted at this point fall prey to the gossip that proclaims loudly that the quality of the connections offered by these services is terrible. This is most often announced in a tone of certainty by people who fell out of the game at step one. So how is a busy girl to figure it all out?

First of all, relax. Breathe. Have a glass of wine. This stuff isn't hard at all. Sure, the service is stuck with a terrible acronym and requires a lot of decisions. But choice is good. Selection is the realm of women. This is where we excel. Sure, geeky guys who are accustomed to choosing between exactly two pairs of shoes (hmm . . . black or brown?) tend to panic when presented with lots of options. But there is no reason for you to panic. This is just comparison shopping.

Do you have a loved one living halfway across the country or the globe that you want to talk to whenever you want without spending a fortune? Do you want to see a nephew or grandchild who lives too far away to visit frequently grow up? Do you collaborate with someone who lives three states away? Maybe you just want to pay less for pretty much the same phone service you have already. Or maybe you want a spare phone number for a fax machine, a teenager, or to give to your ex-husband so you know never to answer it. Maybe you are going to those speed dating parties and want a number to give out that your kids won't answer.

All these things are possible. Some of them are free. All of them are cheap and very easy to explore without making a commitment beyond a few minutes of your time, a few weeks to decide if you like it and, if you don't have a microphone for your computer, maybe $20.

DID YOU EVER HAVE TO MAKE UP YOUR MIND?

We can safely break the way you can look at the world of Internet phones into two basic categories:

Phones that run on your computer and cannot work without a computer
These are often called *soft phones* because they operate on software.

Phones that don't need a computer to operate at all
We'll call these *hard phones* and address them in a moment.

These two options are by no means exclusive services. Those who offer one type may very well offer services for the other as well. It is helpful to think of the two as separate products simply because the two products meet different needs. First, let's talk about soft phones.

TALK TO YOUR COMPUTER

Whenever I explain to my girlfriends that I love using my computer as a phone, the first thing they ask is, "But what about when your computer is turned off? Then you have no phone?" So I'll address that question before I go any further.

Soft phone services are not intended to replace your home phone service. If your phone needs are minimal because you have a mobile phone, though, soft phones could be used as your home service. Hard Internet phones that run independently of your computer *are* intended as a home phone replacement. You can read about those in "Internet Phones Give the Boot to Ma Bell" on page 156.

Soft phones have a few disadvantages. They do turn off with your computer, which makes them useless if you need a phone to be alerted to middle-of-the-night emergencies. Similarly, because they are not tied to a single location (you can use your phone number from

Dear Geek Goddess,

I was chatting over Skype with a co-worker recently, and a she sent me a rather risqué emoticon.

After I recovered from the shock (she does work in accounting, after all), I went looking for that naughty emoticon in Skype's list of emoticons so I could send it to someone else. Not there. Does she have some special NC-17-rated version of Skype that I don't have? How do I get that version?

Playful in Plymouth

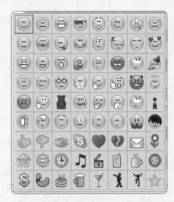

Skype offers a selection of emoticons to spice up conversations. But there are a few secret ones you won't be able to choose from a menu.

· · · · · ·

Dear Playful,

If you like the chat feature of Skype or Yahoo! Messenger (or any of the VoIP soft phones), you will love the emoticons. Why type kisses when chatting with your sweetie when you can send a picture of a smiley kiss instead? Most of the emoticons can be accessed from the drop-down menu, but some are a bit more secret. In Skype, type (bandit), (finger), or (mooning) to get a bit of a surprise. (Search for secret Skype emoticons at Skype's website or Google, or see http://www.skype.com/allfeatures/emoticons/ for more of these.) Don't try these out on your mother! In fact, you might want to first warn whoever you send them to, lest you offend someone. In Yahoo! Messenger, go to http://messenger.yahoo.com/hiddenemoticons.php for a list of hidden emoticons.

any computer with an Internet connection), they cannot be used to dial 911 in emergencies. (If you're interested in learning more about 911 service and VoIP, contact your Internet phone provider, or check out the FCC's page on the topic, *http://www.voip911.gov/.*)

Some of these services, like Skype, aren't even associated with a phone number, relying instead on a username. If you've ever used an instant messaging service, you'll be familiar with this style of interaction.

But just because they aren't exactly like the phone you've been using doesn't mean you should ignore them and carry on as you have been. Email is not exactly

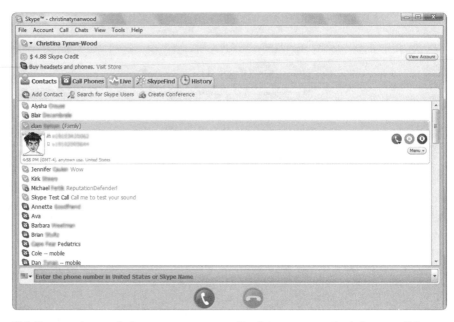

With Skype—and most soft phones—you can see your friends in your contact list before you call them. You can see if they are online or off, see if they are at their computer, read short messages they have posted, and see a picture (if they include one).

like writing a letter and you like that, right? These phone services offer a new (often better) way of communicating. Even though you have adopted email as a means of communication, that doesn't mean you can never write a letter. It's sort of the same thing with these, only now we are talking about voice communications rather than written. So read on.

It takes only a few minutes of using a soft phone to see why this is a cool technology. These services make your communications more intimate, more personal, and more complete. Calls that once started with a dial tone, included only a disembodied voice, and ended with a click now include visual cues, like a picture and online status, and other information your contacts choose to display. I have a friend who lives 3,000 miles and two times zones away. We are close but haven't seen each other much in the last couple of years because of geography. Even so, we "bump" into each other nearly every day on Skype (my preferred soft phone).

When she turns her computer on, a discreet Skype alert on my computer pops up briefly to alert me to her presence. Or if I'm thinking about her but haven't been paying attention to my computer, a quick glance at my Skype contact list tells me if she is around and if she has set her status to *available* or *busy*. It will also remind me of what time it is where she is so I don't goof and call her at 5 AM.

She can post a photo of herself (or any image she feels represents her) that shows up in my contact list. If I decide this isn't enough information and I want to talk to her, I can fire off a few words via instant message to see if she's busy before I interrupt her day with a call. And we can include other friends in our conversations simply by clicking their names in our contact list. So, even though neither of us picks up a standard phone very often to dial the other's number, we manage to stay in touch almost effortlessly. If you wanted to (and if you were willing to style your hair every day), you could also install a web cam so that your Skype conversations include video. This isn't necessary or even always desirable, but it is certainly possible. For many people, this is a great way to see grandchildren or nieces and nephews frequently. The image is choppy, but that's okay. It can allow you to witness some pretty neat things: You'll be able to hear your nephew's first word, see his first steps, or just be able to recognize him at the airport on the occasions when you can find time to visit.

But perhaps the best thing about this type of phone service is the price, which ranges from free to a few pennies per call. Whenever both parties use the same service (as in my Skype examples so far), all calls—no matter the length, location of the callers, or time of day—are free. When I want to use Skype to call a standard landline or cell phone, though, it might cost me a little more.

Call quality can be an issue. You might have heard one of your girlfriends say, "Oh yeah, there was a guy in my office who used VoIP. I could always tell when he was talking to someone on it because I—and everyone else in the office—could hear him shouting at his computer. I think I'll pass." While I agree that shouting to talk is no fun, the problem with this guy in the office was not the service he was using, but his unwillingness to purchase a decent microphone.

So don't be the jerk in the office, and don't scream until you're hoarse. Instead, buy yourself a sweet little microphone or headset to improve the sound quality and give you the feeling of chatting on the phone. All of this sounds very complicated, but it really isn't. I imagine Alexander Graham Bell trying to explain the telephone. I'm sure he had trouble conveying to people why his idea was better than sending a half-starved waif running across town with a note. That is until he got people to sit down at the thing and use it to talk to someone far away. So, to get past this idea that Internet phones are hard to use, you need to dash over to one of those services that are not asking you to sign any contracts so you can get a feel for what it's like. Go to Skype (*http://www.skype.com/*), Google Talk (*http://www.google.com/talk/*), Yahoo! Messenger (*http://messenger.yahoo.com/*), or MSN Messenger (*http://www.msn.com/*) and try it out. It will take a few minutes to download and install the software. If your computer has speakers and a microphone and you've got someone you want to talk to who also has the technology, you can do this right now.

If you aren't sure which service to use and you don't already use one of these services for chat or email, read on for my detailed reviews of some of the well-known services. Alternately, you could take my advice blind and go straight to using Skype.

After that, who knows? You might be willing, as I was, to ditch Ma Bell altogether and use Internet phones exclusively. Before you take this drastic route, though, read the section below on home-phone replacement services. Chances are, at the end of all this, you will be spending less money on phone service, and you'll have a separate phone line for everyone in your family—and one for the fax machine.

Skype

In case you haven't figured this out yet, in my humble opinion, Skype is the best of the soft phones. Feature for feature, it is matched only (at the time of this writing) by Yahoo! Messenger. But it runs lighter (at least on my computer), slowing my computer down less and generally bossing me around less because it doesn't want to take over everything—my web browser, email, online news service, and Internet search—the way Yahoo! Messenger does. And on the whole, I've been very impressed with the sound quality. Add to that a company with a sense of humor without being overly cutesy. It's easy to like. Skype doesn't replace your email or web browser; it is just a phone service, but one that also allows you to instant message, send text messages to mobile phones, add video to your calls, and easily set up conference calling. "Our vision," says Jennifer Caukin, Skype's VP of marketing, "is to better enable the world's conversation."

To take advantage of its rich features—instant messaging, emoticons, video phone, file sharing, and more—you want to sit at your computer with a USB phone, headset, or something with a speaker and a microphone in it and speak to someone else who is also using Skype. Skype-to-Skype calls are crystal clear and completely free. You can keep tabs on people in your contact list at a glance, and ringing someone up is a matter of clicking her name, not fumbling through your address book and dialing.

To call standard phones from Skype, you have to buy SkypeOut credit. The sound quality declines somewhat, because it is no longer a digital-to-digital connection but a digital-to-analog connection. Still, of all the services I've tried, I enjoy the call quality on Skype the most. This can vary due to a lot of factors, so you should try it yourself to see what kind of quality you get with your computer and broadband connection. You can start out by buying a small amount of SkypeOut credit, such as $5. If you're calling a phone number in the same country in which you live, these calls are very inexpensive. That $5 you spent to try it out could very well last you several months.

Dear Geek Goddess,

I bought myself a neat USB headset for my computer, and I love talking for free on Yahoo! Messenger, MSN Live Messenger, and Skype. (I plan to decide which one I like best eventually.) I only intended to use my headset for phone conversations, but it took over all the sound so that now my email notification and error messages—and my music!—play only through the headset, even when I'm not wearing it.

Is there a way to use my headset only for the phone and let everything else play through my old sound system?

Silent in Sausalito

. . . .

Dear Silent,

Windows automatically assumes you want this when you install a sound device, but Windows can be a dolt. You just have to know how to tell it what you do want. Of course you can set it so the headset or phone is used only for your phone service and your computer speakers play everything else.

In Windows XP, click **Start** and then **Control Panel**. In the Control Panel, choose **Sounds, Speech, and Audio Devices**. Now click **Sounds and Audio Devices**, and you will see a dialog. Click the **Audio** tab at the top of this box. The top two choices in this dialog box are Sound Playback and Sound Recording. Beneath each choice are the words Default Device and a drop-down menu that displays all the options for sound devices you have on your computer. Choose the device through which you want your music and all the other sounds on your computer to play.

If you are using Windows Vista, this is only slightly different. Choose Start, then **Control Panel** and select **Hardware and Sound**. From the next list, choose **Manage Audio Devices** under Sound. In the Playback tab, select the device you want to use to play your Windows sounds and your music.

Save your settings and open Skype (if you use one of the other services, it will have a similar option). Choose **Tools/Options** and you will see a menu that allows you to change all manner of settings. Click **Sound Devices** and tell the program to use your headset. Now Skype will use the headset and your music and error message sounds will play through your speakers. And now you know how to change any of this if you change your mind or get a new phone or headset.

You can also receive calls from standard phones into your Skype account by buying a phone number. It's simple to do: Just choose the number at the Skype website, and be prepared to pay for it. A few minutes later, people can call you on your new phone number, which will ring on your computer. Or you can forward it to an actual phone where you want it to ring. (This is a great way to get a phone number you can publish on a website, which is nice if you are Internet dating or running a small business. The number will not reveal your address or other personal information in a reverse search.)

In fact, you aren't limited to your own area code when you buy phone numbers. Maybe your college-age offspring is living abroad. Give him no excuse for not calling home by buying yourself a phone number in the city he lives in. That way when he calls you, it's a local call for him. No matter how many phone numbers you get (got another kid living in New York?), they all come in to the same place. The calls will come to any computer on which you are logged in to your Skype account. Skype has the widest selection of phone numbers of all the services I tried and was the only one that could give me a phone number in my own area code. It offered dozens. Don't worry about having to leave your computer on at all hours to catch the rare call from one of your kids, though. You can easily forward your Skype to your cell phone, home phone, office phone, or all three.

Though Skype does not aim to replace your home phone, the company is working to make your Skype experience complete. You can buy phones that work independently of your computer. (See *http://www.skype.com/* for specific models

When you receive a Skype call on your computer, it looks like this. Click to answer, transfer, or reject a call—or much more. You see the name and picture, if your caller offers one, of your caller before you pick up.

and pricing.) These phones don't just plug into the computer; they let you see your contact list, call people with a simple click, and even get some of the features of Skype-to-Skype calls anywhere you have a wireless Internet connection, even when your computer is turned off.

Skype is a technology that won me over not by its nifty features or even by the opportunity it presents to save gobs of money. It got into my life through the relationships it helped me build.

Shortly after I signed up and started including my Skype username in emails to friends and family, I got a Skype alert from a man I'd never met asking me to add him to my contact list. (This is something to be careful of because of the features that allow you to see what people are up to.) This man wasn't a stranger to me, though. He was my uncle. I had heard his name spoken for years, but my father left Ireland before I was born, and is, other than the occasional letter, estranged from his family. When I clicked "yes" to Donal's invitation, his picture appeared in my contact list, along with the name of the city he was in and his time zone. Five minutes later, my Skype phone rang and it was as if this man—with the most delightful brogue and hilarious tales of his adventures and my father's youth—was in the room with me. These days, we speak often through Skype, no matter where either of us is. Even when we don't speak, we keep loose tabs on each other through our contact list. I know he's around and well when he logs in. Although we have never met, I now count him as a close family member, rather than some dusty ghost of my father's life.

Google Talk

Google Talk is also a nice communication tool, though it is not a comprehensive soft phone the way Skype and some of the others are. It offers no option to call standard phone numbers or receive calls from them. It integrates rather nicely with Google's email service, Gmail, making voice and chat communications part of your email conversations. If you have friends who use Gmail, it's easy enough to download the software and become a user.

Google's chat and phone services integrate nicely into Gmail but don't allow you to get a phone number that standard phones can call or to make calls to standard phones.

If you don't know anyone else who uses it, though, it's likely to gather dust on your desktop. Google Talk conveys a lot of information about people on your contact list at a glance and lets you chat and share files as well as talk. The sound quality is great, as you'll never be connected to a landline. If you just want to talk and you've got a buddy that uses it or is willing to, it doesn't cost anything to add it to your arsenal of communications tools. It's free and easy.

Windows Live Messenger

Microsoft offers a voice service as well, and it offers most of the features that Skype does. But like most things Microsoft attacks after someone else has done a nice job of it, the service is bloated, annoying, hard to use, and—like that drunk neighbor who hangs around the Christmas party till 3 AM—difficult to get rid of once you have invited it in. But for free, you can gab with your contacts who use Windows Live Messenger (the next generation of MSN Messenger) in pretty much the same way you can with Google Talk, except you'll be looking at ads all the while. You are sure to know lots of people who use this service and even if it turns out that all your pals are on Yahoo! Messenger, you will still be able to connect with them due to a new feature.

Yahoo! Messenger

Yahoo! Messenger goes head-to-head with Skype in features, but it also goes head-to-head with Windows Live Messenger in its desire to take over your computer, become your web browser, news source, and email address and load a lot of irrelevant software. With Yahoo! Messenger, you can get a phone number, make calls to regular phones at very cheap rates with no monthly fees, and make Yahoo-to-Yahoo calls for free. But I was frustrated trying to use this service. I spent ages uninstalling and reinstalling it and trying to get it to recognize that it had charged my credit card for minutes.

Once you get the thing working, the calls work fine and it's a reasonable and full-featured soft phone. This service offers a lot of cute emoticons, and a lot of people use it. If it is already your chat and email of choice, it may also be the phone service for you.

I've only scratched the surface of the soft phone universe by starting you in the direction of the biggies. But there are lots of companies out there offering phone service over your Internet connection. Do a Google search and you will see just how many there are. Some of these are bound to be terrific and if someone you want to talk to is a devotee of one of them, that's a good enough reason to try it out.

YOUR VIRTUAL RECEPTIONIST

It used to be that if you wanted someone who would answer your phone and know whether to take a message or transfer the call to your office, car, home office, plane, or boat, you had to hire a secretary. But now that the phone and Internet have joined up, you can get a phone number that can do all this for you without the sensible shoes and nail file. There are a few Internet services that offer this sort of digital receptionist service but my favorite is GrandCentral (*http://www .grandcentral.com/*). It's owned by Google and is in a private Beta version at this writing but you merely have to request a number and wait to get in on the action.

Once you sign up, you get your own new phone number. You get to pick the area code and everything. That number rings into your GrandCentral switchboard where it follows the directions you have set up. You can tell it to route all your calls to your cell phone when you are out of the office and have them ring back into your office when you return. Or you can tell it to route work calls (based on caller ID and your contact list) to your office line and all personal calls to your home number. Or you can tell it to always send your ex, his mother, and that creepy guy from the office straight to voicemail. You can record special outgoing messages for each of your callers—or one for friends and family, another for co-workers, and still another for strangers. It's very cool.

You can also use it to make outgoing calls, which is where things get very handy. Once you have your contacts entered (or imported from your PIM) all you have to do is click on the name to call. GrandCentral rings your phone (whichever one you want it to use) and then it rings the person you are calling. When they answer, you are talking to each other.

There are all sorts of nice little extra features that none of your other phones can do, such as the ability to record phone calls or transfer calls while you are yakking (so you can keep talking on your mobile when you need to leave the house). While it's in Beta, it's free, though there is likely to be a monthly fee once Google deems it ready for primetime.

If you are hesitant to publish your phone number on your blog or in a tag in your email messages, this is a great solution. There is no address information associated with your number, you control where or even if callers can reach you, and the service even includes some phone-spam filtering tools. Sweet.

INTERNET PHONES GIVE THE BOOT TO MA BELL

So now you've tried Internet soft phones and your geek cred just went up immeasurably. You don't need to tell anyone how insanely easy it was while you brag. You are probably considering ditching that bloated bill you get each month from the phone company. It's a natural reaction, especially if you already have a cell phone.

Still, there is something reassuring about that landline. It's simple. It rings when someone calls, and all you have to do is pick it up and talk. Making a call is familiar, comfortable, and you can do it in the dark. No computer, no Wi-Fi Internet. Easy. Still, you can have the best of both worlds. Some Internet phones work almost identically to your old home phone except they send your voice over the Internet instead of over phone wires. They're not free the way Skype or Google Talk are, but they are much cheaper than Ma Bell.

Your cable company very likely offers a phone service that offers to replace your home phone carrier for a lower fee. These are essentially Internet phones that run over the high-speed Internet provided by the cable company. In my experience, they work exactly the same way your home phone does: You call to order service and guys wearing tool belts show up at your house, run around stringing wires, and install a phone jack. You plug in a phone and you are off and talking.

I did notice a few differences. The first was the sound quality, which was often disconcertingly clear, even on my cheap phone. But more noticeable was that my phone went out whenever my broadband Internet did, which is a little more often than my old standard phone line ever did. These phones also don't work if the power goes out, which might have some implications in emergency situations. The price is right though, especially if this is a second line or an office line. The package I got included voicemail, call forwarding, caller ID, and unlimited long distance calling for about half the price I had been paying the phone company for similar services.

But that's just the tip of the iceberg when it comes to Internet phone offerings. Companies like Vonage (*http://www.vonage.com/*), Lingo (*http://www.lingo.com/*), Voip (*http://www.voip.com/*), and a host of others offer Internet phone that come with voicemail, calls to anywhere in the United States and Canada, call forwarding, and a host of other features for a small fee. Over the past few years there have been many more of these that have gone out of business, which your Baby Bell is unlikely to do, so keep that possibility in mind.

In this category, the company with the most noticeable marketing campaign is Vonage. You can buy Vonage products in big retailers, order service and gear from their site, and, just like with the phone and cable companies, a friendly Vonage tech person will come out and install it. "Installation is very easy," says Brooke Schultz of Vonage. "But we do offer home installation for anyone who wants it."

Naturally, as a geek, I opted to install my Vonage phone myself. The package came with a cordless phone, two charging stations, and a router designed to connect the phones to the Internet through my cable modem. The phones were nearly identical to a phone I already own that runs on a standard phone line. And there are routers that allow you to plug standard phones into them.

The morning after I got the phone, the box was staring at me when I stood foggily in the kitchen after pressing the start button on my coffee maker. So I flipped open the quick-start guide. I have a wireless network in my house, which means I also have a router, so I followed the directions for "installing the phone if you already have a router." It told me what color cable to use, where on the router to plug that cable in, and how to plug in the phone chargers. Pretty simple. Just as I finished plugging everything in, the coffee machine gave its last sputter indicating that my brew was ready to drink. I made my first call while sipping that first cup.

I'll admit that I'm a coffee snob. I invested in a fancy coffee machine that claims to brew a pot of coffee in exactly seven minutes to avoid bitterness. If I could install this rig in less than seven minutes, it's pretty darn easy.

CALL QUALITY

I do occasionally get a bad connection or a call starts to develop an echo, static, or a delay with my Vonage (and Skype) phones. But overall my experience with the call quality on Internet phones (all varieties) has been pretty good. Still, I have heard many reports over the years from people who experienced such poor call quality that they gave up on Internet phones and returned to their Ma Bell variety.

My cell phone connection is never perfect either, but I rely on my cell phone. I would put the ratio of good calls to bad ones on my own Internet phones at slightly better than my cell phone. But when calls on an Internet phone are good, they are crystal clear, especially when the other person is also using a digital (Internet) phone. And I can't say that about my cell phone. Still, I do get some dropped calls and some calls that are too poor for communication. On those, I quickly give up and redial.

Brooke tells me that if you have good equipment and a solid high-speed Internet connection, you will more often than not get a crystal clear connection. If you are talking to someone else who is also using an Internet phone, you

Dear Geek Goddess,

I love my Internet phone. I call my sister almost every day because of it. But lately, I've been getting delays, echoes, and other strange problems. We hang up and try again, which sometimes helps. Is there anything else I can do about this?

Can't Hear in Cancun

· · · · · · ·

Dear Can't Hear,

Admit it. You are reading your email, surfing the Web, and playing solitaire while talking to your sister, aren't you? That's one of the great things about talking via computer: There's lots to do to keep your mind occupied while you listen to your sister's latest romance drama for the 97th time. But if you are using a soft phone and find yourself in a poor connection—echoes, static, dropped words—try closing down some of those other programs and let the soft phone have all the processing power and Internet bandwidth it wants. This can often clean up static and cut down on delay.

can expect to be amazed by the call quality. And call quality has been rapidly improving over the past couple of years and I suspect (and hope) that it will continue to do so. "Think about the sound quality you currently get on your computer when you are listening to, say, digital music," says Brooke. "That is the kind of quality you can expect from digital connections in the next few years. Not this year. Maybe not even next year. But we will see it soon."

GOODIES I LOVE

There are a few other little bits that make these phones different from the box-on-the-table version we all know and love. I have touched on some of them already, but I'm going to spell them out for anyone who may still be having a hard time picturing how this works.

Dialing

Dialing is so yesterday. Remember when your phone had a round rotary dial system and you had to wait for the dial to spin all the way back to the starting position before you could dial another number? Quaint. But far from efficient, which is why it quickly became obsolete when "pulse" dialing came along, and all you had to do was press a button. Technology

Dear Geek Goddess,

I know you will call me lazy, but I love the way my soft phone does all the dialing for me. Now I wish I could use my computer to dial my Vonage phone for me too. I have everyone's phone numbers neatly entered into my contact list in my PIM, but I still have to dial that number on my phone's keypad. Is there any way around this?

Languid in Laramie

. . . .

Dear Languid,

Even the so-called hard phones route calls through the Internet, so this really isn't a stupid question at all. In fact, it is quite possible technically for any hard phone to let you dial through your Internet-connected computer rather than through the actual phone. It's also possible for them to do things like record your phone calls to a website, email your voicemail messages to you, and let you log on to choose numbers you want to forward your calls to or choose when you want your phone to not ring at all. Sweet. Whether the service gives you an easy way to do any of this or not is up to them. But since you asked about Vonage, the answer is yes—to most of those things. To dial from your computer, you need to download a little tool first. Go to Vonage's website and click **Features**. There is a long list of features. Choose **Click-2-Call** and then click the download link and follow the directions for installing the software. This little tool will sit in your system tray. When you want to make a call, copy it from your contact list, drop it in here, and click **Place Call**. Your phone will ring as it dials the number for you. Vonage also plans to launch a service that stores all your contacts on its website and it will do all the dialing for you too.

marches onward. Just like cell phones, you can store a digital phonebook of frequently dialed numbers in your Internet phone. I had been using my Skype phone for only a few weeks when I discovered I no longer remembered anyone's phone number or had the patience for writing numbers down in six places, looking them up, and dialing them. I love glancing at a list of names and clicking a name to dial the number. I don't remember area codes, country codes, or phone numbers anymore, and I think that frees up my brain for remembering passages from Yeats and the names of my kids' schoolmates. How much grey matter have I wasted over the years memorizing phone numbers?

Traveling

When you go on a trip, you worry about your phone, right? Will robbers know no one is home if it goes constantly unanswered? Will the memory on your answering machine or voicemail fill up so that when Ed McMahon calls to say you have won a million dollars, he will get a recorded message telling him to go away? My Internet phone comes with me when I travel and rings wherever I am. My callers don't pay extra for this. They won't even know I'm not home unless I tell them. And I pay only pennies for calls to regular phones, whether I'm calling New York or Siberia.

I recently took a lengthy trip to Ireland. Being both a writer and a geek, I took a small laptop with me and a tiny USB Skype phone (I use the FREE.1 USB phone from Ipevo, *http://www.ipevo.com/*). One evening, sitting in a pub with wireless Internet, I called my mother, my house sitter, my editor, and my girlfriends. I even made a few calls to reschedule a kid's music lesson and make a dentist appointment. I listened to all my voicemails and returned calls in several time zones. Much of this would have been too trivial to deal with at the usual international rates but I had a few minutes to kill (while my husband was at the bar getting us a pint) so I took care of it. I spoke at length to people in North Carolina, New York, California, Ireland, and Amsterdam. Some of those calls—those placed to standard phones lines—cost a few pennies each. But the entire night of blabbering cost me less than 50 cents.

Conference Calls

One of the nifty features of Skype (and some of the other services) is the ability to dial several people at once. All you do is select the people you want to include and click to call them. It rings their standard phone, Skype handle, cell phone, or whatever contact ID you have in your address book. No fancy conference services or difficult dialing instructions. It's a great way to have phone meetings, study groups, plan a party, or just get together with girlfriends.

Transferring Calls

Most soft phones (like Skype) and hard phones (like Vonage) can leverage the power of the Internet to do all manner of nifty things. One of my favorites is the ability to transfer calls anywhere. So you can take a call on Skype or Vonage and transfer it to your cell phone when you want to leave the house. Or transfer your mother-in-law directly to her son at work instead of chatting politely or taking a message. How cool is that?

Porting Your Number

As with email addresses, people stay with a phone company, no matter the price, because that company gives them the phone number that is part of their identity. You know you can save money if you flee, but nothing short of moving out of the area code will get you to go through the hassle of changing that number. And that is why the FCC demanded in 2003 that phone companies allow customers to port their phone number if they decide there is a better deal at another company. This ruling was intended to improve competition between cell phone carriers and landline providers, but it works the same way for Internet phone. Just ask before you commit to be sure the company you choose will let you port your number back out again if you decide to leave. The law doesn't necessarily apply to Internet companies, though Brooke Schultz of Vonage assures me that Vonage will let you take your number if you leave.

7 THE WIRELESS HOME

In Angela Freeman's home there are often as many as six members of her family, ranging in ages 2 to 45, lounging about checking email, surfing the Internet, playing online games, and sending instant messages to one another from various parts of the house. They have a wireless network, so no matter where they are in the house, they can connect to the Internet.

"We have a passel of laptops," says Angela, a web content editor for Stanford University. "And at any given time, someone is likely to be using one of them at the kitchen table while someone else is on the couch. I work late from home and can work from the couch while watching TV." Angela's partner Kevin keeps up with colleagues via email. Sophia (age 12) listens to music on iTunes, watches videos on AOL, and does research for school papers. Fiona (age 10) and Isabel (age 6) like Neopets and other online games, and little Carmen (age 2) looks at family photos on iPhoto . . . over and over again.

Angela's family is part of a growing number of households that have decided wireless is the best way to connect their computers to the Internet. The Wi-Fi Alliance estimates that in 2007, 25 to 30 million households in the United States had a Wi-Fi network. Of course, laptops make it possible to take the computer to the couch or kitchen, but it is the lack of tether to a modem that makes the arrangement flexible enough to suit everyone's needs and eliminates arguing over Internet access. "If we need to kick kids out of the common area, they can go work or play online in another room," says Angela. "It just makes things easier."

Wi-Fi also makes it possible to clean up the house by stashing all the ugly hardware—routers, modems, printers, and backup storage drives—out of sight. "We have both base stations and two printers hidden in a big closet in the family room, so it all looks pretty neat," says Angela. "The same closet houses board games, puzzles, and craft supplies." Once you install a Wi-Fi network, all the computers in the house can not only connect wirelessly to the Internet, but they can also connect wirelessly to each other, as well as to peripherals such as printers, back-up hard drives, and fax machines.

"I honestly can't imagine how we would live without the wireless network," says Angela. Every one of my girlfriends agrees. "I have gotten so used to going wireless that I get mad when I have to plug my laptop in to charge the battery," says Annette, my artist and firefighter girlfriend. And since the firehouse where Annette works also has a wireless network, she is able to bring her laptop to work so she can stay connected from her bunk.

"It's like when we went from a wired phone to a cordless one or from cordless to cellular," explains Angela Champness, co-owner and partner at Information Links, a European technology consulting firm. "You wonder how you ever put up with being tied to one spot."

A wireless network does actually work like a cordless phone: The *router* (which is also called a *base station* or *access point*) can distribute the Internet connection to all the computers, PDAs, printers, or other gadgets within range, as long as they have a compatible Wi-Fi adapter in them. That's a bit like the way your cordless phone's base station delivers the phone signal to one or many handsets. Once you get a network up and running, it looks something like this (imagine that's you on the couch):

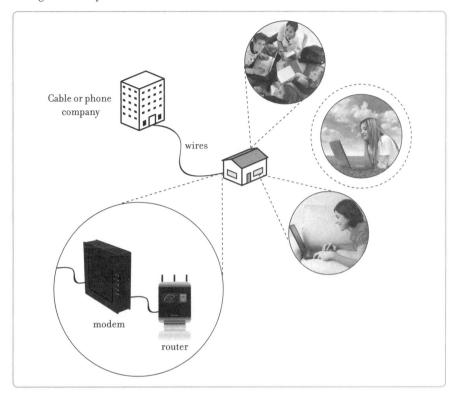

Cable or phone company

wires

modem

router

GETTING YOUR OWN WI-FI

You have probably noticed ads from your cable and phone company and a host of other independent contractors such as the Geek Squad (*http://www.geeksquad.com/*) offering to come to your home and install a Wi-Fi network . . . for a price. While there is no shame in calling someone in to do this if your time is more precious than your money, you might be embarrassed that you did when you see how easy it is. "These days, Wi-Fi is built into the new devices, and setting up a network is a lot easier than it used to be," explains Angela Champness. "You buy a router, and it establishes the connection pretty quickly." For the past few years, the companies that make wireless gear have been very busy tweaking their once insanely cryptic setup tools so that normal people—those who do not relish embracing terms such as *Ethernet submask* and *DHCP configuration*—can buy them, plug them in, and use them. So at this point, hiring someone to install a wireless

WHAT YOU'LL NEED

Here's a quick visual shopping list of everything you will need to set up your wireless network.

Broadband Internet

There is no point in considering a wireless network unless you have a broadband Internet connection.

A wireless router

Sometimes called the base station, or wireless access point, the wireless router allows you to have multiple computers share a single Internet connection. There are lots of these to choose from at electronics stores and online merchants. You want one that is recent and compatible with the gear you get. Read "What to Look for in a Wireless Router" on page 167 for more tips on choosing a router.

*Photo courtesy of Motorola
A Motorola broadband modem: If you have broadband Internet, you already have one of these.*

A wireless adapter for each computer

Each computer will need its own wireless network adapter if it doesn't already have one—this is how your computer will receive wireless signals from the router. If you are connecting a laptop you purchased recently, it probably has one built in. If you have old desktops you want to connect to the network, you'll want to grab an external USB wireless adapter for each one. Read "What to Look for in a Wireless Adapter" on page 169 for shopping tips.

*Photo courtesy of Belkin
You will be spoiled with choices when you shop for routers. Shown is the Belkin N1 Vision wireless router, which not only delivers the Internet to your computers over a 802.11n Wi-Fi network, but looks cute doing it. It even tells you how fast your connection is.*

*Photo courtesy of Belkin
A cute N1 Wireless USB Adapter that matches the N1 Vision router above: It's always nice to get gear from the same manufacturer so it works well together.*

network for you is almost on par with paying someone to buy, plug in, and turn on your cordless phone.

Okay, it must be a little harder than that, or I wouldn't be writing an entire chapter on it. But it really is pretty easy—when everything goes well. Once you find the fortitude to face the technology, it shouldn't take you more than an hour. If you compare that to an hour you might have spent cleaning the bathroom, setting up a wireless network begins to look like fun. "You plug in the cable, plug in the power, and run the setup assistant on the computer," agrees Angela Freeman, whose home network is powered by Apple. "It finds the base station, and you are up and running." That's not to say it's always this easy. Sometimes things go wrong, but don't let that possibility deter you. If something goes really wrong, you can always call in the Geek Squad or another professional to sort it out. Or just unplug all your gear, return it, and try something else.

I run a network built on a Frankenstein-like assortment of parts I've acquired over the years. It is sometimes a learning experience getting these bits to work together. If you want the smoothest possible experience, buy shiny new equipment from the same manufacturer. You will most likely be surprised by how easy this is.

What to Look for in a Wireless Router

There are dozens of wireless routers on the market from manufacturers such as Linksys (*http://www.linksys.com/*), Belkin (*http://www.belkin.com/*), D-Link (*http://www.dlink.com/*), NETGEAR (*http://www.netgear.com/*), Atheros (*http://www.atheros.com/*), Apple (*http://www.apple.com/mac*), and others. Just search on Amazon.com for *wireless router* and see for yourself. They range in price from $40 to much, much more. So how do you decide?

What separates one router from another is usually the wireless standard that it operates on. Understand a little something about this, and all the rest will become miraculously clear. When normal humans set out to install a wireless network, they are often thrown into a tizzy by the dizzying letters and numbers plastered all over the box and product descriptions. As if the word *router* isn't enough to evoke images of skinny guys in thick glasses downing Jolt, everyone involved in the industry has also conspired to give the wireless network system the catchy name *802.11*. But once you get used to the name, most of this geek-speak turns out to be just smoke and nothing to worry about. You don't have to understand what 802.11 means any more than you have to understand what C-3PO is (that's the name of the cute humanoid robot in *Star Wars*). It's just a name. The little letter that follows the numbers is what's really important.

The choices you face when you shop for Wi-Fi gear are defined by that little letter after the name: 802.11*a*, 802.11*b*, 802.11*g*, and 802.11*n*. These are the versions of 802.11 that have, to date, been released by manufacturers. They have been hopping through the alphabet in birth order. So the first one out was a, then came b, then . . . big jump . . . g, and now—the newest on the market—n.

Naturally, as in all things related to technology, wireless gear that supports the newest standard is the most expensive and claims to be the fastest. In fact, the new standard, 802.11n, claims to be faster by two or three times than the older standards.

Keep in mind when making this important decision about routers that you will also have to buy a matching—or compatible—adapter for each computer. (For example, n routers are compatible with g adapters—though they will operate at the g speed of the adapter, not the n speed of the router. Compatibility is explained on the box.) If you have a lot of computers in your home, getting matching adapters for them all can add up, especially if you choose the newest and fastest standard—though it is often a good investment to do just that. 802.11n is, at the moment, pretty new, and it's much faster than g. As of this writing n is still in the draft stage; it isn't final. But what the heck does that mean?

Well, that brings me to one thing that's cool about Wi-Fi: It has a governing body! A group of geeks from all parts of the technology industry oversee the equipment and make sure it all works together. In fact, Angela Champness was a founding member and Secretary of the Wi-Fi Alliance from 1999 to 2001, which is why I asked her to weigh in on Wi-Fi for us. The Alliance makes it its mission to educate consumers and businesses about Wi-Fi and its equipment. Best of all, it puts a stamp on gear that passes its tests. Simply look for this logo when shopping:

Or check the Wi-Fi alliance website (*http://www.wifi.org/*). As well as certifying specific products, the site also offers tutorials and other information. And if a newer standard ever comes along, it will be explained there.

But what about those other standards, 802.11a, 802.11b, and 802.11g? For the home network, I recommend at least 802.11g. The 802.11a standard routers are speedy but not very compatible with other Wi-Fi gear. They also don't have nearly the reach of signal that the others can achieve. Getting a signal to reach the distance of even a small apartment might be a challenge—though if you live on a boat or in a studio apartment you might be okay if *all* your gear is 802.11a and your computer is still running on XP. The 802.11b standard, while it has plenty of reach, interferes with lots of equipment you are likely to have in the home, such as cordless phones, remote controls, and maybe even the microwave. Some of this older equipment may have trouble running under Vista. It's also not as fast as 802.11a or 802.11g.

Still, if you are operating older computers, are on a tight budget, and you see an 802.11a or 802.11b router priced so low that it would make Wi-Fi possible for you when otherwise it would be just a dream, I say even 802.11a or b is better than no wireless at all. Just make sure your router and adapters have the same letter after 802.11.

What to Look for in a Wireless Adapter

The Wireless adapter is the receiver that lets your computer (or other gadget) pick up the Internet signal put out by your router. You can buy one for your computer, be it a laptop or desktop, for about $20—maybe more for one that is compatible with 802.11n. You may even be able to buy a Wi-Fi card for your PDA or digital camera that will fit into its memory slot and will connect the device to a Wi-Fi network.

Before you spend any money, though, make sure you don't already have an adapter. Most new computers (and many PDAs) have a Wi-Fi adapter installed at the factory. The box or technical documentation that came with your computer or gizmo (or the manufacturer's website) will say if the device has Wi-Fi. It was probably prominent in the marketing materials and perhaps the reason you chose this particular device. But if you aren't sure and can't be bothered to get up from the couch to look for the answer, your computer knows itself pretty well. Just ask it.

If you don't already have a wireless adapter, you'll need to purchase one. You have a few choices. First question: Are you buying the adapter for a laptop or desktop? (If you are trying to connect a PDA or other gizmo to a wireless network, check with its manufacturer to see how to do this.)

A PC Card Wi-Fi Adapter

LAPTOP

Nearly all new laptops these days already have a wireless adapter. Adapters for older laptops come in two styles: one plugs into the USB port, and one slides into the PC Card slot (formerly called a *PCMCIA* Card slot).

If your laptop has an available PC Card slot and available USB ports, you should be able to use either type of adapter. Your decision should be based on cost and convenience. The PC Card adapter slips neatly into the laptop, so you will be able to leave it there when you move your laptop around. You'll hardly know it's there, and you probably aren't using the PC Card slot for much else anyway. But this option will usually only work

A laptop's PC Card slot and a PC Card: Look for the arrows that show you how to insert it correctly.

Dear Disorganized,

I completely understand. Sometimes it seems like buying something new is easier than finding something in the house. Fortunately, you don't need that old paperwork.

In Windows XP, click the **Start** *button, and choose* **My Computer**. *Then select* **View System Information**, *and click the* **Hardware** *tab (at the top of the dialog that appears).*

Now click **Device Manager**, *and you will see a list of all the hardware in your computer.*

In Windows Vista, choose the **Control Panel**. *Click* **Hardware and Sound** *and then* **Device Manager**.

Once you are in the Device Manager, look for Network Adapters. It will tell you what you have, right down to the brand name. Is there a network adapter that has the word wireless in its name? If so, you have a wireless adapter, and you should be able to get some information about it here.

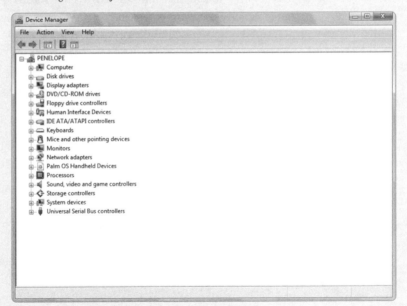

The Device Manager in Windows Vista shows all the hardware on the computer.

on a laptop; desktops by and large don't have PC Card slots. A USB adapter will work in virtually any computer, but it usually sticks out or is connected by a wire. It also takes up a precious USB slot that you could for another device.

DESKTOP

You also have essentially two choices when it comes to purchasing a Wi-Fi adapter for a desktop: internal or external. An internal one will come on a motherboard-like card. You will have to open up the computer's case, pop it in, and plug in some cables. I'm guessing you don't want to do this if you have another option. And fortunately, you do.

You can simply get an external USB adapter. Not only will you be able to install this very easily, but you can move it from computer to computer, even from laptop to desktop. And if you have your computer tower stashed under a desk that blocks your signal, you can set the adapter up on a shelf or desk to improve your signal quality.

Once you have settled on an internal or external adapter, you have to decide on the 802.11 standard and the manufacturer. Have I already made it clear that all your gear has to run the same standard? There are also lots of good reasons to choose an adapter from the same manufacturer as your router. One reason, aside from ease of installation, is speed. Manufacturers are able to maximize the speed between the devices when they build both the router and the adapter. But if you do end up with a Wi-Fi adapter from a different manufacturer than the one that made your router, don't panic. As long as the letter that follows the 802.11 matches your router, everything should work just fine.

PRINTER

If you are working on your laptop in bed and realize you need to print some-thing, you may feel as if you just ran into the flaw in your otherwise brilliant Wi-Fi system. But you don't have to run downstairs and plug your laptop into the printer—you just need to connect your printer to the Wi-Fi network. "I have wire-less printing, so I can sit my booty on the couch and print out my travel plans, maps, invoices, or whatever without stirring," brags Annette. Because most printers don't come with Wi-Fi adapters installed, you will likely have to buy one if you want to place your printer somewhere other than next to the computer. Or if you have a compatible printer, you can plug it into the router—or into one of the computers on your network—and it will show up as one of the printers avail-able to your computer, though this can be tricky. (See "Setting Up Your Network" on page 175.) Look for something called a *Wireless Print Server* that will connect to your printer. Once you install it (follow the directions that come with it), you will be able to choose it as a printer from your laptop and print to it just as if it were connected to your printer, only without getting out of bed. Of course, you will eventually have to get up to retrieve your printout.

Or if you don't mind your printer being near the router—and you don't have a printer you can plug into the router (this will be clear from the plugs available to you)—you can get a USB hub that attaches to your router and allows you to plug all sorts of USB devices into it. Then anyone on the network can access the USB devices as if they were plugged into their own computer. This is good not only for printing but also for backup hard drives, storing music and video so everyone can access it (look for something called *network attached storage*, or *NAS*), and all sorts of extras.

Photo courtesy of Belkin
The Belkin Network USB Hub lets you attach a printer, hard drive, scanners, and any USB device to your router so you can share them with everyone on your network.

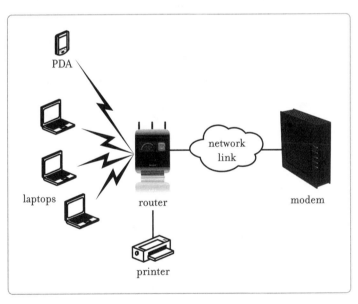

Your Wi-Fi network will look something like this. There are wires connecting the modem and the router, but everything else is wireless as long as each laptop or PDA has a Wi-Fi adapter. Your printer—or network USB hub—will probably be plugged into the router.

Dear Geek Goddess,

I got my wireless network up and running, but I've heard all about these people who accidentally steal their neighbor's signal. I don't want to be one of them. I'm in enough trouble with my neighbors because my dog likes to dig up their begonias. I can just imagine what would happen if I started stealing from them.

On Eggshells in Englewood

• • • • • •

Dear On Eggshells,

Your neighbors aren't likely to notice if you steal their signal, but it's easy enough to check. Is your computer connected to the Internet right now? If so, here we go.

In Windows XP, look in the system tray for an icon that looks like this:

Right-click it and choose **View Available Wireless Networks**. *You will see all the networks within range. Click yours and choose* **Connect**, *like this:*

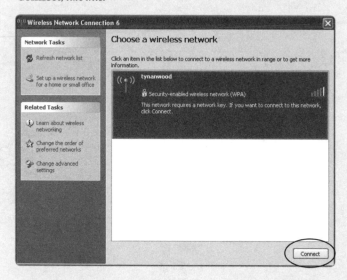

In Windows Vista, look in the system tray (at the bottom-right of the screen) for that same icon.

Right-click it. That will bring up this menu:

Choose **Connect to a network** *to see all the networks available to you.*

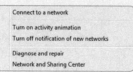

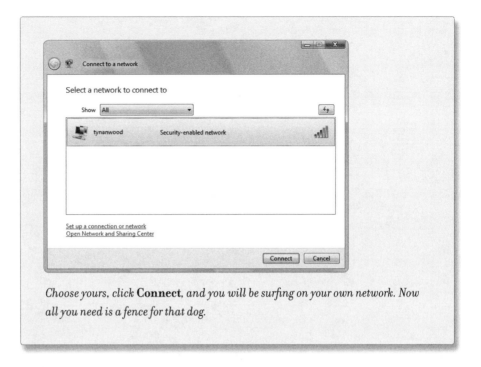

Choose yours, click **Connect**, *and you will be surfing on your own network. Now all you need is a fence for that dog.*

SETTING UP YOUR NETWORK

As several of my girlfriends have already said, installing a Wi-Fi network is easy. You run the software that came with the hardware, connect the router to your computer to adjust its settings, plug the router into your broadband modem, plug an adapter into your computer(s), and connect. If all goes well, it should take less than an hour. If all goes really well and you only have one or two computers, it could take just 20 minutes.

If your computer currently has a broadband Internet connection and you are simply adding wireless to your setup (which is likely), your manufacturer will ask you to first run the CD that came with the router. That CD will install the drivers your router will need, walk you through the setup, and help you secure the network. The gear will come with step-by-step instructions.

Once you get the router set up, install the adapter(s). This is even easier. Again, start with the CD that came with it and follow the on-screen steps. If you bravely purchased an internal adapter, you will have to turn off the computer and open up the lid after the drivers install. That—and locating the right place to put the thing in that swarm of chips and cables that make up the guts of your computer—is the hardest part of the process. Installing an upgrade card to a PC once you have the case open is just a matter of snapping it in.

Dear Geek Goddess,

I have a new wireless network in my house, and I love it! I want to set up a desktop for my son in an enclosed porch that's rather far from my router, and I'm worried the signal won't reach that far. I don't want to get the entire computer set up only to find it won't connect to the Internet. Is there a way to see how strong the signal is using my laptop—or even my husband's PDA—so I can pick the right spot for my son's computer?

Wireless in Wichita

. . . . . .

Dear Wireless,

Yes! There are countless ways to detect a Wi-Fi signal and measure its strength; you don't even need a computer to do it. There are keychain-sized devices that do nothing but tell you how strong the Wi-Fi signal is where you are standing. My husband recently wore a t-shirt around our neighborhood on Halloween that glowed in the dark and displayed the Wi-Fi signal emanating from the houses. (That was embarrassing for me and the kids. It was embarrassing for him, too, though he didn't seem to realize it.) Check out ThinkGeek (http://www.thinkgeek.com/) if you want one of these.

Photo courtesy of ThinkGeek

A Wi-Fi detector t-shirt for geeks with absolutely no dignity: The more bars that glow, the stronger the signal.

If you are installing a PC Card or USB adapter, just plug it in when the manufacturer's instructions tell you to—usually after you have used the CD that came with it to install the drivers. It will probably go right out and locate your wireless network and connect to it.

When I installed my recent 802.11n network, the setup could not have been easier. I followed a series of stickers with big arrows, clicked OK a few times in the software, waited a little bit, chose a password, and was up and running.

If you want to use your laptop, simply bring it to the place you want to put your son's computer and follow the directions I gave to On Eggshells in Englewood. But when you are viewing the available wireless networks, take note of the bars to the right, as in this screen:

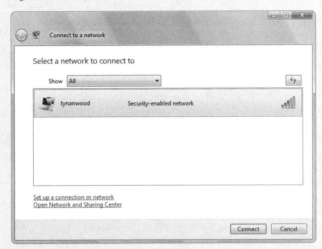

These bars tell you your signal strength. It looks like the signal-strength indicator on your cell phone, right? The more solid bars you have, the stronger your connection. If you have a Wi-Fi—enabled PDA, it can also be used this way. Whatever tool it uses to find a Wi-Fi connection will probably also show you the signal strength of those connections. Or you can download software for a PDA that does nothing but sniff out Wi-Fi connections. Look on the manufacturer's website for wardriving tools, Wi-Fi sniffers, or Wi-Fi detectors.

I started it when my husband decided to run out for beer, and I was surfing—and feeling like celebrating—when he got back 20 minutes later.

Where to Put Your Wi-Fi Router

Geeky men love to talk about stuff like "signal attenuation," which is a euphemism for lost signal strength. You've probably noticed that this sort of thing worries men. They fret a great deal about where to place the router so that it will provide a strong and manly signal. Some men advise complex tests to figure out the optimal placement of a router so that the signal doesn't go limp before it

Dear Geek Goddess,

I have a Wi-Fi network in my home, but I'm suddenly having a lot of trouble with it. It's constantly telling me I don't have a connection, and then 20 minutes later the connection is back. I live in an apartment building. Do you think maybe someone has hacked into my network? Did I get a bum router? It's very frustrating.

Intermittent in Ithaca

. . . .

Dear Intermittent,

Don't return your router yet. I'll bet the problem is much simpler than that. In fact, I'll bet money that you or one of your neighbors is using a cordless phone that uses the same frequency as your network. If it's you, you will notice that your network kicks out when you're on the phone. If your cordless phone has a channel button, press it to get it to change channels. If that doesn't fix your problem, or if the problem keeps coming back, you can force your network to use a different channel. Your router has a private web page you can use to make changes to security settings and change the channel and other geeky whatnot. The setup program you used to install your network made these changes for you, but you can log on and do it manually too.

gets to you. There are even (expensive) devices on the market that you can carry around to measure signal strength from various vantage points.

I've even listened to geeky guys suggest a flashlight test: Stand in the spot where you plan to put the router and shine the light around, observing where the signal is likely to be weakened by reflection or absorption. Metal, concrete, and water are the Kryptonite of wireless signals, rendering the signals useless for getting online. The flashlight thing sounds like fun, and if your guy wants to do it, I say pour yourself a drink and watch. His efforts, especially if he's handy with a drill and Ethernet cable, might even result in a stronger signal. But I'm pretty sure the real reason guys do this is they like those big flashlights and look for any opportunity to wave them around while shouting stuff like, "The TCP/IP protocol on the submask on the DHCP configuration procedure uses a subnet algorithm that allows consecutive transmission of tachyon rays through the buffer net, Jim. We are looking at a complete breach of the plasma coil! She's gonna blow!" They enjoy it, and there is no harm done. It even makes for a good show.

But while the men are marching around waving flashlights and speaking their made-up language, let's face facts. The router has to plug into the

A common web address for home networks is 192.168.0.1. Try typing that into your browser's address bar. These addresses can vary by router, though, so if that doesn't work, look for the right address in your router's manual. You will know you are in the right place when you get a router configuration menu. (You may need a username and password; if so, crack out the manual. It will be in there.) The look of these tools varies by router, but here's how it looks for a Linksys router:

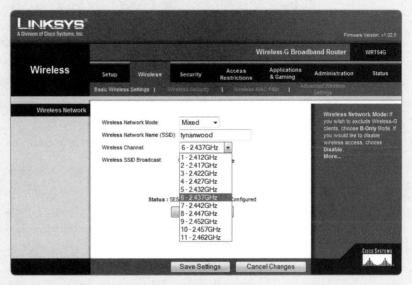

Next to Wireless Channel *is a drop-down menu. From here, you can change the channel. This is not unlike finding a good channel on broadcast TV used to be back in the days of rabbit ears. Feel free to mess about. Channels 1, 6, and 11 are widely considered the sweet spot among network geeks, but since channel 6 is usually the default (and is awfully close to those 2.4 GHz phones that you can pick up for $6 at Target—did you do that?), it's best to start with either channel 1 or 11.*

broadband modem, so—unless you want to run a lot of cables behind the furniture or under the house—you are going to park the router right next to the modem, right? And that modem is probably right where your cable guy or DSL installation dude put it. So, decision made. Enjoy your drink, wait for the men to stop playing, and get on with your life.

Of course, if you are planning ahead here and have not yet had your broadband installed, you might want to ask the installation guy to get out his big flashlight and wave it around before you settle on a place to position the modem.

It will give you something to talk about, make him feel important and manly, and perhaps even improve your network's speed. If you leave the placement of the router entirely up to him (without the flashlight flattery gambit) he'll just put it in the spot that is easiest to wire.

Even if your router has limited mobility because of modem location, you need not accept a limp signal as your lot in life. There are a few things you can do to boost it. If you put the router on top of a bookshelf instead of under a chair, for example, that will do a lot to increase the signal you get by letting it fly right over many of the obstructions in your house.

Moving the router only a few feet away from something that might cause interference (such as a cordless phone, microwave, or anything else that puts out radio signals) can also help. But unless you live in a mansion and want to get a signal out by the pool, your 802.11g router will probably give you a completely acceptable signal even if you do nothing more than plug it in and set it down in the spot that looks least offensive to you.

BOOSTING THE SIGNAL FOR A PALATIAL ABODE

Now, if you do live in a mansion and want to surf out by the pool, I'm all for it. Why even have a pool if you can't lord it over your coworkers that you are checking your email while lying next to it? There are a few ways to go about this. Which one you choose will have to depend on how much enhancement your signal needs and how much trouble you want to go to.

One way to increase the signal is to add a second wireless router. You can add a second router by simply plugging it into the first one. Routers have extra Ethernet ports so you can add computers and other devices such as printers, hard drives, routers, or VoIP phones directly to them. Adding a router, though, requires running wires—a hassle or an expense, no doubt about it. In some places (like really big houses) this can't be avoided. If you don't relish crawling under the house clutching Ethernet wire in your teeth, get the cable or phone company or an independent party who specializes in this sort of thing to come out and do the wiring for you. (Don't forget to make the installation guy use the flashlight!)

Photo courtesy of Linksys
A Linksys Wireless-G Range Expander

A simpler way to go about this, though, is to buy a signal booster, or *range extender*. These grab the Wi-Fi signal you already have and fling it a bit further. They work surprisingly well, require only a power outlet, and cost about $70.

You want to place the booster near the computer in need of a stronger signal (as long as that's somewhere within the scope of your router), rather than close to the router. Using one of these will also avoid some of the conflict hassles you might run into if you decide to run two routers. (This doesn't always happen, but having two routers can be a challenge to troubleshoot.) You can get several boosters if your house is sprawling.

Locking Up Your Network to Keep Out Thieves

Unfortunately, the same thing that makes your Wi-Fi convenient for you makes it convenient for others. You turn on your laptop, let it search for an Internet connection, click *Connect*, and (woo-hoo!) you are surfing. Your neighbors might never thank you, but they, too, might love the way your Wi-Fi network makes surfing the Internet something they can do from the bathroom, family room, or porch. They might not even intend to swipe your connection, since computers often choose the strongest signal to connect to on their own without even asking for permission first.

When my friend Tracy DuBay set up her wireless network at home in the Netherlands, she became an inadvertent Wi-Fi pirate. "I got a new router and thought I had it all figured out," she explains. "It was easy. Voilà! We were all connected. But we weren't connected to my system! We were connected to the neighbor's two or three doors down. They had a much stronger signal than we did." Noticing only that everything was working fine, Tracy and her family surfed happily on this signal. Of course, when she did notice what was going on, she remedied the situation. Tracy's neighbors may not have willingly shared their network with her, but they probably never noticed that she was using it, either. In fact, some people don't mind sharing their wireless connection with neighbors. If you believe the Internet should be free, leaving your Wi-Fi network unsecured could be like your own personal revolution. (Just be sure you don't have a black hat hacker for a neighbor.) Most of the time, one or two average people surfing on someone else's Wi-Fi uses so little bandwidth that it won't bother you any more than letting your neighbor's passion-flower vines grow on your fence or letting him take advantage of your porch light to illuminate a little-used walkway.

There is a geographic limit to how far a standard in-home wireless network will reach, so if you are sharing yours, you are doing so most likely with your immediate neighbors only. But if you live in a high-rise or a densely populated area, that could mean a lot of people. I live in a neighborhood of houses where we all have big lawns and yards, so when I set up my network, I walked around the

Dear Geek Goddess,

I was bragging at a family get-together about my new wireless network, and my brother-in-law, who has something negative to say about everything, told me that my neighbors can now read all my emails and see what websites I've visited. That doesn't really bother me, since I'm sure my neighbors don't care about my shopping habits or correspondence with my sister. But he says they can also access the files on my hard drive. I'm not sure I trust the world that much. Normally I ignore my brother-in-law, but this has got me worried. Tell me he's wrong.

Scared in Schenectady

• • • • • • •

Dear Scared,

There is a killjoy in every crowd. First of all, yes, these things are potentially possible. But they are things you can control, which I'm sure your brother-in-law failed to point out. I explain how to secure your Wi-Fi network in "Going into Lockdown" on page 184; this would lock out any access to your emails or anything on your hard drive. If you want to share your Wi-Fi with your neighbors but not your files, you can do that.

perimeter of my lot with a Wi-Fi detector to see if my neighbors or people parked on the street would be able to log on. It turns out that my Wi-Fi connection ends at about the same place my dog's fence does. Since he barks whenever someone sets foot inside his perimeter, he got a quick promotion to Internet Security Hound. (I'm thinking of getting him one of those jackets like FBI agents wear.) So the urgency of locking down your Wi-Fi connection depends somewhat on where you live and how much you trust your neighbors. "My brother lives in a downtown area," explains my friend Melissa Lavengood. "He had wireless set up in his house but couldn't be bothered with security. He was having all kinds of problems with his Internet connection but only during the day when he was trying to work from home. Finally he hired a technician to come check it out. That's when he discovered that the medical practice next door was using his Wi-Fi and hogging all his bandwidth, which explained why everything went back to normal after 5 PM when the medical practice was closed." Setting up the security on his network quickly fixed the problem and may have been the first signal the medical practice got that it wasn't using its own connection.

*In Windows Vista, click the Start button and choose **Network**. Then click the*
***Network and Sharing** tab at the top of that menu so it looks something like this:*

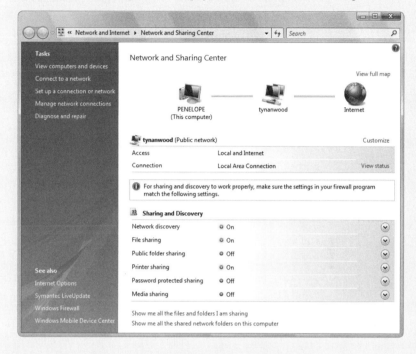

If you have an unsecured network, turn file sharing off.

*If you are using XP, I explain how to set up a workgroup later on in this chapter. At the step where you are asked to click **Turn on File and Printer Sharing**, you should choose to turn it off if you are not planning to secure your network.*

With a little know-how and some tools that are freely available over the Internet, though, your neighbors—be they so inclined—could get access to anything you send over your Wi-Fi connections. This private revolution of yours entails a certain amount of trust. Anyone who would take the time to listen to what I send over my Wi-Fi connection would be quickly bored to death. But if you happen to be, say, selling secrets to a foreign government or engaging in any activity over email that you consider confidential (especially if you think your neighbor might be secretly a spy like the Arnold Schwarzenegger character in *True Lies* or a private detective hired by your husband), or if you simply don't like flying with the doors open, take that final step and lock down your network. It isn't hard.

GOING INTO LOCKDOWN

There are several types of wireless security to choose from. Which one you use will depend on the equipment you have, the software tools that came with it, your own security needs, and the level of effort you are willing to put forth. Some people will go to any geeky length to protect their network and live in fear of a breach. For example, it is possible to configure a network so that only certain computers can access it and even so that some of those computers can only access it during particular hours of the day. But that involves knowing some pretty technical stuff about Internet protocols and typing long strings of numbers into cryptic network administration menus. (Each bit of networking hardware has a unique and cryptic string of numbers called a *MAC address* that you can use to name the devices allowed onto a network.) If you want to get deeply into security and protecting your privacy, there are lots of books on the subject. Wireless networking is a complex subject, and something you can spend a lot of time on if you're so inclined. Of course, you can always hire someone to do this for you if you are a spy or if you need something super-secure but don't want to become a paranoid geek.

But most of us, myself included, take a more laid-back attitude toward network security. I don't do anything on my computer that involves state or corporate secrets, nor do I operate a high-profile website. I figure, for the most part, that a hacker would have to be a pretty unmotivated loser to be spending his time listening to me yack about technology with my girlfriends when there are so many bigger fish to fry. So I take the usual precautions (as in, I turn on security in my Wi-Fi network and operate a trained and jacketed canine security force) and don't lose any sleep over it.

I'm going to assume you aren't too paranoid, either, and explain only the two basic types of security that can protect your network from anyone who doesn't know your password. Your router's setup program will walk you through the process. If you can follow a basic recipe in the kitchen, you can do this.

Wired Equivalent Protection

Wired Equivalent Protection (WEP) is the more common of the two widely-used encryption standards. It is the less secure of the two, but it is the one that works with nearly all equipment. When you turn it on (using the software that came with your router), WEP generates a key that you will use like a password on each computer you want to allow on your network. You won't have to type your password every time; you can set it to log in automatically. (But write your password down somewhere safe anyway.)

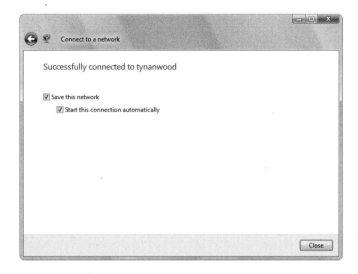

Once you get your network secured, simply check those two boxes (**Save this network** and **Start this connection automatically** in Vista), and your computer will connect automatically from then on. A *WEP key* is a cryptic bunch of numbers. The more numbers the key has, the more difficult it is to crack. You can choose from 64-bit encryption, which gives you a 10-digit number to type in on each computer, or 128-bit encryption, which offers a higher level of security but means typing 26 digits into each computer. Go with 128-bit if you can handle all those numbers.

Wi-Fi Protected Access

The other encryption standard, *Wi-Fi Protected Access* (also known as *WPA*) came out after WEP and is much more secure. This is most likely the security that your shiny new router will recommend and help you to set up. You will only run into problems if you have an old adapter that's trying to access your spanking new router and can't. Some older equipment can't "speak" WPA security. If one of your computers can't connect, you will have to either resort to WEP security or upgrade the offending adapter.

AND NOW FOR THE FUN PART

Getting onto the Internet from the couch is one of the great things about having your own Wi-Fi connection, but it isn't the only benefit. And now that you have security set up on your network, you might find you are brave enough to try some of the more advanced features.

Maybe you have already tried sending instant messages around the house. It's fun. But once you get past bombarding the kids with silly emoticons, you might discover that it also serves a real purpose. How sweet would it be, while you are shopping online from the comfort of your bed, to send an IM to someone in the kitchen asking for a glass of water or some chocolate? And what do you do when you want to have an argument with your spouse (or even talk naughty) in a house where you are always surrounded by eavesdropping kids? "Kevin and I use instant messaging to have conversations we don't want all the kids to hear," says Angela. (Trust me: She is not the only one.) If you haven't tried IMing around the house, just download Skype (*http://www.skype.com/*) or Google Talk (*http://www.google.com/talk/*) and give it a go.

Instant messaging tools use the Internet to let you reach someone on another computer. But you don't have to be on the Internet to reach the computer in your kitchen. You just have to turn on the feature that lets you see the kitchen computer—or at least the files the kitchen computer's owner has decided to share with the rest of you.

It sounds intensely geeky, but follow a few simple steps and you'll be surprised at the results.

* warnInG: *You don't want to do this if you haven't set up security on your network. So go back to "Going into Lockdown" on page 184 if you haven't locked your Wi-Fi network down.*

To set up file sharing in Windows XP, first make sure your computers are all connected wirelessly to the Internet.

Next, think of a name for your in-home workgroup. This is a name for all the computers connected together, so something like Smith Family or your street address will do just fine. It can be anything you want, and it doesn't need to be a secret or hard to figure out. You just have to be sure you spell it exactly the same way on every computer, so jot it down once you pick it.

Now, click the **Start** button and choose **My Network Places**. Click **Set Up a Home or Small Office Network**.

Click **Next**, and then click it again. Now you will see the screen that sums up the network hardware in your system. Tell it to ignore any disconnected hardware by checking the box.

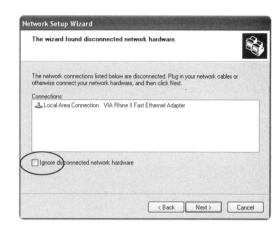

Click **Next**. Choose the middle option: **This computer connects to the Internet through a residential gateway or through another computer on my network**. It is probably the choice your computer has preselected. Now click **Next** again. In this screen, name your computer and give it a nickname as well, if you want. Choose a name that lets other people know which computer it is. You might say *Kitchen* if that's where it is or *Stanley* if that's the name of the person who mostly uses the computer. Click **Next**.

Okay, now you get to enter the nifty name you came up with for your workgroup. Where the screen now says *MSHOME*, replace that with your workgroup name.

Click **Next**, and choose **Turn on File and Printer Sharing**. Click **Next** again, and you will get a summary of everything you just did. Click **Next** again. Now you have to watch an animation meant to convey that computers are sharing information. In the last screen choose: **Just finish, I don't need to run the setup on another computer**. Then close the dialog.

Follow these directions for every computer you want to connect to the workgroup.

To see if it worked, go to **My Network Places** and click **View Workgroup Computers**. It should show you the name of your workgroup and an image of every computer on your workgroup.

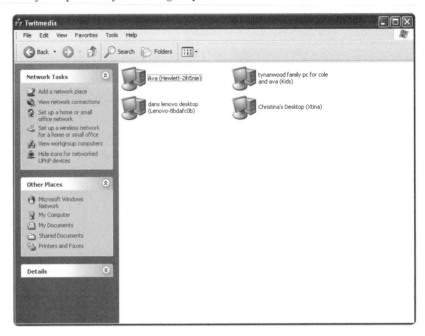

Now click **Printers and Faxes**. You should see every printer (and fax machine, if you have any of those) connected to every computer that you have connected to the workgroup. Go ahead and print something to a printer on the other side of the house: love notes for your husband, chore lists for the kids, a recipe for yourself, whatever you like. Pretty neat, huh?

If you're using Vista, click the Start button and choose **Network**. That should bring up a list of all the computers on your network, because Vista aims to do this all automatically. If you see nothing here, click the **Network and Sharing Center** tab at the top of this menu.

Now make sure that the Network Discovery option is activated:

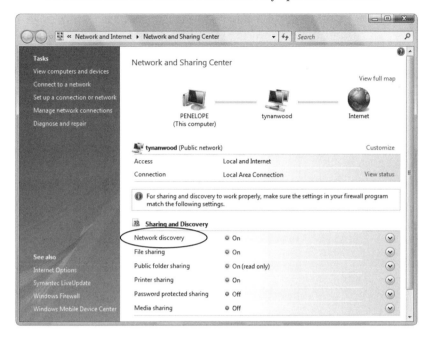

You may need to restart your computer, but now you can see all the devices in your house that are connected to your wireless network. If a computer is missing, it may not have network discovery turned on.

You can use these same tools to use printers anywhere in your house. If you want to print something from the printer in your dining room but are in bed with your laptop, click the **Add a Printer** tab right next to the *Network and Sharing Center* tab, and ask Vista to find that printer for you.

GEEK CREDENTIALS

If you got your Wi-Fi network set up, got a workgroup running, and are able to print wirelessly, you can consider yourself one of an elite group of technologically savvy members of society. But you better enjoy it fast, because JupiterResearch predicts that by the year 2010, you won't be quite so special. By then, 56 percent of families will have a wireless network. For now, though, you are well on your way to being a geek goddess yourself. And you should be proud. You don't have to tell a soul how easy this was. Just bandy the term 802.11 around casually and watch the Luddites flinch. Or when some man makes a condescending remark about your technical prowess, raise the possibility that it is his network that is suffering from signal attenuation and suggest he try the flashlight test.

It was a typical workday. I was writing, talking on the phone, carrying on a sporadic email conversation with my sister, and doing research online. Then my sister's emails started coming with an extra feature: Each statement was punctuated with hilarious emoticons and goofy icons. They jumped up and down, ran across the screen, and did all kinds of comical things. Suddenly this email conversation was a lot more fun, and I was laughing out loud. She sent me a link to the website where she got the free software and strongly recommended it. She said a friend had sent her the link, and even though I know better, I didn't think twice about heading over to the site and downloading the cute tool. My antivirus software warned me not to download software from sites I didn't trust, but I ignored it. I sent the link to my husband, and he downloaded it too. The software took only a few seconds to install, and we had a lot of fun firing stupid missives back and forth to each other till the charm wore off. At the same time, though, my Web research was becoming nightmarish. Every time I went to a web page, dozens of ads popped up. I had to restart my computer more than once as it bogged down in what I can only describe as an increasing ad storm. Even though there was a clear cause and effect here, it wasn't until the next day that a little light bulb went off over my head. That stupid email icon tool was, in fact, *adware*: a bit of code that sits on your computer and pulls ads to you. I would never have downloaded it if it hadn't come from someone I knew. But in this case, like that famous Trojan horse, I wasn't suspicious of it, because I had invited it in myself. I called my sister and asked, "Lots of ads on the Web today?" And she started ranting, "I had to turn my computer off. It's insane. Is it everywhere?" So I explained that her cute icon tool was adware, and she should also call the friend who sent it to her. Not only did she feel silly for inviting this trouble in, but she also felt guilty for visiting it upon me. "I feel like Typhoid Mary," she said glumly. My husband, too, had noticed the problem and, when I called him, was in the midst of finding a fix (which wasn't easy). We all recovered, though the solution was geeky and time-consuming, and I would have had a much better week if I had never downloaded that bit of code. My sister had an even worse time because she isn't as comfortable with technology, so implementing the fix was scary and confusing for her. She also believes that if I hadn't told her, she would never have figured out what was going on and might have simply started to hate her computer.

Adware is just one of the hazards of connecting a computer to the Internet. It isn't the worst of the hazards, but it alone is enough to warrant taking preventative measures. You also have to watch out for *phishing scams* (which trick you into giving out personal information), *spyware* (which tracks what you do on your computer and passes on this information), and many other evils. Preventing *malware*—a general term for all bad code—is a matter of installing some software and learning some safe surfing habits. Prevention is key, because getting rid of malware is every geek's nightmare.

If you are wondering if your computer is adequately protected, you are in good company. Dena Haritos Tsamitis, Director of Education, Training, and Outreach for CyLab (*http://www.cylab.cmu.edu/*) at Carnegie Mellon University, performed two studies with women over 30 years of age that showed a disconnect between what experts know to be risky online behavior and what average people do. "Half of the parents said that they had no need to monitor their kids," says Dena. "Fifty-four percent felt that they were safe from online threats. Only 20 percent thought that email, browsing, and shopping held any risk for them." This is probably not because these women are stupid, ignorant, or any more blasé about their safety or that of their kids than you or I. They simply think they are safe. But are they? According to a study done by McAfee and the National CyberSecurity Alliance (NCSA), Americans are in near-universal agreement (98 percent) that it is important to keep security software up to date, and 93 percent believe their home computers are safe from viruses. But the facts don't support these beliefs. Only 51 percent of those same people surveyed actually had current antivirus software on their computers. And though 73 percent of those Americans believed they had a *firewall* (a barrier that guards your computer from attacks via a broadband connection) installed, only 64 percent did. The results were similar for phishing protection and spyware guards. In fact, according to this survey, less than one in four Americans is fully protected against viruses and malware.

How about you? Do you update your virus protection weekly? Can you claim with certainty that you have a phishing filter and that it's working right now? If you do have all these things completely under control, good for you! If you don't, you may think all of this stuff is too difficult, confusing, time consuming, and

Dear Geek Goddess,

I spent the last three weeks listening to my sister tell me about the enormous hassles she went through to get her brand-new computer working right after she "foolishly" (her word) failed to set up any antivirus protection on it. I just bought myself a brand-new laptop and don't want to make the same mistake. But I find this topic simultaneously terrifying and incredibly boring. Also, I have a full-time job and four kids, so I can't spend all day on this. Just tell me how to protect myself in as few words as possible. Please!

Rushing in Rockford

· · · · · · ·

Dear Rushing,

A few words? Now there's a challenge I'll take: First, install a security suite or an antivirus program. (See "Use Protection" on page 194 for more on this.) Set your antivirus program to get frequent updates. Use it to scan your hard drive for problems on a regular basis. Use complicated passwords for everything you do online. Never follow links sent to you via email that ask for passwords or personal information. Be careful when downloading anything from the Internet. When you have time, read the rest of this chapter.

How did I do?

irritatingly boring. I know. I know. I know. But you know what is really time consuming and boring? Fixing a computer that's been invaded with adware, viruses, and other malware or regaining your identity after it's been stolen. You just want to turn on your computer, do what you need to do, and get back to your life. That's what we all want. But to do that, you have to take care of this first.

USE PROTECTION

"Going onto the Internet without wearing protection," says Marian Merritt, Symantec's Internet Safety Advocate, "is like having unprotected sex with strangers." You really don't want to do that. "I like to tell my mom that though there are dangers, you don't have to become the tech expert yourself," she says. "You can rely on experts to keep up with some of this stuff for you. You can turn to your operating system manufacturer—Apple or Microsoft—for essential safety measures. To protect you from viruses, bots, spam, and other risks, you should get a good security suite."

Naturally, Marian recommends Symantec's own Norton 360, a suite that covers everything from virus protection to parental controls. But there are oodles of choices out there, from tools available via a free download to hardware that protects every computer on your wireless network. Your choice should depend on your needs (how many computers do you want to protect and what kind of a surfer are you?) and your budget. Here is a list of some popular options to get you started.

McAfee (http://www.mcafee.com/us/)
McAfee offers a range of products and services, from a simple virus scan to a full-blown security suite (McAfee Total Protection with SiteAdvisor Plus). It is a big player in the market and has been protecting corporate and personal computers since 1989. If you are afraid your computer may already be riddled with malware, you might want to ante up for the company's remote virus removal service (available from its website). Log in, pay up, and then watch their experts take control of your computer via the Internet and tidy up your mess.

Symantec (http://www.symantec.com/)
Symantec makes Norton 360 (the cover-all-your-bases suite) and a host of lighter security products for the home user. Norton 360 also includes backup capabilities and an optimizer tool that helps with disk cleanup and other computer maintenance chores. This is the best-selling security product on the market, and it's quite likely that your new computer came with a free trial. Just make sure you ante up when that trial ends, or you

won't be protected at all. Norton 360 also includes a parental control tool, but you have to install it separately.

Panda Security (http://www.pandasecurity.com/)

Panda makes a host of security products, including a suite that protects you from "identity theft, viruses, spyware, hackers, and other Internet-borne threats." The site offers a free scan of your computer before you download the product (which is available for a free trial), so stop by if you are fretting.

Trend Micro (http://us.trendmicro.com/)

TrendMicro offers a complete security suite and will secure up to three computers in your home for one price. The tool also includes parental controls. You can try the product for 30 days and get your money back if you don't like it. Also check out Trend Micro's online tool HouseCall (*http://housecall.trendmicro.com/*). It's a free computer scan you run right from the Internet.

AVG (http://free.avg.com/)

If money's an issue or you simply want something right now and don't have a credit card handy, download this free basic anti-virus tool. Since it runs lighter on your computer and takes up fewer resources than some full-fledged suites, it's a great way to protect an older computer that you may not want to spend money on. If you don't like it, it cost you nothing. If you love it, you can always upgrade to the AVG Internet Security Suite.

SWORN ENEMIES

Now that you have employed an expert (in the form of an antivirus program or security suite) to protect your computer, you don't need to get very familiar with all the bugs and nasties that are out there trying to infect your computer any more than you have to know how to diagnose strep throat once you get yourself a good doctor. But you might want to know a bit about it, so here is a quick rundown on some of the well-known forms of malware—and how to prevent them.

Adware

* WHAT IS IT? *Adware is a bit of code that, once it gets on your computer, causes ads to pop up when you are online.*

* THE PREVENTION: *Be careful what you download, and know the source of emails you open. Make sure you have a pop-up blocker working on your browser. Run a good anti-virus program or security suite. Be sure it's current, your subscription is live, and that you run frequent scans of your computer for adware.*

Dear Geek Goddess,

My computer is brand new, and it came with a fancy security suite already on it. I saw the icon on the desktop, so I'm fine. Don't all new computers come with this already installed?

Confident in Cody

· · · · · ·

Dear Confident,

Operating under the assumption that you already have virus protection is like assuming that he's handling the birth control. We know how that turns out. So before you assume anything, make sure you are actually protected.

Look in your system tray (that's in the bottom-right corner of the screen in Windows XP and Vista). There are a lot of little icons there. If you are protected, one of them will be for your security software. Not sure what they all are? That's easy. Simply move your mouse cursor over them slowly, and an informative bubble will pop up. If you right-click the icon, a simple menu will pop up.

All the worry and hoopla over adware might sound silly. "What's the worst that can happen?" you might ask. "I am tempted to buy a new pair of shoes? I see a preview for *Lost*? Ads are part of life, right?" Well, that may be true for television, where there are governing bodies overseeing what's allowed in ads, but it's not so on the Internet, where anything goes—even software that makes you look at so many shocking ads you can't do anything else. If that—and my story about the adware my sister convinced me to try—have not yet persuaded you that adware is an evil, consider the case of a substitute teacher in Connecticut whose life was very nearly ruined by adware in 2004.

She made the mistake of leaving her classroom to use the bathroom. When she returned, according to the news reports on her trial, her middle-school students were crowded around a computer looking at graphic pornography that kept popping up in new browser windows. She couldn't close the windows fast enough

If none of the icons on your computer indicate you are safely using protection, but you know you purchased something, look for it in your programs list. Then load it, turn it on, and make sure that all the features you want (and paid for) are activated.

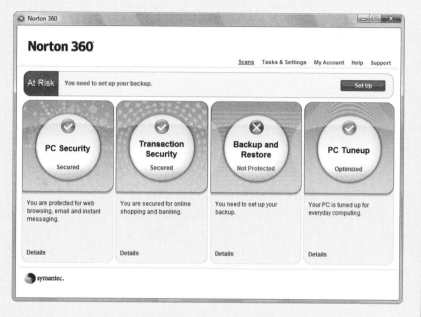

Norton 360 offers reassuring green check marks to indicate that your security (if not your backup) is working just fine.

to keep the shocking images off the screen. In desperation, she threw a sweater over the monitor and called some other teachers and the vice principal to help her. But there was likely nothing she could have done to stop the onslaught, short of turning off the computer.

The truly scary part of this story is that a jury found her guilty of child endangerment, which carries a possible sentence of 40 years in prison. This demonstrates a deep misunderstanding of the invasive nature of adware among everyone involved in the trial. (A judge finally asked for a retrial because of the faulty technical information given to the jury before her sentencing.)

According to one computer expert who later examined the computer in question, an adware program had been downloaded by the classroom's regular teacher before the substitute got there. And that is exactly how it happens. Adware lies in wait and hijacks your browser, redirecting it toward sites (usually ads) that it wants you to see—in this case, pornography. Any sane geek would hand walking papers to the technical administrator (not the teacher) who allowed unprotected computers into a classroom. But, unfortunately, there are not enough good geeks in our school systems.

Most security suites will block pop-up ads, but some do a better job than others. In addition, the newest versions of just about any browser you use will usually come with a pop-up blocker. Be sure this protection is turned on.

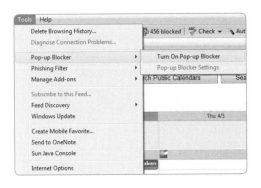

The browser you use will have a menu choice for this. In Internet Explorer, you will find it under Tools. Simply turn the pop-up blocker on.

In Firefox version 2 and later, pop-ups are blocked by default. Look in **Tools**, then **Options**, and finally **Content**. Make sure the checkbox next to *Block pop-up windows* is checked. You can download one of the toolbars offered by Google (*http://toolbar.google.com/*), Yahoo! (*http://toolbar.yahoo.com/*), or Earthlink (from *http://www.earthlink.com/*, click the **Software and Tools** tab). These all block pop-ups and offer other features as well.

Spyware

* WHAT IS IT? *Spyware is a bit of code that sits on your computer, looking incognito, while it follows you around and tracks everything you do. By definition, it was installed and operates without your knowledge or consent. It tracks your activities—right down to the keystrokes you enter, the websites you visit, and more—and sends detailed reports back to the agency it works for. Spyware can even hinder your control of your computer. It can install software, redirect your browser to sites it wants you to visit (those that download other viruses, for example), or even change the settings on your computer.*

* THE PREVENTION: *Be careful what you download, and know the source of emails you open. Spyware often rides in on a Trojan horse or from insecure peer-to-peer file-sharing applications like Kazaa. Use a reliable antivirus software program that claims spyware protection, and perform frequent scans. If your antivirus software does not specifically target spyware, you can also get a tool that does.*

There are certainly shady organizations out there using spyware for harmful purposes, but not all spyware is nefarious. It's always sneaky, yes, but it's not always evil. If you are a teen with parents who are worried about what you are up to on the Internet, it may be sending reports (as Bond did) to someone named M (only this time it stands for *Mother*) about your Internet activities. Or, maybe your spy is a digital detective your spouse hired (or rather, installed) to find out if you are cheating and communicating with your paramour via computer. Some corporations use spyware to keep track of their employees' Internet antics as well. Or maybe you willingly signed up for a service that uses some form of spyware to provide you with technical support. It's certain that the US government has used spyware to track criminals.

Viruses

* WHAT are THEY? *A virus is a bit of code designed to do something you probably don't want your computer to do. This can be anything from erasing data to sending your financial information to some criminal in Russia. The term covers a wide range of malware.*

* THE Prevention: *You can pick up viruses through any unprotected contact with the Internet: via email, file sharing, downloading, or instant messaging. You can also get viruses from removable disks. Be careful what you download and stick in your USB or floppy drive, and know the source of emails you open. Since that won't protect you from all viruses, use a reliable antivirus software program, update it often, and let it do frequent scans of your computer.*

There was a time when you could tell when your computer came down with something. Like a sick person, it would show symptoms. "People think, 'My computer is running fine. I don't have viruses,'" explains Symantec's Marian. "And it used to be that the computer would run slowly or something funky would happen. But the modern criminal is very smart, and his very survival depends upon his victims not noticing his code on their computer, so that isn't as true as it used to be."

You may have heard stories of viruses that reset your computer clock or show goofy pictures before deleting files. Ah, the old days when computer miscreants were a community of boy geniuses flexing their geek muscles and having a bit of fun at the expense of the corporate world. Hackers these days aren't playing around—they are all business.

Well, sure, there is still the occasional silly virus. "Last week I published a malware definition that was funny and cheeky," says Olaiz Urrutia, Virus Encyclopedia Director at Panda Software International in Bilbao, Spain. "Once you run the virus file, your computer talks to you. A polite voice tells you that you have been infected, your files have been deleted, and to have a nice day. It is hurting you and also has a funny side. There was another that was romantic: When you opened Notepad [a software program], it started to write messages like, 'My dear princess, I need you a lot.'"

"But nowadays," explains Olaiz, "most malware is not interested in damaging the computer or files but in gaining [its creator] some economic benefit. People must be aware that there is malware in circulation that has the goal of stealing money or personal information. That is the more common type."

"Dangers aside, there is also a social embarrassment element to catching a computer virus," says Marian. "I had a friend who was doing freelance work for a law firm, and she hadn't installed antivirus on her computer. She sent an email with a Word document attached to her client, and it infected the entire firm's computers with a virus she didn't know she had. She had to tell everyone she was the cause so they would stop opening her email attachment. Not only was she embarrassed, but her professionalism fell into doubt with her clients."

A good virus-protection program works by analyzing your computer and identifying code designed to do something malicious, or identifying programs that are doing things they probably shouldn't be doing (like a game that starts sending email to everyone in your address book). On the package this will be phrased as "recognizes emerging threats," or something else that indicates the software can think on its own, rather than simply eliminate threats that others have already identified. The world of malware evolves so quickly that programs which only identify known viruses won't be very effective. Also be sure that your virus protection software is scanning the emails you send and receive.

Worms

* WHAT are THEY? *A worm is a form of virus that can replicate itself and use your computer to infect others.*

* THE prevention: *Be very careful when opening emails with attachments, especially if you don't know the source. Because you can get this bug from people you do know who may not be aware they have a worm, use a good antivirus program, make sure it's running, and do frequent scans. Also make sure you keep your operating system, browser, and other software up to date. Software vendors issue patches that are meant to protect against these threats.*

A *worm* is a pernicious brand of virus that you typically catch through email or through flaws in your software browser or other software. Once it's on your computer, it starts emailing itself to everyone in your address book. If you have ever gotten a strange email with an attachment from a friend, and he doesn't know he sent it, it's is probably the work of a worm.

Botnets

* **WHAT ARE THEY?** *Botnets are large groups of hijacked computers working together—without the knowledge of their owners—to do the evil bidding of their creator.*

* **THE PREVENTION:** *You can prevent your computer from becoming a part of one of these armies by using a good antivirus program, updating it frequently, and letting it scan your computer at regular intervals.*

Here's the idea: A malicious coder sends his code out over the Internet to infect susceptible computers everywhere. In this way, he builds an army of evil robots (called *bots*) in the form of ordinary home computers with his bit of malware on them. These bots ride in on Trojan horses, are attached to email, or ride worms to get to your computer. Protecting yourself from all these forms of malware is the best way to stay out of this army. Once a bot lurks on your computer, it waits for instructions from its malevolent master, sometimes called a *botnet herder*. It sounds like something out of a science fiction movie involving pod people and space ships, but it's quite real.

"My friends laugh at me, roll their eyes and say, 'So you are telling me that there is something on my computer making it into a zombie?'" says Symantec's Marian. It does sounds crazy, but these zombies have become a serious epidemic. Some experts, including the so-called father of the Internet and Google's Chief Internet Evangelist, Vinton Cerf, call it a pandemic, estimating that one in four computers is infected. "The last count I heard is that they infect 6 million computers worldwide," says Marian. "And that number is growing rapidly."

Bots can do anything their creator tells them to do, but they usually use your computer to send spam and host phishing sites. They are also used to identify and infect other computers and even shut down websites by overwhelming them with traffic. "But you will never know the bot is there," says Marian. "These [coders] know what they are doing."

"A bot can use stealth techniques to hide on your hard drive," says Dan Tynan, my pedantic, know-it-all husband and the author of *Computer Privacy Annoyances* (O'Reilly Media, Inc., 2005). "It might disable your antivirus software, or it may be so new that your software hasn't caught up with it yet. If you run an antivirus program and keep it up to date, you are better off than if you don't. But keep in mind that security software is a bit like flossing your teeth: It's better than not flossing, but it doesn't guarantee you won't get cavities. You also have to watch what you download, where you go, and be careful online."

Dear Geek Goddess,

My son's computer is acting crazy. I suspect it has a nasty virus because we forgot to subscribe to an anti-virus program for it when the free trial ran out. Is there a way to start from scratch?

Sickly in Syracuse

. . . .

Dear Sickly,

If you believe your computer is horribly infected, you may indeed want to go beyond an antivirus program to a more rigorous option. (But first read "Rejuvenate a Tired Friend" on page 26. Sometimes a computer that's slow and crashes a lot simply needs a little TLC.) Remove all your important data from the computer first (and scan it for viruses) and store it on an external drive. Then consider a couple of drastic options: Completely wipe the hard drive clean, and reinstall the operating system and all the software. Or, if the computer is a bit older, replace the hard drive altogether, since hard drives spin and eventually wear out, anyway. I recently replaced the hard drive on a computer for which the repair had become too burdensome. (Kids with gaming habits have a tendency to collect malware by sneakily downloading "free" games—even when they have been warned not to.) It was like a brand-new computer afterward and cost less than $100 to update. None of this is overly difficult, but it is no fun at all and quite time consuming. Consider hiring the Geek Squad or some other professional do the work for you. This is a good project for a teenager—if you have one of those—looking for geek street cred as well. It's a good learning experience, not too expensive, and pretty easy.

THE SOCIAL HAZARDS

And that brings me to the next step in your safety plan. Now that you have all your ducks in a row when it comes to protecting your computer, you need to go look in the mirror. Looking back at you is the biggest flaw in your personal security system. Just like in spy movies, hackers more often get through bullet-proof computer security systems by exploiting the people who run them than through fancy technical mumbo jumbo. In the world of security, breaking through human guard posts to compromise a computer is called *social engineering*. "Social engineering is the most frightening of the hacking tools," says Dena of Carnegie Mellon. It's called this because a hacker uses social tricks (rather than technical

Dear Geek Goddess,

I recently bragged to my brother about all the great open source software I had discovered online (Thanks BGGs!—best geek girlfriends). I thought he'd be impressed, but instead he turned suddenly disapproving and made it sound as if I was taking my life in my hands and somehow funding the coffers of warlords by downloading anything off the Internet. Now, he's my big brother and has always treated me like I'm an idiot, and he's also—between you and me—a bit paranoid. But usually there is at least an ounce of truth in even his most insane propaganda. So I'm not sure what to believe. Is all this great software I discovered turning my computer into a Machine for Evil (as my brother put it), or has he gone completely off the deep end?

Vexed in Victoria

. . . .

Dear Vexed,

Well, your brother has a point. You can catch a lot of bad bugs—and even turn your computer into the minion of some spammer—by downloading code from the Internet. But the Internet is also full of terrific software that seems too good to be true but really is great software for free. (See "Like the Idea of Free?" on page 71 for more on this.) You just have to be careful. Even if you have an excellent antivirus program running, you can override its warning and download anything you want.

The solution? Get protection, and use it. Know the source of anything you download. Do a little background check before downloading. Google the name of the software or the website, and see if there are any warnings out there. Read reviews at geeky websites or shareware vendors such as Tucows. Be sure that your security suite or antivirus program also offers protection against Trojan horses. Keep up with the patches issued for your browser, and increase its security settings. To counter your own human tendency to fall into traps, be sure to do a full system scan of your computer frequently. Weekly is a good idea—and daily wouldn't hurt.

ones) to get you to give him what he wants. Maybe you will tell him enough about you that he can guess your passwords or find other personal information. Or maybe he can get you to actually tell him your passwords and usernames, credit card number, social security number, or other information he can use for financial gain. Instead of trying to sneak past your antivirus protection, he gets you to override it and invite his code in by promising you some stupid game or cute icons for free. So until you put your defenses up against this sort of invasion, you can't quite set your virus protection and forget about the other hazards out there. A little prevention goes a long way.

Defending the Gates

∗ WHAT'S THE PROBLEM? *Passwords that are easy for you to remember might also be easy for someone else to figure out. If your password is breached, you stand to lose your money, your identity, or your privacy.*

∗ THE PREVENTION: *Use complicated passwords, and guard them closely. Never use something that has a lot of meaning to you like a child's name, middle name, birthday, anniversary, or pet name. This is information you might give up without thinking much about it if someone calls, emails, or asks you to fill out a form online. Use numbers in your password, or intersperse numbers into words that you can remember.* **If your password can be found in a dictionary, it's not strong enough.** *And don't use the same password for every account. If one account gets compromised, you'll be in deep trouble. Don't email passwords to anyone, and don't write them down on the desk in front of your computer.*

You entrust a lot of your life to the Internet and other computer systems—whether you think about it or not—and so do companies that you do business with. It's convenient. You can log on to pay your cell phone bill, check your balance due at the phone or electric company, read email, listen to voicemail, check your calendar, and a host of other essential services. Often a username and password are the only things keeping that private information yours alone, so it is essential to choose your passwords carefully. It can seem like an enormous hassle to keep track of complicated passwords for what can be dozens of different accounts. But this is not something you should take lightly.

Talinda Bennington and her husband Chester made a very public example of why it is important to take your choice of password seriously. She and her husband—frontman for the popular rock band Linkin Park—started receiving very strange phone calls and emails in 2006. In the life of a rock star, this isn't too unusual, but this stalker knew so much about her life that Talinda doubted it was a stranger. The messages were creepy and the stalker was also messing around in her accounts—changing her voicemail password, sending emails to her friends and family from her personal email address, and more. No financial damage or violence had occurred, but she was nonetheless frightened and angered by the invasion. Then she got a call that really rattled her. "I know where your children are right now," said the now-familiar voice of her stalker.

Talinda's life was starting to look like a movie starring Neve Campbell, and she didn't want to wait for the scene where everyone gets stabbed. So she called Gus Dimitrelos, director of WhoHackedMe (*http://www.whohackedme.com/*). Gus is a retired US Secret Service agent who specializes in cyber-stalking and providing digital evidence to state and local law enforcement agencies. Because of his rare combination of law-enforcement and technical skills, Gus is a very busy man. (He and I spoke about cyber-stalking in a general way since he did not want to talk about a client; I took the Bennington's story straight from the headlines.) "Hackers, identity thieves, and cyber-stalkers are the lions, tigers, and bears of the cyber-world," he told me. "They don't exist until you become the victim."

Gus tracked down Talinda's stalker, who turned out to be a female Linkin Park fan—a single mother, not a knife-wielding maniac. She just wanted to be part of the Bennington's lives. She wasn't a particularly skilled hacker either; she simply knew a lot about Chester Bennington, had a lot of free time at work, saw his email address somewhere, and guessed at his password—his middle name. Once she started reading his email, she had access to enough information to allow her to guess at all his other not-so-carefully-chosen passwords and eventually to have access to every detail of the Benningtons' lives.

But if you are thinking this could never happen to you because you aren't famous, think again. "In 2007, various surveys put the number of identity theft victims in the U.S. alone at between 700,000 and 9 million," says the Better Business Bureau (*http://www.bbbonline.com/*). And identity theft and other means of financial gain are more common reasons for hackers to try and get into email, voicemail, bank, and other accounts than obsessive fan devotion. So come up with a scheme for your passwords that does not rely on personal information that is easy for others to discover. Then make it even more difficult to guess at your password by adding some numbers to it. And change your passwords periodically. You should guard your passwords the way you do your social security number, bank account numbers, and other important personal information.

Don't Take the Bait

* WHAT'S THE PROBLEM? *Phishing scams lure you to a website and trick you into giving away important information such as bank account numbers, credit card numbers, passwords, and social security numbers.*

* THE PREVENTION: *Never follow links sent to you in email that ask you to fill in forms, enter account passwords, or require any personal information unless you are sure of the source. These are usually phishing scams. Legitimate companies should not be asking to confirm credit card information, social security numbers, passwords, or other personal info at whim or via email, but con artists are very good at creating emails that look like*

they came from a legitimate source. When in doubt—or always—give customer service a ring or simply open your browser, type the web address of the company in question, and check your account details that way. Many security suites (and email programs) will alert you if they think an email is a phishing scam. Listen to them.

A *phishing scam* is an email that appears to be from a company you might do business with—such as a bank, PayPal, or eBay—with the goal of getting you to click a link in the email. That link then takes you to a fake site—that looks like the real thing—and asks you to enter your account name and password, or other information. If you have ever gotten spam emails, you have probably seen these efforts in action and perhaps even fallen for one. Phishing scams sent via email are so common that I get at least 10 a day. The email might say your account has been compromised or suspended, or that someone has made a charge to your account. Or it might ask an innocent-seeming question. It might say anything to get your attention and trick you into clicking a link to get to the site and correct the problem, deny the charge, or answer the question. When you do, you end up at a dummy site—a phishing site—which asks for personal information. Thinking your bank or some other legitimate business is asking for it, you give up account numbers, passwords, addresses, credit card numbers, social security numbers, and who knows what else. The real people behind the site are thieves, trying to steal the very account numbers you just gave them.

If you have fallen for one of these, you are not alone. (See "What to Do If You Think You Goofed" on page 207.) These schemes are clever. "I teach cyber-security for a living and was almost duped," Dena explains. "When phishing scams first started a few years ago I had just upgraded to DSL at home. I got an email from my ISP congratulating me on updating my service and asking me to confirm some details. I followed the link in the email to a website that looked like my ISP's site. I was entering my credit card—and about to click Submit—but something felt wrong. I had already given them this information over the phone. Why did they need it again? I paused and thought about it; I looked closer for clues and I saw that the web address looked wrong. So I called my ISP instead. It was a scam, and my ISP dealt with it." In the few short years since this happened to Dena, though, the clues she saw when she looked more closely have become much harder to spot.

"These days the bad guys will take the time to make [phishing sites] look perfect," says Marian. But a good security package will tell you if it thinks a site or email link is suspicious and suggest that you not follow the link. It will probably flag legitimate emails along with the phishing scams, but sometimes all you need is a reminder to stop, like Dena did, and think before you give up any important information.

WHAT TO DO IF YOU THINK YOU GOOFED

Let's face it, everyone makes mistakes. Even geeks fall for socially engineered come-ons meant to lure them to a website and enter credit card or account information. If you realize you have been conned, here's what you can do to recover.

* If you gave out your password to a site that you aren't sure about anymore, change the password. Fast. Before the hacker does it. If you get there and the password has already been changed, contact the fraud protection department for the account that has been compromised. There should be a link on the site.

* If you think you may have given out your credit card number to the wrong person, watch your statement like a hawk. In fact, you should examine every charge to your credit cards as a matter of habit. This is the best way to avoid rampant fraud being perpetrated in your name (and on your tab). If you see bogus charges—even small ones—contact your credit card company immediately. Chances are it has gotten very good at handling these complaints. If you are certain you goofed with your credit card numbers, call the issuer immediately. The company can put an alert on your account, which means you have to authorize every purchase made to it. This can be a hassle for you—you might have to call to authorize your own purchases—so do it only if you have good reason.

* Since a growing trend in ID theft involves stealing identities to get medical care or prescription drugs, watch your insurance claim statements as carefully as you would watch your credit card statement. And be sure to report a stolen or lost insurance card or medical ID card immediately. Having your identity stolen for medical reasons can result in even bigger problems for you than having your financial identity stolen, since you will not only have bills that aren't yours, but your medical records will no longer be accurate— and that can be very dangerous.

* Get help! If you are sure your identity, social security number, or credit card numbers are compromised, go to the police. This is a crime, and the police can help you get information you can't get on your own. Also contact Call For Action (*http://www.callforaction.org/*) for assistance with getting the mess straightened out.

* Go to the Federal Trade Commission's site (*http://www.ftc.gov/*) and file a complaint. You will also find advice, alerts to current online scams, and forms for automating your complaints to the police and your financial institutions.

Don't Trust a Con Man

＊ WHɑT'S THe PROBLeM? *A con man has a very specific skill: gaining trust and exploiting it. And, for this, he has many weapons in his arsenal. Maybe he's good with numbers, speaks several languages, has access to a helicopter, dresses like Frank Sinatra, loves Las Vegas, adores kittens, and has been waiting all his life for you. But then one day he, and your money, are gone, leaving you with only a sinking feeling and an empty bag. In the real world, he's been around forever. On the Internet, he's exactly the same guy, only now his job has gotten a lot easier.*

＊ THe PReVenTion: *Never wire money to anyone unless you know for certain it is someone you know and trust. Don't believe anything that's too good to be true—jobs, princesses who need rescuing, get-rich-quick schemes, and so on. Be very wary of work-at-home ads. Keep abreast of the scams out there by visiting the Internet Crime Complaint Center website (http://www.ic3.gov/). You can subscribe to its news (or RSS) feeds so that you are aware if a new scam turns up or if there is a sudden rush in a particular brand of phishing scam.*

There was a time you could spot a con pretty easily on the Web. On closer inspection, websites thrown up by crooks looked cheesy and unconvincing. The URL was suspect, involved a lot of numbers, or looked nothing like the website of a bank or any legitimate business. Those days are gone. There are brilliant coders working on the dark side who have the time and the skills to create sites for their scams that won't set off a single red flag in your mind as you happily enter your credit card number, social security number, email password, cell phone number, and voicemail password—exactly the goods these bad hats need to get a paycheck. Your con man doesn't even need to be a brilliant coder anymore. Brilliant coders are also making a living by selling do-it-yourself fake website kits to con artists, so setting up an online con isn't for the hacker elite anymore.

"These criminals are very good at what they do because they are making real money at it," says Marian. In fact, studies have shown that phishing scams decline on weekends and after hours, indicating that there is a cadre of coders out there for whom this is a day job. (Or maybe all the zombie computers they use shut down after work.)

Phishing scams are rampant, but they aren't the only way you can get caught in a scam. An absurd number of people wire money to people all over the world for reasons that they believe in—often passionately—until they realize they have been duped. Finding people to run cons on has also gotten a lot easier with the increase in blogging, social networking sites, and online dating. People volunteer all kinds of information about themselves in an effort to meet friends, get dates, and increase work connections. For the most part, these trends are exciting, and many women love them for good reason. (See Chapter 11 for more on social networking.) But you do have to be wary of strangers.

"People put a lot of information about themselves online," says Gus Dimitrelos, the retired Secret Service agent who caught the Linkin Park stalker. "You have the right to do that, but you have to remember that that information is available to everyone. You are suddenly like a movie star. If you put up a site that says you are into soccer, and I'm running a con and want to get close to you," explains Gus, "I will tell you that I'm a Brazilian soccer player. I'll send you a photo of me in a game. We will discover we have all kinds of things in common and, pretty soon, I'll be your best friend. And I'll know everything about you."

Would you wire money to a stranger? Probably not. To your best friend or perhaps a person you believe you are in love with or to purchase something you desperately want? People certainly do. This con can take many forms. Maybe you find exactly the rare, antique car you have been looking for online (perhaps because you advertised that fact?), but the seller lives overseas and can't take a check or money order. The only way to get the car of your dreams is to wire the money. Trust me—that car doesn't exist. You will never get anything, and you will never see your money again.

Or perhaps you believe that a poor Nigerian princess can't get any of her millions out of the country without your help. Again. No princess. No millions. No percentage. You just gave up your bank account number.

Maybe it is an investment you can't resist. Or maybe you have been informed that you've won a huge lottery payout . . . but there are these processing fees. Be careful of debt-elimination sites as well. These require a lot of personal information, and the goal here is often identity theft.

Or here is a good one: You are looking for a job online, preferably one that will let you work at home. You find one that seems perfect and apply. As part of the application process, you cough up your social your security number, address, and a copy of your birth certificate. You are hired! And the job is so easy. All you have to do is ship the items they send you to an overseas company. And then your first paycheck arrives. And it is huge, much bigger than your agreed-upon salary. They contact you immediately to explain that a mistake has been made and ask you to wire the overpayment back to them. Only after your "refund" has transferred does it become clear that the check was a fake—and so was your job. Now they have your money and your identity.

HOW TO FIGHT BACK

Maybe it seems as if policing the Internet should fall into the job description of the police (and it does), but that's no reason to take a passive role. The Internet is made up of people. Those of us with good intentions outnumber the bad guys. And you don't need to become a crazy, gun-wielding vigilante in order to help make it a safer place for all of us. Not being a dupe is a very good place to start. And if you have just installed a security suite, learned not to respond to phishing schemes, and cleaned the bots and Trojan horses off of your computer, you can pat yourself on the back. You have already taken several great steps toward cleaning up Dodge.

    You now know better than to click a suspicious link in your email. "But if you get an email from, say, your bank that includes a link that, for whatever reason, you think might be legitimate," suggests my husband Dan, "call the bank to names of your kids or pets. Don't use your anniversary, birthday, or any other information that's easy to guess or that you might willingly give out if some charming telemarketer calls and chats you up.

* Whenever you get rid of a computer, be sure you wipe the hard drive carefully and use a digital shredder to make sure hackers can't resuscitate your data. (See Chapter 1 for details on how to do this.)

* Watch your credit report carefully. There are three national credit rating organizations: Equifax (*http://www.equifax.com/*), Experian (*http://www.experian.com/*), and TransUnion (*http://www.transunion.com/*). You are entitled by law to one free credit report per year (see *http://www.annualcreditreport.com/* for help on acquiring it), but you might want to make it a part of your smart financial plan to check your credit reports more frequently. The more time an identity thief has to operate without you noticing, the more damage he will do. Even if you never shop online or surf the Internet, you probably give your credit card to hotels, stores, and restaurants. The dangers are not that different. "My identity was stolen by, I think, someone who got my personal information from one of the hotels I stayed at," says Marian. You can even sign up for a plan that emails alerts to you whenever there is activity in your credit report. If you see something amiss, call one of the three credit agencies so they can put a fraud alert on your credit report. This will stop the thief from opening any more accounts.

find out if they sent it. If it turns out that they did, treat them to a lecture on what a dangerous practice that is. My bank just sent me one. I called them and gave them an earful." If we all do that, they will eventually stop sending out email that causes confusion between legitimate bank inquiries and phishing scams. This is contributing to the problem.

If the email that appears to be from your bank turns out to be fake, let your financial institution know about it so it can alert other customers and take action. You can also forward any suspicious email to the Better Business Bureau at *nophishing@cbbb.bbb.org*.

Take one more step and report the crooks to authorities and organizations that can use that information to warn other consumers. You can fill out a report detailing the fraud you encountered at the National Consumers League Fraud Center (*http://www.fraud.org/*), or simply call the Fraud Hotline at 800.876.7060. Don't limit your tattletailing to Internet frauds; this site also tracks phone scams and other forms of fraud.

If you are offended by some particular spam, find you are getting a lot of the same phishing scams, encounter an Internet fraud you would like to report, or feel you may be the victim of identity theft, contact the Federal Trade Commission. You can forward spam directly to the Commission at *spam@uce.gov*. The FTC collects these spam messages in a database, which it then uses to pursue legal action against the most egregious spammers. If your fraud requires more explanation, use the FTC's online complaint form at the FTC website.

Also contact the ISP of whoever appears to be sending the email. You can often figure this out from the email address. Simply type the part after the @ symbol into a web browser. If it is a legitimate ISP, it will have a fraud department listed somewhere on its site, or you can guess and forward the email to *abuse@ ispname.com*. (Use the actual name of the ISP, of course.) Keep in mind, though, that spammers rarely reveal the real source of their email. They have nifty tricks for creating email addresses that appear legitimate but that don't lead to them. But don't worry about that. ISPs can use information in the email you send to find bots that are sending email. And they like to take those down.

All of these issues are also good reasons to use your Internet connection to stay abreast of the policies of the people you vote for. Privacy and the Internet are big political issues and will only become more so in the future. We need tech-savvy legislators who are aware of the dangers and willing to vote for policies and laws that protect us.

GEEK PARENTING

One summer evening, I was dining with my family at the home of my girlfriend, Jill, and her husband, Jeff. There were two other families in attendance; the food was great; the weather was fabulous. We ate Jill's excellent cooking and drank Jeff's carefully selected wines out on the deck overlooking the Intracoastal Waterway. After watching the sun set over the water, the grown-ups retired to the living room to gab while the kids went to their rumpus room to play. It was an idyllic evening out of a *Martha Stewart Living* photo shoot.

Or at least it was until a 7-year-old belonging to one of the other couples ran into the living room shouting, "Mom! Dad! There are naked men and women on the computer and they are doing really gross stuff!" It seems that along with the toys and TV in the kids' rumpus room, there was also a computer connected to the Internet with no Web filtering controls. The 7-year-old had not exaggerated. Some of the "gross stuff" on the screen shocked the married adults. The kids were horrified and the parents mortified.

Jill (whose name has been changed to protect her) believed her kids were so unsophisticated about the Internet that they wouldn't know where to find trouble with both hands if they were looking for it. I'm sure she knows her kids. But she underestimates the Internet. Sometimes ignorance is bliss, but not in this case.

This incident was more than just embarrassing to Jill and frightening for the children. She was responsible, through neglect, for exposing these children to hard-core pornography. It is no doubt something she will lose sleep over for a long time, and I'd be lying if I said the other parents present that night aren't angry about it. But the mistakes she made are extremely common. The first was to locate a kid's computer in a place where she couldn't easily *supervise its use*. When Mom herself is not a geek, this is a common mistake. The Pew Internet & American Life Project found in a study that overall, 73 percent of teens who go online from home have the computer in an open family area, but among families where the parents do not go online, 40 percent of teens have the computer in a private space, such as a bedroom.

The second mistake Jill made was letting the kids use the Internet without establishing *clear ground rules* (beyond the time limits she applies to TV). Jill's third mistake was failing to install any *parental control software* to block unsavory content. As awareness of Internet dangers has risen, so has the use of filtering to help kids enjoy the Web while shielding their eyes from smut. But a lot of kids surf without a filter: Pew found that only 54 percent of parents of online teens have a filter installed on their home computer, though that number is up from 41 percent in 2000.

Kids don't need to know anything about the Internet to find trouble, just as they don't need to know anything about water to drown in it. In this case, it was one of the kids who led the others to trouble. (He had heard the name of a website from a friend's older brother and, showing off, told the others to check it out. He had no idea what it was.) But it might just as well have been an innocent Web search that led the kids into trouble.

Geek lore abounds with tales of innocent searches or website names that seem like something familiar but that lead directly to the gutter. At one time, according to popular geek legend, *http://www.whitehouse.com/* was a hard-core porn site, misspelling *Barbie* in a Google search would take you straight to triple-X porn, and searching for *Titanic* led directly to a (graphical) gay homage to actor Leonardo DiCaprio. None of these examples are true anymore (if they ever were) because the Internet underbelly changes as quickly as the weather, but today's dangers are just as easy to find as the stuff of lore. (That 7-year-old didn't have to look too hard to find the hard-core porn my 8-year-old daughter saw, did he?)

In other ways, Jill is a responsible parent. She taught her kids to swim at an early age so they would not be in danger around water. She taught them the names of the all the parts of their bodies so they would be able to communicate if something untoward happened to them. She taught them not to take candy from strangers, how to cross the street, and to memorize their phone number and address. She makes sure they read age-appropriate books and watch movies with a kid-friendly rating. But she bought a computer, connected it to the Internet, and installed it in the kids' playroom (where she goes only to check up on them and clean up) without first making rules, offering instruction in avoiding the dangerous parts of the virtual world, installing parental control software to block dangerous material, or even understanding the dangers herself.

Don't make this mistake. Maybe the technology does seem confusing and difficult. But learning to swim, getting a grasp on middle-school math, and getting food on the table seven nights a week are hard, too. These are fast times, but there is no excuse for sending your children out into the wild to fend for themselves. The Internet is an amazing social and educational resource, but kids need your help to learn to use it safely.

IN PLAIN SIGHT

Honestly, the trouble that Jill's kids found on the Internet may have high shock value and untold consequences for those innocent little minds but, technically, it is one of the easiest things to guard against. (See "Safety Gates" on page 234.) There are less shocking dangers that children need just as much—or more—guidance to negotiate. The Internet is a portal to the real world. And with that portal comes all the hazards, hurts, pitfalls, and challenges associated with going out into that world. To think that young children—or even many teenagers—can handle it alone is either irresponsible or very naïve. That's why I think the first rule of letting kids on the Web is to make sure they do it where you can keep an eye on them. They may not need to sit in your lap (unless they are very young) but you should be at the ready in much the same way you are when they are playing ball in the yard.

My own children are no more likely to go in search of trouble online than Jill's are, though they are both pretty tech savvy. My eldest is the kind of kid who builds computer games and learns programming languages in his spare time, but he's innocent of the world in the way that tweens are. I have coached both of my children for years about what to be careful of on the Internet: They know not to give out their physical address or phone number, name their school, offer up passwords even when the request appears official, or reveal any other information about themselves. We have logged many hours surfing together where I have taken the opportunity to point out what looks to me like a scam (but they might think will lead to free candy), the tricks that persuade kids to download dangerous files, and how not to be conned. I have established clear rules, mostly having to do with downloading files, giving out information, opening emails from people they don't know, and avoiding sites they might find scary or shocking. And they follow these rules not because they are afraid of punishment but because these are safety rules—just as looking both ways before crossing the street is a safety rule. I have never tried to scare them nor have I ever taken away their Internet privileges if they make a mistake. I'm now pretty confident they won't give out any personal information or meet up with strangers they've met online. and I have content filtering installed on both of their computers so I know they won't accidentally stumble into smut. But even with all this, I don't let them go on the Web unsupervised.

A lot of parents dismiss this advice, telling me that their kids know more about the Internet than they do, and keeping an eye on them is not going to help. I'm certain those kids *are* smart surfers. This generation of kids is growing up on the Internet, and they know it well, but that doesn't change a thing. Kids who are facile with technology still need their parents. And the essential rules here have nothing to do with technology. In fact, they are just like the rules you probably already have for the real world: Know where your kids are and who they are with. But when it comes to the Internet, you need to know not only where their bodies are (that's easy—parked in front of the screen) but where their mind and eyes are. That is much harder. Sometimes that means kids should ask permission to go to a site. (Filtering software can help you with this; see "The Web Filters" on page 235.) At other times it means you have to literally watch over them while they surf. Or it means you are simply at hand, checking in occasionally and asking what they are up to. And sometimes it might even mean you spy on them a little bit. This depends on how old they are, how much independence they have, what they are interested in, and how much they tell you. But it always involves you paying attention.

There will probably come a time when I will have to let go of this supervisory role with my own children. I will have to let them drive the car too. And they will, hopefully, grow up and go off to college. But like everything else with kids, that time will come after a long road involving much coaching, learning to trust, and passing the mantle of responsibility once it's been earned. I don't know if there is an age, height, or milestone that should mark the moment when it is suddenly okay for a kid to move his Internet connection to the privacy of his

Dear Geek Goddess,

My 14-year-old son is a very smart surfer, and I have content filters installed on his computer so I know he won't "accidentally" look at pornography. But sometimes I leave him home alone, and I'd rather he didn't go online when I'm not there. Got any suggestions?

Careful in Carlsbad

· · · · · · · ·

Dear Careful,

In my house, we have a wireless network that my kids use to access the Internet. So if I want to leave my son home alone for a few minutes, I drop his wireless adapter into my pocket and take it with me. This way, he can still play computer games, but he can't go online. There is also a product that locks down the computer (or the TV) entirely so that you need a password to use it. It's called BOB: The Screentime Controller (http://www.usebob.com/).

bedroom, but I will say that this is certainly something that requires a lot more thought than it often gets. Even a child that is capable of negotiating scam artists, dealing with strangers who might try to lure them to private meetings, and avoiding pornography (perhaps with the help of content filtering) may not be quite ready to handle the school bully who can now reach him via instant messaging or the lure of sites that feed a dangerous interest or obsession.

When the computer is in plain sight, you can walk past and glance at the screen, you will notice a look of horror or shock register on a kid's face, you will be there to intervene if smut flashes onto the screen, and you will be able to easily glance through emails or IM contacts to make sure you know who your kids are communicating with. You will notice furtive behavior and attempts to post photos, and you will know if your son is using a webcam and what he is saying or doing in front of it. Having the kids at hand as they use the Internet for schoolwork or to chat with their friends also affords you the opportunity to teach them how to handle themselves. It's easy for kids (or anyone) to forget that a strongly worded email will cause hurt feelings—especially if they never have to confront the recipient. If you offer suggestions and guidelines, share a philosophy of kindness online and off, talk about empathy, and ask how your kids would feel if they received that missive (instead of jumping straight to punishment), you can build their trust (in you) and their etiquette skills while providing this necessary supervision.

If your kid starts to develop an obsessive dependence on an online virtual world or a compulsive need to communicate with a friend, you might not notice for months if she does all her surfing alone in her room. If your child is drawn to hate sites, those that encourage eating disorders or suicidal thoughts, or those that feed other dangerous obsessions, you will never have a clue if he is allowed to do it privately and with plenty of warning before you enter the room. Even if your kids are innocent in their interests, computer addiction is a serious problem for kids who often find online virtual worlds so engrossing they have a hard time leaving them. Sometimes it takes a parent to insist, "Get up! Go outside!" to break the spell. I do this frequently to my little geeks and am usually met with strong resistance. (This is when I do threaten to take away their Internet connection altogether, which usually stops the resistance.) But my Internet addicts thank me after they have spent a delightful afternoon playing with friends or building a fort outside.

Still, I'm writing a book on technology, and you may feel that you aren't up to the task of supervising a kid who is as comfortable in the virtual world as you are in the real one. I encourage you to rethink that. Rather than put your head in the sand and hope for the best, make some popcorn for the both of you, sit down, and ask for a tour. Your child has put a lot of effort into finding his way around the Internet and he'd probably love to show you what he's up to. My 11-year-old son is seriously geeky, borders on addictive when it comes to online virtual worlds, has friends in different time zones he schedules quests with, sells stuff he has created in Second Life, and downloads gaming code from forums so that he can mod it. Compared to kids like him, *I'm* a noob. But he loves it when I pull up a chair and ask for a tour. He loves to show me the things he has built, introduce me to the personalities he uses in various forums (yes, playing with other personalities is something this generation gets to do—he speaks entirely with an Irish accent in one forum), and let me watch in wonder as he shoots his way out of a galactic battle. In these discussions, he has expressed his interest in learning things I would never have expected (programming), his ideas for online empires (he would not be the first pre-teen to make a fortune online), and some of his favorite YouTube videos (they were pretty funny).

I have no interest in learning to do most of the stuff he likes to do online, but his skills (and his spelling and typing speed) never fail to impress me. I can see that what he's doing is pretty innocent, that he is sensitive to the feelings of other players in games and forums, and that he can steer his way around anyone who might ask him for inappropriate information with both ease and humor. (He even reports people who break the rules.) In short, he demonstrates that I have taught him well. Getting a kid-driven tour of the Web is much better than worrying about what horrors may be happening to him when I'm not paying attention. Also, it not only improves my own understanding of what happens online but also improves my understanding (and appreciation) of my kids. Most of the time, I walk away proud of them. And I like to believe they will trust my judgment on matters I do know about if they know I have actually seen what they are doing and might, thanks to them, actually know something about the Internet. Though sometimes I do offer a gentle correction—on manners, not on programming—during my son's tours. This is the reason I sat down, after all: to be the parent.

Even if your kids know what Second Life is and you don't care, and even if they can create an avatar and trick it out with a virtual sword, and you don't know (or care) what an avatar is, they are still the kids and you are still a parent. You bring a great deal to the table, even the virtual one: They need your help. So what if they bring the technical savvy? You bring your vast knowledge of the world, of manners, and of appropriate behavior. You can see how their actions might have future repercussions they can't imagine. You can see how posting a picture of herself in a bikini might embarrass your daughter later. You can suggest that your son might want to wait until he's calm before he sends that angry email to someone he might later want as a friend. And you might be able to stop him before he breaches some other law (written or unwritten) of etiquette, privacy, manners, or sense. Just keep in mind that this should be a learning experience for you and your children, not the moment when you sweep in and start taking privileges away. If there is something that sends up a red flag for you, by all means discuss it. But if you come away from this dishing out punishments, your next tour won't be very friendly. Later on, you may wish you had kept these lines of communication open.

As your kids get older, this all gets much harder to do, just as all supervision gets more difficult as kids get older. Teenagers, for example, are fond of social networking sites and may be completely unwilling to share what they do there with you. Even if they are computing in the family room (which will also be harder to enforce), they may be quite good at hiding what they do. This may be a perfectly innocent desire for privacy, or it may be a clue that your kids are doing a lot of things they don't want you to know about because it would scare you. You know your kids, and their particular warning signs, best. A lot of parents get their own MySpace and Facebook accounts so they can search for their kids' profiles and scan them for inappropriate photos, hostility, inappropriate language, and other dangers. I encourage you to do whatever you can to supervise your kids, but you might take heart in knowing that most victimization of teens happens offline and that most kids who find trouble on the Internet as teens went looking for it. That's not to say you should relax about what your teenager is up to. Teens who go looking for trouble and engage in risky behavior online and off need your help in understanding the real-world implications of their actions. I'm simply saying this is not a problem that's specific to the Internet—though the Internet does make it a lot easier for them to locate trouble in the real world.

Just like with younger kids, parenting is what teens need, not technical lock-downs. (Though a forced disconnect from the Web may be appropriate or necessary in some cases.) Parenting teenagers is a very difficult job since it requires you to be able to discuss sex, deal with growing independence, and supervise young people who may be able to drive and have a lot of personal freedom but very little real-world experience. Adding the Internet to the mix doesn't make your job easier, but keep in mind that it often does make the teen years easier for kids. It allows them to express themselves, learn about topics they may be too embarrassed to discuss, find communities that may not exist locally that help them feel as if they belong in the world, and play with different personalities as they discover who they are. In some cases, teenagers are able to become someone in the world (by selling things they design or forming small businesses online) before they even get to college. And the Internet is an essential tool for getting into college since all pre-visit research, college applications, and communication with admission officers now happens online.

Fortunately for me, this isn't a book about parenting teens, but I do believe that your best tool here is an open, understanding, caring, and honest relationship with your teen. If he wants to deceive you, he certainly can, unless you are very tech savvy. So I encourage you to consider the ways the Internet might be able to help you rather than harm you. Even if you can't keep your teen in plain sight anymore when she is on the Internet, you can move online with her by becoming part of her online community.

The Internet provides an easy way for kids to communicate with each other and, if they are so inclined, with strangers. That can be extremely frightening, just as imaging the trouble your kids can get up to in a car can cause you to break out in a cold sweat. But the Internet also allows you new ways of communicating with your kids you never had before. You simply have to choose to embrace it. Rather than spying on your kids' MySpace or Facebook profiles, get a page of your own and send them a friend request. If your kids use tools like Twitter to update their friends on their day-to-day lives, join the action. And use text messaging and instant messaging to communicate with them—they like it.

Hopefully, you will find that you enjoy your kids' company in the digital world as much as in the physical one. And just as when they were little, you can offer friendly advice about indiscretions or risky behavior. If you are facing bigger challenges with your youth than a few online *faux pas* and hasty photo postings, technology might actually become your best friend. You can buy cell phones with GPS tracking in them, black boxes you can put in your teen's car that use GPS tracking and then email to alert you if they are parking at Lover's Lane or driving too fast (*http://www.alltrackusa.com/*), and spyware that you can install on your kid's computer to track what your teen is up to online (*http://www.spectorsoft.com/*). I'm not necessarily saying I recommend any of this but, like you, I was once a teenager, so I can fully understand the temptation to go this route as a parent.

MORE GUIDELINES THAN ACTUAL RULES

When you take your kids to the playground, pool, a friend's house, or let them do any of these things alone, you probably send them off with a set of guidelines: no biting, don't get in a car with someone you don't know, stay where I can see you. Your rules are yours. They are formed in response to your own beliefs and fears, your kids' ages and abilities, where you live, and where your kids are going. You lived in the world for quite a few years before becoming someone capable of coming up with these rules, and you are probably borrowing a few from your own parents. Well, your parents didn't have rules for Internet surfing, and you may feel like you haven't lived in that world long enough to come up with rules for it. So you might want a little help getting a handle on this.

If you yourself don't know how to swim, you might take your kids to the YMCA or the local beach or municipal pool and sign them up for lessons. They will not only be safer around water, but it will allow them to enjoy swimming, boating, surfing, and many other activities. This is a good plan that works just as well for learning to surf the Internet. If you yourself don't feel you know enough about the Internet to teach your kids, get help. You are reading this book, and that's a good start, but there are lots of resources at your fingertips if you have an Internet connection. There is some good general information at the federal government's Internet safety education site (*http://www.onguardonline.gov/*) as well as at sites established by private enterprise. Or you (and your kids) can take a training class through i-SAFE (*http://www.isafe.org/*). There are classes all over the country, or you can attend an online class without leaving your house. They are free and comprehensive. Or watch the instructional videos geared to kids (with cute characters and silly humor) at NetSmartz411 (*http://www.netsmartz411.com/*). Or troubleshoot your problems, get up to speed, and get parenting advice at the education site run by Dena Tsamitis (see Chapter 8) and Carnegie Mellon, My Secure Cyberspace (*https://www.mysecurecyberspace.com/*). You might also want to check out GetNetWise (*http://www.getnetwise.org/*) and Be Web Aware (*http://www.bewebaware.ca/*). WiredSafety (*http://www.wiredsafety.org/*) offers advice for both parents and kids, including an Internet safety booklet you can download or read online. And SafeKids (*http://www.safekids.com/*) offers a complete list of rules for pre-teens that you can print out and post near the computer (*http://safekids.com/kids-rules-for-online-safety/*).

To get you started, though, I will outline the major online dangers so you can gauge your own response and set rules and safeguards accordingly.

The Danger: Cyber Bullying

I mention this first because it is such a serious concern for kids, even though most of the noise about protecting kids online focuses on sexual predators and porn. Online bullying appears to be about as common as acne for kids these days. According to an i-SAFE survey of kids in fourth to eighth grades, 58 percent of kids admit someone has said mean or hurtful things to them online, 53 percent of kids admit to having said something mean to another kid, and 42 percent of kids have been bullied.

There was a time when home was a place safe from the assaults of the school bully, but technology has given the bully seemingly limitless resources. A bully can reach right into your kid's bedroom, which is one excellent reason not to let the kids surf unsupervised. Being bullied is something kids tend to keep secret, and being a bully is something they certainly don't admit to. But if they are being bullied through email, instant message, or by having malicious things said about them on websites, you will see the anguish on their face if they are sitting nearby at the computer. This might lead you to learn about a situation you may otherwise have missed. There is a heart-wrenching story by the father of middle-school student named Ryan Patrick Halligan at *http://www.ryanpatrickhalligan.org/* that details how important it is to know who your kids are communicating with online. Though his parents were pretty savvy about the Web and he was well versed in Netiquette, Ryan was being bullied via instant message, websites, and email for a long time. Though he had a good relationship with his parents, they didn't learn about the 24/7 reach into Ryan's bedroom that his bullies had until after Ryan took his own life.

Technology has even made bullies out of kids who, in an earlier time, would not have been physically big or scary enough to dominate the playground. In fact, technology is particularly suited to the special skills of the social bully, who is often a girl. A social bully uses her influence to gang up on one girl and trick her into revealing secrets, and then uses that information to humiliate her victim publicly. Or she isolates one girl socially and, once that girl feels alone and friendless, threatens her.

The social bully loves all the new tools she has in her arsenal. Whispering, note-passing, and calls to a home phone are weak weapons compared to instant messaging, text messaging, email, and websites. These communication tools are rarely supervised by adults, give access to the victims at any time of the day or night, and are often anonymous for bullies. They are also extremely powerful and invasive. For example, a bully could use a cell phone to snap an embarrassing photo of her target in the shower at school, post it to a website, and email or text message the photo (or a link to it) to half the school before her target is done with the blow dryer.

Since the divide is split pretty evenly between kids who do the bullying and those who are bullied in the virtual world—no doubt in part because victims frequently retaliate with the same tools that were used against them—don't assume your kids are too nice to be the bully. Again, education is the key. Teach empathy. Ask kids to imagine how they would feel if they got the email or message they are about to send. And remind them that there are serious real-world implications of these actions, something kids are often clueless about. Invasions of privacy (like the shower scenario), online harassment, threats, and much of this behavior that kids think is just "funny" is actually illegal or at least banned by their school and can result in serious consequences for the bully. Also, most bullies don't really want to drive another kid to take their own life or go on a shooting spree and may

Dear Geek Goddess,

I recently found my 13-year-old daughter sobbing in front of the computer. I am so glad that the only Internet-connected computer in our house is in the family room, or I might never have come upon this heartbreaking scene. Because she couldn't hide her tears, I managed to get her to tell me what was wrong. It seems she has been receiving what I can only describe as hate mail from a girl she once considered a friend at school. She showed me the email that made her cry, and it was nasty. There were lots of other emails from this girl in my daughter's inbox. I want to stop this girl from ever being able to reach my daughter through email again, but I'm not sure how.

Mad in Madison

· · · · · ·

Dear Mad,

Good for you—not only for being a responsible parent but also for taking your daughter's dilemma seriously. (If there are threats or if you believe this situation is dangerous, also read my response to Incensed in Ithaca on page 226.) There are certainly ways to block this nasty girl from contacting your daughter in the future. If your daughter is using an email address provided by your ISP, it may allow you to create a whitelist of email addresses that are the only ones allowed through or a blacklist of email addresses that are blocked from getting through while allowing all others through. This will depend on your ISP, so you should ask it for details. Most email software and online email services also offer filtering tools that allow you to sort your email as it comes in. The specific method for blocking an email address will vary by the email software or service your daughter is using. Some are as simple as right-clicking the email address and choosing **Block**. Most require you to create a filter. If she is using a Gmail address, for example, you can create a filter by opening the email from the mean girl and clicking the **More Actions** drop-down menu at the top of the inbox. Choose **Filter Messages Like These.** *This will bring up the Create a Filter window:*

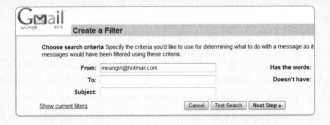

The email address you want to block will already be filled in. Click **Next Step** *to bring up these options:*

Here you can delete any future messages from this girl as they come in to your daughter and, if you like, forward them to yourself so you can keep an eye on this relationship.

But filters are very easy for an Internet-savvy kid to turn off. So if you think your daughter might find herself sucked back into this relationship, you might prefer to get her a full-featured safe email account from a service such as Kid Safe Mail (http://www.kidsafemail.com/), ZooBuh (http://www.zoobuh.com/), or Safe2Read (http://www.safe2read.com/) that will clean out spam, run any new contacts by you before allowing her emails to be sent to them, allow only email from contacts you pre-approve, send a copy of every email to your email address, and all sorts of other safety features, which you can configure to suit your preferences and the ages of your kids. There is nothing stopping her from using a different email address if she really wants to, though. While you are fired up, you might want to consider your daughter's cell phone as well. Many carriers offer parental controls that allow you to block calls and messages from certain callers. Contact your cell phone provider for more information.

never expect things to go that far—though there is a lot of evidence to support the connection between bullying and both of these responses. There is a handy guide to these matters that details all the many forms cyber-bullying can take at Cyberbully.org (*http://www.cyberbully.org/cyberbully/docs/cbctparents.pdf*).

Talk to your kids about cyber-bullying, give it a name, let them know you are aware of it, can help, are on their side, and that you take it very seriously.

If your kids have an online journal or a MySpace, Facebook, or Xanga page, read it. (According to The Pew Internet & American Life Project, 55 percent of teens have one of these.)

Do a search for your kid's name in Google and MySpace to make sure no one else has put up a page to harass your kid.

Ask questions and read your kids' email and instant messages if you suspect a problem. Help your kids block the bully's missives. (This depends on your situation and how old your kids are.) A determined bully can easily get a new email address or screen name, though, so you have to be vigilant.

The Danger: Bad Company

There are a lot of scary stories in the news about kids meeting people online, maintaining virtual relationships with them for a while, and then going off to meet up with them in public, never to be seen again. Though this is not the most common danger kids encounter, it is certainly terrifying and has gotten a lot of attention in the media. The fact is, this doesn't actually happen very often, but

Dear Geek Goddess,

My son is something of a geek. He loves online role-playing games, eschews sports, and is a bit socially awkward. I adore him just as he is and so do his many friends, but I have always worried that he might become the target of bullies. Well, it finally happened. He didn't admit this to me willingly. But I noticed that he stopped using his computer and seemed sad and emotional. So I asked him. Gently. He broke down and told me that some kids at school had been saying nasty things about him on a blog, posting embarrassing photos of him on MySpace, and pestering him on his instant messaging software and email. I don't know what to do. I plan to talk to the school about the in-school harassment, but I don't know what to do about the virtual stuff.

Incensed in Ithaca

. . . .

Dear Incensed,

This is some pretty serious stuff. I would not limit my response to the technical if this were my son, but it sounds like you have the real-world stuff under control, so I will focus on the Internet harassment.

Most online services have rules about using their service to harass others, so contact the ISP the bully is using. If the ISP agrees with you, the bully may have that's no reason to be blasé about the potential danger. The biggest safeguard against online predators—never give out personal information—is good general advice and it also protects kids from other, less horrifying, dangers like spam and junk mail.

The problem is that it's not enough to simply tell kids to never give out personal information to strangers. Young children and tweens often don't have the same understanding that adults have of what a stranger is. And older children have a very different idea of what constitutes personal information than we old-school adults do. These are both concepts you have to define very carefully. Simply saying, "Don't talk to strangers" is not enough, because lots of people that kids do talk to—the tutor, a new teacher, everyone at school—are strangers until they talk to them. So they may assume that someone they have been chatting with online for a while is also not a stranger. Fortunately, there are some great resources for getting this message across. Check out the Internet safety videos at The Safe Side (*http://www.thesafeside.com/*) and the videos at Netsmartz411.

his account terminated. You can find the service provider in several ways. If the harassment takes the form of email, use the email address to track down the service provider. For example, in the email address bully@hotmail.com, Hotmail is the email provider. (See also my previous tip for blocking emails on page 224.) Go to the service provider's Contact or Acceptable Use page and send an email with any documentation of the harassment you can provide. Similarly, if the harassment comes in over instant messaging, contact the IM provider. Certainly you should also use that program's privacy controls to block this bully. Most IM tools also allow you block any IMs from people not in your son's contact list. I would choose that setting, since it's easy enough for the bully to get a new IM identity. If the bully is using MySpace, Xanga, or a blog tool such as Blogger or Typepad, alert that service to the inappropriate content as well. There is an inappropriate content button at the bottom of every MySpace page. And the Parent Page of Xanga has some helpful advice and tools. If you simply have no idea how the bully got that website up on the internet, go to http://www.whois.net/ and look up the website address. This will tell you who hosts it and sometimes who owns the domain. Website hosts will take harassment through their service seriously. But if your child receives a threat over email or IM, contact the police. That's illegal. The bully should be, at the very least, alerted to the fact that what he is doing is illegal and that there could be real-world consequences.

Kids are also very gullible. It's part of their charm. So even if they seem to completely understand why not to give out their address to some stranger in a gaming site, they may need a lot more instruction when it comes to giving out information that's requested by, say, someone disguised as a cartoon character on Disney's website. Granted, these hazards are not as scary as some pervert trying to find out where your innocent baby lives for horrible nefarious purposes—these come-ons are trying to gather personal information about them to sell them things, steal their identity, or just to mail them junk—but they are very common and pretty slippery. If anything, this concept is getting harder to convey to kids who live in an age where posting every thought and personal experience on the Internet is part of being friends.

Even at MySpace, though, where talking openly about intimate topics that previous generations might not even have discussed with a spouse is common, posting a phone number is still against the site's rules. But lots of kids do it

Dear Geek Goddess,

My daughter is a serious student and I'm very proud of her academic accomplishments. She is just starting to think about the college application process. I do have a concern that I want to ask you about before I confront her with it. She uses MySpace, Facebook, and some other social networking sites a lot. In fact, I would say she is a bit addicted to them. I have never liked it, but all the kids seem to do it. Now that she's applying for college, shouldn't she stop all that nonsense? Surely the college admission people peruse those when they review applications. I would hate to see all her hard work ruined by a bad habit that everyone in the world can see.

Disapproving in Delaware

· · · · · · · ·

Dear Disapproving,

Your concerns are well-placed, but hold on just a minute before you yank your daughter out of her social networks. First of all, college admissions officers don't scan kids' MySpace pages very often—if at all (though employers often do when they are considering job applicants). "We rarely consider information we find in social networking sites in the application process," explains Thom Golden, Associate Director of Undergraduate Admissions at Vanderbilt University. "We don't really have the time to do that sort of search, but, more importantly, when we get an application, the student and a counselor have signed it to verify that the information in it is accurate. The Internet provides no guarantee of accuracy.

anyway. And even if your kids are too smart to post a phone number, they might reveal a lot of information that you wish they wouldn't: They might use real town names, name their school or teacher, and refer to a restaurant or other locale that gives a clear picture of where they are in the real world. Be very specific when setting your guidelines about giving out personal information. And revisit the subject frequently.

The Danger: The Internet Never Forgets

Facebook, Xanga, MySpace, Friendster, and other sites are all about getting together with friends and talking about your life. Kids seriously buy into that. What they may have missed is that these friends may not be who they say they are and that when you "share" your innermost thoughts, fears, and dreams, any

Anyone can set up a Facebook profile for anyone they want, so there is no guarantee that the page we are looking at actually belongs to this student."

In fact, a lot of colleges use social networking to recruit students. Some colleges create Facebook or MySpace pages so that students and potential students can get to know each other before coming to visit the college or applying. And admissions officers have been known to use these sites to field questions and to get to know students. There are even social networking sites designed specifically to help students find colleges and colleges find students. At Zinch (http://www.zinch .com/), for example, your daughter can create a profile that includes all sorts of things about her interests that would never be captured in a standard college application. And colleges use those profiles to find students who fit criteria they otherwise find very hard to fulfill. "Colleges are looking for diversity," explains Mick Hagen, president and co-founder of Zinch. "When we started brainstorming this idea, we met with the Dean of Admissions at Princeton, and she told us admissions officers often have very specific needs. For example, maybe they need more brass players. It is very difficult for her to seek out brass players in the standard application process. Zinch allows students to put up a page that says who they are and the skills they have and, through those pages, colleges can go looking for the things they need."

So you see, social networks aren't a bad habit; they may be a skill your daughter can use to great advantage. Just be sure she understands how to behave in public and that she knows her social networks are a public place, and then encourage her. She sounds like one smart cookie, and I'll bet she knows what she's doing.

one of the site's 95 million members can read them, whether you count them as your friend or not. (Some sites allow kids to create pages that are not shared with the world at large. Be sure your kids understand this difference.) You and I may know that this is not the place to unload stuff we might be sensitive about or to post photos we will probably someday want to forget we ever took, but don't assume your kids know this. It simply may not have occurred to your innocent 13-year-old that 1 or 2 of her 200 best friends at Xanga may not actually be a pink-wearing, pigtailed, cute 13-year-old girl who is really, really into soccer. Some of them might be a 56-year-old overweight man with a shady past, the school bully who is collecting these confessions for later use, or, in the future, it may be someone interviewing her for a job.

These confessions can have lasting consequences since the Internet has remarkable staying power. Even if you delete that photo or confession, it may have been picked up and posted elsewhere by the time you do, or it may be cached somewhere that's still searchable by Google. (See the Internet Archive at *http://www.archive.org/* for proof of this.) It's a sure thing that your teen doesn't have the foresight to imagine how she is going to feel when she shows up for a job interview in a few years, all scrubbed and college-graduated, only to be faced with a high-school photo of her and her BFF wearing only thongs—or she would never have posted that picture in the first place. The tell-all journal, photos posted on Flickr (a social network based on photographs), and all manner of personal publishing is the mode of expression du jour, and it has spawned an army of experts (such as *http://www.reputationdefender.com/*) who get paid well to scrub the Internet of these embarrassing moments.

The Danger: Malicious Downloads

Kids love to download games, cute little tools, and even stuff they don't need or want just because it's there, they found it, and it's free. They don't see the downside. If a site says, *Click here for free Yu-Gi-Oh cards*, they click. Why not? Well, the "why not" is that those bits of code are often Trojan horses or other malware that's designed to collect personal information (for identity theft and similar purposes), hijack your Internet connection to turn the computer into a spam-sending zombie, or perform all manner of evil digital actions. These little bits of code are designed to be sneaky so that neither you nor your child will notice what they are up to until there is so much junk on the computer it slows to a crawl or you're so inundated with pop-up ads that you can barely surf the Internet. And then someone (that's you, Mom) will have to find a way to clean up that mess—and it's not easy. I'm sure that's not how you intended to spend your day.

The best prevention for this mess it to never download anything from a source you aren't sure of. Educating your kids as to the dangers of indiscriminate downloading is a great place to start. Kids being kids, though, will still download that game (just as they will sneak that cookie that's off limits) as soon as you turn your back—no matter how clever and tech savvy they are. So you should also set up safeguards to prevent them from downloading anything without your permission. In Windows XP, you can't stop them from downloading programs, but you can stop them from installing what they download. Do this by creating a user account for your kids (or for each of them) that does not have administrator rights. From the Control Panel, choose **User Accounts** and you will see the menu shown here.

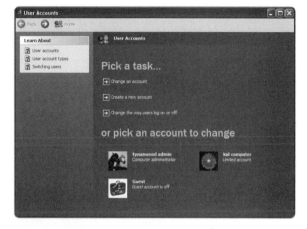

Click **Change an account** (or **Create a new account**), choose the account you want to change, and select **Change the account type**. You will get the menu shown here.

Select **Limited**, as I have done here, and then click **Change Account Type**.

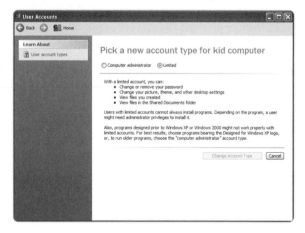

In Vista, you have more options for user accounts, including one that won't let kids download files at all. From the Control Panel, choose **User Accounts and Family Safety**, then **Set up parental control for any user**, then select the kid's account (if you haven't set an account up for your kids, you can do that here). Click the account you want to restrict. Choose the **Windows Vista Web Filtering** option to get this menu:

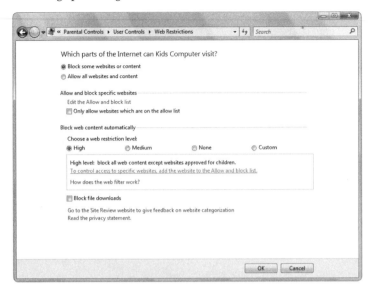

Simply click the **Block file downloads** check box, and you will regain control. Also be sure the computer is running a firewall and a virus protection program, and set up frequent scans of the hard drive.

The Danger: Smut, Drugs, Hate, and Bombs

No matter how you slice it, there is bound to be content on the Internet you don't want your kids to see. When they are very small, this could include medical and health sites, teen pregnancy advice, trailers for scary movies, blogs, and, well, about 90 percent of the Internet. When they get a little older, you want them to be able to research school papers and learn everything they can on a subject if that's what they want to do. That could include a lot of sites you didn't allow them to see when they were smaller. And when they get even older, you want to know that they have access to the health information, teen pregnancy sites, relationship advice, and more mature art and literature that you might not want a youngster to see. But you still don't want them happening onto sites that extol hatred, eating disorders, racism, brutality to women, violence, pornography, or snuff films—all of which is out there. In fact, even if you are over 50 you probably don't want to slip accidentally into a lot of this smut. (Even if you do like stuff that's a bit saucy; much of this content is beyond comprehension.) In all these matters, you the parent are the judge of what's right until the kids get old enough to make their own decisions. Because of the wild variety of material on the Internet, there has been a lot of talk recently of censoring the Internet. But I strongly believe these choices are far too personal to leave to regulation—even if someone does come up with a way to do it. And the Internet is, of course, too valuable to consider banning it for your youngsters entirely. But no matter how savvy you are, it is possible to find inappropriate material by accident. (Just ask my friend Jill.) What's a shocked parent to do? I've already stated my case on keeping an eye on your kids while they surf for as long as you can manage it. Even if you are diligent about this, though, I also recommend you install some age-appropriate Web filtering.

Dear Geek Goddess,

My 6-year-old loves the computer, and I'd like to let him take advantage of the Internet to get some of his seemingly limitless questions answered. I use Google to get answers to my questions, but a lot of the results I get there are a bit mature for him. Can you suggest a way to let him search on his own?

Overwhelmed in Okeechobee

· · · · · ·

Dear Overwhelmed,

Google is an amazing resource, and your son may be ready for it any day now. But until then, I recommend you start him at Yahoo! Kids (http://kids.yahoo .com/) or Ask for Kids (http://www.askkids.com/). Or use Google's own content filters: On Google's main page, click **Search Preferences** *just to the right of the search box. That will bring up, among other things, Google's SafeSearch options. Simply select the* **Use Strict Filtering** *option as I have done here:*

SafeSearch Filtering	Google's SafeSearch blocks web pages containing explicit sexual content from appearing in search results. ◉ Use strict filtering (Filter both explicit text and explicit images) ○ Use moderate filtering (Filter explicit images only - default behavior) ○ Do not filter my search results.

This won't help with ideas that are too hard for him to understand, but it will filter out words and images you don't want him to know. Also considering setting him up at BrainPOP (http://www.brainpop.com/) or Cosmeo (http://www .cosmeo.com/). Kids with questions are often happy, informed, and entertained at these sites for hours or days, and the material is targeted right at the kid with questions.

SAFETY GATES

Even if the computer is in the family room and you have established rules and guidelines, content filtering software is like wearing a seatbelt in the car, goggles when you use power tools, and a life vest on a boat. Accidents happen. In fact, some of the nastiest sites out there are so pernicious that accidentally landing on one can start an explosion of disgusting pop-up ads that you will have a hard time stopping. If you have been following my advice up until now, you probably already have some sort of pop-up, virus, and malware protection (if not, please read Chapter 8—don't go out there naked!). But if you have kids in the house, having a stronger brand of protection that makes sure they stay clean by standing guard over browsing, chats, and perhaps email is almost a necessity. These tools are not a replacement for education, but they act as safety alarms, training wheels, and parental assistants. They are also handy for enforcing time limits and other rules you've established.

Unfortunately there are a lot of tools out there, and it's difficult to determine which is right for your needs. To this end, Adam Thierer of The Progress and Freedom Foundation has written a definitive study (available at *http://www.pff .org/parentalcontrols/*) of all the tools available to parents to monitor and control what their kids are up to online. Thierer is a strong advocate for education rather than regulation when it comes to Internet safety and is lobbying for an education campaign much like the government-sponsored campaigns to raise awareness of forest fires, car seat safety, crime awareness, and physical fitness. I completely support this cause. He also suggests installing parental control software. "There is no substitute for teaching kids how to behave online, but that's no reason you can't put up some safety gates," he says.

In his report responding to suggested regulation on this matter, "Rep. Bean's 'SAFER NET Act': An Education-Based Approach to Online Child Safety," he explains more fully:

> Government officials feel that more needs to be done to help parents shield
> their children from content they find objectionable while also helping
> to root out serious threats to child safety, especially online predators.
> Regulation, however, is not the only answer. In fact, it's not even the most
> effective answer. *Education* should serve as the cornerstone of any serious
> effort to deal with the issue of protecting children from either objectionable
> content or various cyber-dangers.
>
> In 2002, the National Research Council of the National Academy of Sciences
> brought together a blue-ribbon panel of experts to study how best to protect
> children in our new Internet world . . . The report discussed a sweeping
> array of methods and technological tools for dealing with potentially

objectionable media content and other online concerns. Ultimately, however, the experts used a compelling metaphor to explain why education was the most important tool that parents and policy makers should rely upon:

Technology—in the form of fences around pools, pool alarms, and locks—can help protect children from drowning in swimming pools. However, teaching a child to swim—and when to avoid pools—is a far safer approach than relying on locks, fences, and alarms to prevent him or her from drowning. Does this mean that parents should not buy fences, alarms, or locks? Of course not—because they do provide some benefit. But parents cannot rely exclusively on those devices to keep their children safe from drowning, and most parents recognize that a child who knows how to swim is less likely to be harmed than one who does not. Furthermore, teaching a child to swim and to exercise good judgment about bodies of water to avoid has applicability and relevance far beyond swimming pools—as any parent who takes a child to the beach can testify.

Though they are by no means a complete solution or a replacement for knowing what your kids are up to or teaching them to surf the Web safely, these tools can be very convenient—the same way putting alarms around the pool allows you to go in the house rather than stand vigil over the water.

A Web filter—any Web filter—would have kept that evening at Jill and Jeff's house clean and happy. These stop a kid from accidentally landing on a site that contains content in areas that you have designated as inappropriate. Oh, and if you have an Internet addict in the house (child or adult), they can help you set time limits or block a site that's become a particular problem. I have a kid who is devoted to MMORPGs (massively multiplayer online role playing games, said really fast like the Comic Book Guy in *The Simpsons* would). So I use a Web filter not only to keep him from stumbling onto the dark side but also to block this particular distraction until he has finished his homework, played outside, practiced his music, lived in the real world, and asked permission. Then I unblock it. Used in this way, it becomes a motivator rather than a distraction, and we are both happier for it.

THE WEB FILTERS

I like to look around the house before I buy something in the hope that I might already have something that will suffice. This works here too. Your ISP quite likely offers some parental control tools that might fit your needs. In fact, if you have kids in the house and all other things are equal, you might want to let this feature influence your choice of ISP. For example, EarthLink offers website filtering, kid-safe email, and controls to boot kids off the computer when you deem they have used up their time allotment.

If your ISP doesn't offer parental controls, you may have some in your security suite. If you sprang for the full-blown suite from McAfee or Norton, there are some tools in those, though they are not as complete as the tools designed strictly for the purpose.

Since you may find you want a stronger brand of protection (if your ISP doesn't offer anything you find up to snuff), I have taken a look at some of the specific parental control tools generally available to you below. But keep in mind that things change in the world of software, and a feature that was not available when I looked at it may have been added since. Fortunately, you can take any of these for a trial run by downloading them to your kid's computer before you commit any money.

Windows Vista

If your computer is brand spanking new, it is likely running the Windows Vista operating system, meaning it already has some very nice parental controls. This is one of the major improvements in Vista over Windows XP.

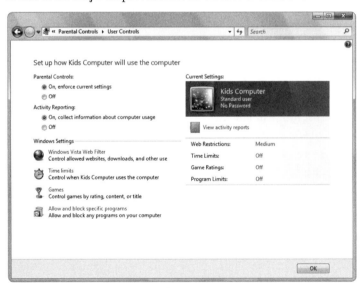

You can access the new parental controls in Vista through the Control Panel.

Vista allows you to set up a user login for every person who will use the computer. That way you can set the computer rules you want each user to live by. So if your teen shares a computer with a 10-year-old, you can allow games, websites, and time controls that are appropriate for each of them. Vista is the only tool I looked at that allows you to set a game rating for each user. That way, at least, the younger child won't have access to the first-person shooters you can't stop the teen from playing. Even if your youngster takes his laptop to school or a friend's house, he won't be able to install and play games (on his own computer anyway) with a higher rating than you have approved. In fact, if he's grounded, you can block games altogether.

In Vista you can allow kids to play games based on their ratings.

Vista is pretty flexible when it comes to blocking Internet content as well, allowing you to select an option to simply let Vista decide what a "high" level of protection is or going in and customizing—by categories such as hate, weapons, adult content, or by particular website—what you want to filter out. You can also block file downloading completely so your kids won't be tempted by every offer and "free" game they happen upon—at least until they can tell the difference between legitimate downloads and those that are more likely adware or Trojan horses. You can always override this if you want to allow him to download the latest Virtual Villagers from Pogo or Yahoo! Games.

Windows XP

While the parental controls in Windows XP are not as sweet as those in Vista, they do exist. If your kids use Internet Explorer (part of XP) to surf the Web, you should quickly turn on some basic filtering before you let the kids have at it if you

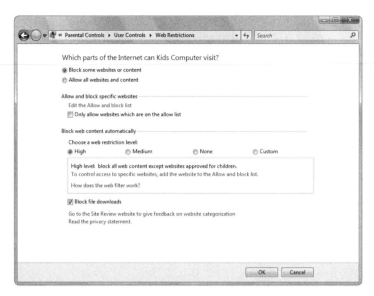

In Vista, you can block all file downloads when your kids are using the computer—until they are old enough to tell the difference between a game and a con.

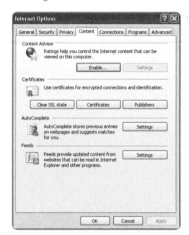

aren't ready to install something more effective. Choose **Tools**, then **Internet Options** and, in the menu that pops up, choose the **Content** tab. You'll get the menu shown here.

Click **Enable** to get a slider bar you can use to dial up the protections. You can set up a password so that your tot can't simply override these filters by choosing the **General** tab within the content filtering menu shown here.

Then click the **Create Password** button and follow the directions.

In the General tab, you also have the option of allowing sites that have no rating, but the rating system Content Advisor uses is not very effective. So if you choose that option, you'll be letting through a lot of smut (including the site that spoiled my dinner party at Jill's). But if you don't allow those sites through, you will have to manually approve (by typing your password) nearly every site your kid wants to get to. Since many websites are made up of hundreds of sub-sites, you'll be at this all day. This tool may be better than nothing, but it is hardly ideal, so don't stop here.

Net Nanny

Net Nanny is probably the best-known name in parental control tools. I use this program on the computers in my house that aren't running Vista. I like that Net Nanny lets me manage the kids' Internet access from my own computer via the Internet and is willing to send me an email anytime a kid requests an override or gets blocked or warned away from a site.

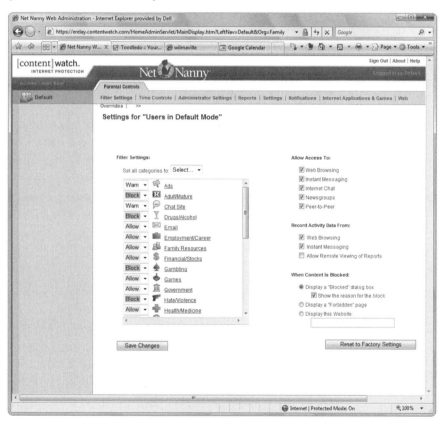

You can choose what to allow and what to block in Net Nanny using a rich set of criteria, but if something is blocked that you would allow, it's easy to override it.

In addition to letting Net Nanny protect the kids from net nastiness, I frequently log on from my own computer to block gaming altogether until I decide the homework, chores, and other real-world responsibilities are completed. It also shows me reports on what the kids are up to so I can see how much time they spend on IM, for example. This allows me to make informed decisions about what to block or limit. And I love setting time controls so that my daughter gets kicked off the Internet an hour before her bedtime, essentially fighting that fight for me. This program only blocks Internet use, so it doesn't stop my little game addict, but it's a nice control.

SafeKeeper

Some parental control tools rely on technical tools such as keywords or little software robots that search the Internet for words, phrases or other indications that an image or content includes nudity or offensive material. But the best of them rely on people looking at websites to maintain a list of sites that are banned under each category. According to Phil Worms of Netintelligence, the company that makes SafeKeeper (*http://www.mysafekeeper.com/*), "We have rather a large team of people who do nothing but look at websites that have come in through the bots or other means. A bot will block family photos of a beach vacation or allow nasty content because the colors in the photographs are murky. A person knows better."

I like SafeKeeper because it allows me to manage not only the Internet but other programs on up to three computers via the Internet for one price. I can sit at my computer and change time controls, block sites, or look at logs of my kids' online outings. My desk happens to be at home, but this would work just as well if yours is at work since you can access your account from any computer that's connected to the Internet.

SafeEyes.com

While most filtering tools will let you set blocks of time when the Internet (or sometimes particular programs or the entire computer) is either off limits or allowed, some will let you give each kid a time allotment. With SafeEyes installed, for example, you can tell your kids that they are allowed an hour a day on the Internet and—even if they haven't used that up—they have to log off an hour before bedtime. The software will back you up.

I like that feature, but SafeEyes wasn't for me. It was always asking for a password from me, which reminded my kids that I was using the tool to monitor their Internet use. I found this frustrating because I already have too many passwords to remember, and it caused the kids to whine—and I don't need more of that. It also only regulated Internet use, not other software on the computer, and my son will simply switch to a game on his computer when booted off the Internet. The stuff he gets up to on the Internet (usually) is more educational than computer games, so that wasn't an improvement. Still, it's a functional filter at a reasonable price.

CyberPatrol

One thing I liked about this program is the quick-override option. Say you want to use the kid's computer—or lend it to an adult guest—and you don't want to play by the rules, you simply type your password and tell it how long to allow all the rules to be broken. In fact, this program lets you manage particular programs. (Got a game-addiction problem or excessive IMer?) It will let you set a time allowance as well as times of the day where Internet or particular programs are off limits, and the tools for setting this up are very easy to use. It will even let you set a weekly time limit for Internet use, which I thought a rather nice feature. (I considered installing that one on my husband's computer.) The only downside, in fact, that I found was that this program doesn't allow remote management features. So if you want to change the time allowance or block a particular website or program, you have to sit down at the kid's computer to do it.

CYBERsitter

I found this one a bit geeky, asking intimidating questions and expecting an understanding of filtering tools that a typical user may not immediately possess. Again, this one blocks only Internet access, so if you are looking for something that helps you limit all computer use, this software isn't it. But it has some impressive Internet reporting features and keeps a log of both sides of every chat conversation in case you ever need to do some detective work to find out what your kids have been up to. It does block MySpace and other social networking sites—a good thing if your kids are under 13, I think. But you can turn this feature off when your kids get older.

CYBERsitter does an initial scan of material already on the computer, in case your kids have been downloading nastiness, but it found so much stuff on my daughter's computer that was innocent that I found it to be of marginal use. I'm too lazy to sort through 200 false negatives, so I ended up just ignoring its findings altogether.

You only pay once for CYBERSitter, though, rather than having to ante up for an annual fee. Like many of the other programs here, it is not a simple matter to uninstall, which will keep the kids from just turning it off but also might aggravate you when you decide to take off the training wheels.

AOL Parental Controls

If you have (or don't mind getting) an AOL screen name for yourself and each of your kids, you can get your parental controls free from the AOL website. Click **Downloads** and then **Parental Controls** at *http://www.aol.com/* and follow the directions. Once you get it all set up, your kids will have to log into their computers with their AOL screen names. This does remind them that you are monitoring them, which—as I said—wasn't ideal for us because it led to complaining. Also, it offers only a few choices in terms of protection (low, medium, high). But hey, free is free.

LET THEM HAVE FUN

The Internet is an amazing resource for kids. A kid not old enough to walk to the mall can meet other kids from all over the world, have boundless learning at her fingertips, play interactive games that teach concepts that once required boring evenings repeating sums or spelling words, watch educational movies, get immediate answers to the most trivial or pressing questions, and converse instantly with a relative living on another continent through any instant messaging program. The Internet isn't the easiest entertainment, communication, or learning tool for a parent to manage, admittedly, but it is by far the most worthwhile. I am proud that both of my kids prefer to spend an hour at BrainPOP or chat with a cousin on Skype to watching just about anything on TV, which to them is nearly boring. I do spend more time and effort monitoring what they do online than I do on movies, TV, books, or even computer games, but I consider my efforts well worth it. I never have to tell them to turn off that drivel on the TV. (Though I do have a checklist of real-world activities they have to do before they can log on.) I am faced instead with arguments like, "Mom, I won't learn medieval history by playing outside! Why can't I do this?" So overall, I consider the Internet—even with the extra effort—the best weapon in my parenting arsenal.

10 Groovy Gear and Gadgets

"I was meeting a girlfriend for lunch recently," says Susan Trainer, founder and CEO of Trainer Communications, "but she was late. Instead of getting mad and wasting what is to me very precious time, I fired up my BlackBerry and used the time to go over numbers and discuss a project with a colleague." As an executive and a mother of four, Susan is busy. This sort of idle time—waiting in doctor's offices, at kids' sporting events, for late lunch engagements—was once a major source of stress. But she has managed to use a collection of gadgets to harness that time instead. When Susan's lunch date that day finally arrived, she found Susan embroiled in her work. It took Susan a few moments to wind down so she could partake in the lunch date, which her friend saw as a reason to feel sorry for Susan. She called Susan's BlackBerry a leash and announced that she herself would never get one. This is a surprisingly common female sentiment. Most of the women I know who have embraced technology have been told something similar.

"I don't see it that way," says Susan. "I used those 10 minutes being productive instead of getting annoyed because my friend was late. That was work I otherwise would have been doing that evening when I would rather be spending time with my kids." When Susan's friend's employer offered her a BlackBerry, she refused it. "She was proud of herself about that," says Susan. "But I know that she just guaranteed that she will not be the best she could be at her job."

Gadgets may smack of masculine energy, evoke fears of never being able to turn off the electronic leash, and even bring out anger in women who believe that those people obnoxiously chattering and texting on cell phones have let technology cloud their judgment. But I'm with Susan. I have managed to squeeze in work while waiting for my daughter outside a gymnastics class instead of discussing the latest episode of *Heroes* with people I barely know. I don't consider it a leash. Without it, I might have had to go to an office and let a babysitter watch my kids take their first steps or learn to ride a bike. But I use gadgets for more than just time management. I use them for entertainment, to keep track of my hobbies and exercise, and just to keep my sanity. Like most women, I have laughed more than once at a man for the silly array of gadgets he wears on his belt or for his affection for the TV remote. But like most women who have embraced gadgets, I find they often make the impossible possible—though I keep them in my purse rather than wearing them like some geek badge of honor. Perhaps the women who have not embraced them simply don't need to use gadgets to stay organized? But I suspect they are simply not giving the idea a chance.

CAMERAS

"Life is all about the moments," says Angela Crickman, a registered nurse in California. "The cute things your kids say, their cute looks. Knowing you have pictures of your kids doing all those silly things you love and actually knowing where those photos are is a great thing!" No one understands how fleeting life's events are quite the way a woman does. The wedding that took months to arrange will be over in hours, and the baby wrapped in pink will be piercing her navel before you can blink. Is it any wonder women like cameras? And digital cameras are the best. Digital cameras allow you to delete embarrassing shots before anyone sees them or even upload compromising photos of your ex to a Flickr account before he downs yet another Scotch (though this is a really bad idea). The market is flooded with digital cameras that are tiny, cute, and make all manner of promises. That's the problem with them—how do you choose?

Shopping for a digital camera is a frustrating exercise in temptation, confusion, and dizzying choice, which probably accounts for the pile of emails I have from girlfriends asking me to recommend the perfect camera so they don't have to sort out the choices on their own. But all the important choices about cameras are personal, despite the plethora of confusing specs and acronyms. Let your lifestyle and the things you want to take pictures of determine what you want in a camera, and you will do well. Here's a list of features to consider as you shop.

Convenience

If you just want to take the occasional vacation photo, aren't planning to make frame-worthy prints of your photos, and don't want to become a pack horse for your gear, the camera in your cell phone may be all you need—and it will have the added advantage of always being in your purse. If you find you want a camera capable of taking photos you want to display, you can still find a camera small enough to keep forever stashed in your purse. Even professional photographers keep one of these tiny point-and-shoot models on hand, because the camera that's with you takes the most pictures. You'll find some sweet cameras on the market for not much

more than $100 that will fit in your smallest evening bag without skimping on features. They'll let you zoom in on your subject, capture images at respectable 6 to 8 megapixels (keep reading for more on megapixels), edit out red-eye automatically, and review your shots on the camera's screen. For a little more money, you can get a lot of fancy features packed into a very small package.

Photo used by permission of Sony Electronics, Inc. The Sony Cyber-shot DSC-T2 comes in five fun colors (black, white, green, teal, and pink), can shoot in 8.2 megapixels, and has 4GB of internal memory.

Simplicity

Think of cameras in dating terms. Have you ever found yourself out with a man who looked great on paper (and in that suit) but was impossible to crack? Nothing he said made sense, he didn't get your jokes, you felt like you should like him, but you just couldn't get interested. You and your camera need to click. (Sorry.) This is especially true if you hated your last camera or are new to digital cameras. A camera that you can pick up and start taking photos with right away will get a lot more use than one that frustrates you. This is a personal matter, so pick up every camera that appeals to you for whatever reason, and see if you can make sense of it. Are the buttons clearly marked? Does the menu system make sense? Do you need to crack the manual to take a picture? If you get an immediate feeling of "What the #$@#@#$%#!" move on to another camera. You will eventually find one you love, a feature that should not be underrated.

Good looks

Women are often told we are silly for caring about the way things look. I think the way gadgets look and feel is important. Their color is also important. Call me superficial, but I wouldn't carry a purse that I thought was ugly, and the same goes for gadgets. The marketplace is full of adorable, colorful, and easy-to-use cameras. If these appeal to you, let them. Just like with a man, though, make sure this toy runs deeper than its looks. Make sure the camera is easy to use and a size you are happy with. Then scan the specs to make sure they meet your requirements.

Dear Geek Goddess,

I'm shopping for a camera and keep running into the term "megapixels," which—if you can judge from the way the salespeople start jawing on about it—is the most important feature any camera can have. Unfortunately, I'm pretty fuzzy on what the term means. Do you think you can bring it into focus for me?

Blurry in Burgaw

． ． ． ． ． ． ．

Dear Blurry,

Despite sounding like some sort of arty superhero, this term describes something pretty simple. A megapixel is a million pixels. When it's used to describe cameras, it means that the camera has that many sensors capable of recording pixels. So the bigger the number describing a camera's megapixel ability, the more sensors the camera has and the more detailed the photo it takes will be. A 3-megapixel camera has approximately 3 million sensors. A photograph taken at 3 megapixels won't be as dense or detailed as one taken at 8 megapixels. Megapixels are an important part of your camera choice but not as important as most men make it sound. Men enjoy tossing numbers around, but women know better. Big is good, but even a camera that can boast 10 megapixels is a lousy camera if you don't like it.

Megapixels

Many people start with a camera's megapixels when camera shopping, but, despite the impressive terminology, this isn't that big of a deal.

In the non-professional photography world, you will encounter cameras that come with somewhere around 2 megapixels (your cell phone camera, for example) and go up to about 10 megapixels or more. The higher a camera's megapixel capacity, the more expensive it's likely to be. Cameras with more megapixels allow you to take detailed photographs that are good for poster-sized blowups. These high-resolution photos are going to be large; probably too large to email or post to an online photo site. A camera that has 10 megapixels will have a setting that allows you to take photos at lower resolutions, but a 3-megapixel camera will not let you take photos at higher resolutions.

If you don't plan to make posters from your photos, you don't need the highest resolution available. A 6-megapixel camera will take sharp photos that you should be able to blow up to crisp 11-by-17-inch prints, which is enough for most people. One cool thing about having a high-resolution camera is that it gives you more room to edit your photos on your computer later (with Adobe Photoshop or some other photo-editing software). So you can cut smaller parts out of your photo—just the faces, say—and that cut-out section won't be as grainy or blurry as it would be if you cut it from a low-res image. Even if you are in the market for more serious camera, you can save money by getting one that shoots at 8 megapixels instead of 10 or more. Consider what you plan to do with your photos and your budget; if poster-sized art is not part of your plan, a camera with 6 to 8 megapixels should be fine.

Battery life

This is a big deal with most gadgets. Short battery life is particularly frustrating with cameras, because you just want to take the thing out and shoot photos, not spend your life making sure it gets a power meal. Be sure your camera has a rechargeable battery. Take a look at the claims the manufacturer makes for expected battery life (taken with a grain of salt), then use these claims to compare models. If you plan to use your camera on a vacation where you don't want to worry about battery life, consider buying an extra battery.

Autofocus

Let's face it, autofocus is easy. But you may also find that you want to be able to easily turn the date and timestamp, flash, and red-eye features on and off without going to school first. Some cameras come with easy-to-access presets for shooting scenery or portraits, and some bury these handy features deep in an onscreen menu. Check that out before you buy. Also, if you imagine that you will one day evolve into the Ansel Adams of digital photography or even want to learn one or two snazzy effects, be sure you can turn off the autofocus and presets completely and that manual controls for setting aperture and shutter speed are available. Some point-and-shoot cameras don't let you choose any manual settings.

Zoom

That shiny, red camera in your hand claims it has *7x zoom*, but what does that mean? It means that the camera can magnify an image seven times, which is nice. A zoom lens can save you from having to shimmy up to your subject on your belly to get that close-up. But most digital point-and-shoot cameras offer some sort of zoom, and somewhere the specs will say which part of the zoom is *optical* and which is *digital*. Given the choice, you should opt for higher optical over digital zoom. *Optical zoom* is handled by the camera lens, and the results should be crisp and clear. *Digital zoom* relies on software in the camera (not the camera's lens) to enhance the image, and the results are usually not as good as you'll get from optical zoom.

Shutter lag

It's your daughter's birthday. Everyone is singing "Happy Birthday," and you want a picture of her blowing out the candles. You find the perfect moment, press the shutter, and nothing happens. The flash doesn't go off, your daughter blows out the candles and looks darn cute doing it, and you have to find a knife to cut the cake. You set the camera down, angry at it, and then it decides to take a picture, getting a photo of someone's elbow. That is what's known as *shutter lag*, and it is one of the main reasons people move up from point-and-shoot cameras to a digital single-lens reflex camera (DSLR). (See "The Semi-Pro Digital Camera" on page 249.) Shutter lag varies by camera and is hard to evaluate in the store, which is why your camera's return policy is important. If your camera never gets the shot you want in any kind of light, return it. You may not need a DSLR; perhaps a higher-quality point-and-shoot will do. But shutter lag is not exclusively the fault of the photographer and is often a function of the processor speed in the camera. If you are still experiencing it in bright light, it's not going to improve.

Memory card

Most digital cameras have a slot that accepts a small memory card that can hold lots of photos. For example, while your camera's internal memory may only hold two photos taken at the camera's highest resolution, a 2GB memory card can hold hundreds of images. You can get memory cards that hold much more than that, but low-capacity ones are cheap. Do not buy a camera that doesn't accept a memory card: You will hate it instantly.

The Semi-Pro Digital Camera

Digital cameras have made photography accessible to scads of people—myself included—who would never have gotten involved in putting a darkroom in their house or wearing a vest stuffed with hundreds of rolls of different film and seven pre-loaded cameras strung around their neck. These days, taking photography a bit more seriously is within easy reach of anyone willing to spend a bit of money on a nicer camera and a lens or two. If you are the parent of a sport-playing child, are frustrated with the quality of the pictures you've been getting with your point-and-shoot camera, feel the artistic pull of photography, or simply want to take better pictures, consider upgrading to a digital single-lens reflex camera (DSLR).

Photo used by permission of Sony Electronics, Inc. The Sony Alpha DSLR-a350 ($799) is a great example of a DSLR rife with features for amateur photographers: a live-view that swivels for easy framing, easy-to-access presets, and long battery life. This one shoots at a maximum of 14.2 megapixels, but you can find DSLRs that take shots at lower resolutions and start at about $500.

Until rather recently, the DSLR was considered a professional camera. DSLRs use a lens and mirror arrangement to expose the "film" instead of using a processor the way point-and-shoot cameras do. And using one is more like using one of those serious old-style professional film cameras. They are smaller than a pro-level film camera but much bigger than the tiny point-and-shoot you can drop in your pocket. DSLRs are making professional-quality results available to just about anyone who can afford them. They have autofocus features and handy presets for shooting portraits and fast-moving subjects, just like the point-and-shoots. Not all DSLRs have a live-view feature (though almost all point-and-shoots do) because you need to look through the viewfinder to frame your shot with the lens. But some offer a live preview, which is not as accurate as the viewfinder but still very handy. So if you are planning to take pictures of kids—who like to see Mom's face without the camera in front of it—look for this feature. All let you look at the shot after you've taken it so you can quickly see how your photos are turning out.

But the cool part is that DSLR cameras allow you to change lenses (actually screw one off and replace it with another lens), which means you can buy specialized lenses to take macro shots (big pictures of small things), wide-angle lenses, and more. If you're in the private detective business, you could even get a giant zoom lens that allows you to see details your eye can't even register, so you can get the money shot from the building across the street.

Dear Geek Goddess,

I recently bought a DSLR camera, and I love it. It's big—I need a camera bag for it—but I take such great shots with it that I'm considering starting a business taking baby portraits. In fact, I feel as if I have a relationship with this camera—a really powerful one. Who knew? I'm ready to take it to the next level, though: out of the autofocus setting. Do you have any advice?

Daring in Detroit

· · · · · · ·

Dear Daring,

I love my DSLRs too. The next step up from the autofocus setting is the presets. Most DSLRs have a dial at the top or side of the camera with aperture, f-stop, and other presets for the different sort of pictures most people want to take: portrait, landscape, fast-moving subjects, portraits in low light, and more. They have funny little icons you have to sort out, but once you get those (look in your manual for a description of the presets on your camera), you should be off and shooting. I strongly recommend that you also visit the website of one of my girlfriends— photographer Me Ra Koh at http://www.merakoh.com/home.php. She not only offers tips for women like us, but she has created videos of her photography workshops for women. The second in her series is called Beyond the Green Box: Understanding Your Digital Camera, and it offers hands-on instruction for getting out of the autofocus setting.

I have two DSLRs, and my photography made a huge leap when I moved up to them. In less than 30 minutes with one of these, I have watched women go from "I hate photography! I never get a single good photograph!" to "Wow! What's the cost of a macro lens that would allow me to get a close up of my daughter's face and blur the background?" Some more things to consider when shopping for one of these are how it feels in your hand (they tend to be heavy, especially if you add a zoom lens), where the buttons are, and the type of battery that comes with the camera. Battery life on these—because they rely more heavily on a standard-camera view finder instead of the LCD ones—is often much longer than with a point-and-shoot, but you still want a rechargeable one. When comparing prices, be sure each camera you are considering includes a lens—this might be called a *kit*—because some prices are for just the camera body. Lenses are expensive, but the one that comes in the kit is a good, versatile starter lens. Once you use it for a while, you will have a better sense of what other lenses you might want (if any).

Accessories

What's the first thing a woman does when she gets a new gadget? Accessorize. Once you get your new camera settled into a new camera bag (try eBags—*http://www.ebags.com/*), you'll want to trick it out with some gear of its own.

Memory Cards

Like popping in a new roll of film, extra memory cards allow you to keep right on shooting after your camera gives you the "Out of Memory" message. It's always a good idea to stock up on these, especially if you are going on vacation and don't want to bring a laptop along to dump your photos on when you run out of memory.

Photo courtesy of Lexar

Wireless Card

If you are a devotee of posting your photos to online photo albums like Flickr, Snapfish, and Picasa, or to your Facebook profile, consider popping a wireless card like the Eye-Fi (pictured) into your camera's memory slot. That Wi-Fi connection will allow you to send your photos wirelessly (whenever you have a connection) directly to your computer and to your online photo album.

Photo courtesy of Eye-Fi

PORTABLE PHOTO PRINTERS

You probably already have a printer for your computer, but you might want a dedicated one for your camera. While many inkjet printers do a good job with photos, small, portable photo printers give you instant prints on photo paper without a computer, which makes these a lot of fun at parties. You plug your camera (or memory card) directly into the printer and print straight to it. The print quality is nice—probably better than your desktop printer—and the glossy image will be long lasting, but your choice of paper size is limited.

DIGITAL PICTURE FRAMES

These are essentially just an LCD screen that stores and displays your photos—hundreds if you like—in a frame you can set on the mantle or hang on the wall. You load your photos onto the frame's internal memory and tell it how often to change the photo and whether to use fade or other effects. Some frames will even play music to accompany your slide show and come with a remote so you can flip through your pictures while your tail is parked comfortably on the couch. The frames are inexpensive enough these days that you might even consider loading one up with photos to give as a gift.

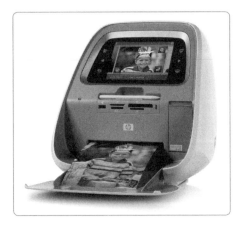

Photo courtesy of HP

The HP Photosmart A826 Home Photo Center even lets you create personalized greeting cards without ever connecting to a computer. Pop in your camera's memory card and edit your photo, add text and clip-art, include a frame, and print, all from the 7-inch color touch screen.

Photo courtesy of Pandigital

An assortment of Pandigital's digital photo frames

VIDEO CAMERAS

Once one of the most expensive personal electronic purchases the average consumer would ever make, video cameras are now as universal and accessible as cell phones. Tiny cameras that pack features we once would have marveled at in a $1,000 camera now cost little more than $100. It is now easy to buy your middle-school Tarantino wannabe his own camera, pick one up on the way to a wedding, and get a high-definition direct-to-digital video camera capable of filming uninterrupted for 15 hours so you (or, more likely, he) can record every second of a birth. There are also new ways to use video, thanks to sites such as YouTube that make owning a video camera something normal people consider even when they aren't about to have a baby or get married.

The first thing to look at when shopping for a video camera is the storage media used to hold your footage. How many people still have videos of their kids on a hulking camera that records to VHS tapes? (A show of hands, please?) Well, some things never change. Video always requires a lot of storage space, so devices with new storage technologies are the trendiest and most expensive of these babies. VHS tapes went by the wayside long ago and have been replaced by a succession of innovations: MiniDV tapes, MiniDVDs, DVDs, memory sticks, and hard drives. I'm sure this will keep changing well into the future, but the hard-drive option we have now is a big improvement over bulky tapes.

Direct-to-digital storage, today's cutting edge, stores life's moving moments on a hard drive inside the camera. Some cameras store 20 hours before you need to transfer the video to a computer to free up space. Others store only 20 minutes. And that storage capacity—as well as fancy zoom features, high definition, and the ability to shoot in challenging lighting conditions—accounts for most of the wild variation in price among video cameras. For little more than $100 you can buy a cute little Flip video camera that holds 60 minutes of video and fits in your pocket. For many people, that's enough.

Photo courtesy of Pure Digital Technologies
The Flip Mino (http://www.theflip.com/) is a pocket-sized camcorder (4" by 2" by 0.6" and only 3.2 oz.) that records up to 60 minutes of video. It connects to your TV for instant viewing or uploads to your computer via the built-in USB port (shown flipped up).

But if you want to make full-length movies, capture complete soccer games, or record your jaunt through Europe, complete with charming interviews of Nordic sheep herders, you might want to spend a little extra to get a camera that will do more.

Some feature-packed video cameras won't set you back much more than the little Flip, especially if you are willing to store your video on last year's storage media. Look hard at how important the storage media options are to you and how they will actually affect your use of the camera. While it can mean a difference of hundreds of dollars to get a camera with lots of hard-drive storage, direct-to-digital really is an improvement over the previous options (tapes and DVDs). It's much easier to get your footage off the camera and onto your computer where you can edit it, upload it to your blog, or share it via your broadband connection with distant relatives or colleagues.

Most video cameras offer some sort of zoom. The one I recently gave my son has 40x optical zoom, which lets me take really tight close-ups of my kids playing in the surf without ever getting up from my beach chair. That can transform not only the way you take film, but your actual memories, because it allows you get closer even than your own eye can see clearly. Who wouldn't like to have their memories enhanced by technology? These babies have come a long way from that camera that's gathering dust in your family room.

Photo used by permission of Sony Electronics, Inc. The HDR-SR5 High-Definition Hard Disc Drive Handycam Camcorder records up to 22 hours of video straight to its 60GB internal hard drive and shoots in high definition.

As with any camera, look for ease of use before you make up your mind. I have tried cameras that are so easy to use that I could hand them to an 8-year-old and expect good footage. Others are so difficult to use that I accidentally—and repeatedly—deleted all my footage.

Accessories

While we are on the subject of video cameras, I want to recommend one of my favorite accessories for them—and for your living room—the Sony DVDirect Multi Function DVD Recorder. Plug your video camera, VCR, or digital camera into this little baby, and it will burn your footage directly to a DVD so you don't have to connect it to a computer at all. Not only will it handle the footage you just shot with your new camera, but it will take all those family videos that are gathering dust on old storage media (like VHS) and transform it all into a handy collection of DVDs. It's simple to use and does not require a computer, so you can keep it right there in the living room.

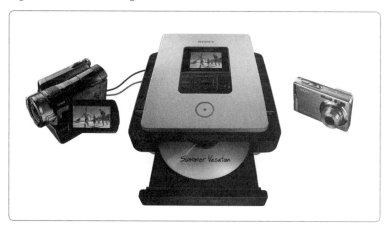

Photo of Sony DVDirect Multi Function DVD Recorder used by permission of Sony Electronics, Inc.

PERSONAL DIGITAL ASSISTANTS

"I love my iPhone," says Allison Schwartz, Life Coach at Allium Coaching. "My boyfriend gave it to me as a gift, but even he didn't know how much I would love it. I have my schedule with me at all times. I can record notes and send them to myself via email so there are no more small papers floating around in my purse. It has a great camera and screen for viewing photos. The map program replaces my need for a GPS (global positioning system for maps and directions), and the Internet access is great. With this little device I feel more organized and prepared."

Keeping track of the stuff of life is one area where technology can be a tremendous help—making possible what was once too mind-boggling to attempt (managing a small business with children in tow, for example). In this, PDAs and smartphones can be a tremendous help. They keep you organized, connected, and on top of the million things that are threatening to go off track in your life. They let you capture small moments, time that otherwise might go wasted, and actually save time by eliminating redundant tasks like writing phone numbers down in several places or comparing calendars with a spouse or work associate. But they are confusing to buy, in part because there are a lot of features to consider, but also because the decision is so clouded by the influence of trends. A friend recently asked me if I thought a Palm Pilot would help her keep on top of the million details of her landscaping business. Before I could answer, everyone in our small dinner party laughed at her and flashed their respective

BlackBerries, Tilts, or iPhones. She was shamed by her own ignorance of the current technology and skulked away before I could answer her question, which was a good one. Okay, Palm devices are no longer called Palm Pilots, but she was approaching things in the right way: She was starting with what she needed—something handy that she could use to capture ideas, make notes to herself, take pictures, keep track of people, and get her email on the go. And the current version of the Palm—the LifeDrive, Palm T|X, or even the mobile phone and PDA combos Treo or Centro—was probably exactly what she wanted.

I know people who rely entirely on their smartphone the way Allison does. Others use a laptop, an ultra-portable computer (a very tiny full-fledged computer), a separate PDA and a cell phone, or just a simple PDA with no ability to connect to the Internet or make phone calls. But this is another realm where your work, buying habits, and style preferences are more important than what the current "it" device may be. I know people who grabbed an iPhone the minute it came out only to discover later that they needed some of the tools they had been using on their older Treo and ended up carrying both devices around. Think about yourself first, then get what you need—even if iPhones are the look this season. (Unless getting this season's look *is* what you want; in that case, go for it.)

One complaint I hear often from women who do not want to move to a PDA is, "I love my paper agenda. I won't give that up." Well, I have a PDA, but I love my paper agenda, too. I love the ritual of buying a new one every year. I love the feel of pen on paper. But writing things down is not the same as capturing phone numbers as you dial, entering all your repeat appointments for the year in just a few minutes, having your health information in your purse when you're at the doctor's office, or looking up something on the Internet while waiting to pick up a child from school—all from a device that will play music and audio books and fit in your pocket.

The best time to consider buying a PDA is when you are shopping for a cell phone. But you can also get a PDA that is not a cell phone, and some of these are very good. Following is a breakdown of features to help you evaluate what you want.

Keyboard

Manufacturers are getting mighty tricky when it comes to sneaking keyboards into PDAs with sliders that hide the keyboard, onscreen keyboards, and phones that spin around to expose a keyboard. Take a very hard look at the keyboard, because no matter how innovative it seems, the type of keyboard you choose is both a personal and very important decision. The size of your fingers, how fast you type, and even where and when you type will affect what you want in a keyboard. Some people love onscreen keyboards. Others are fanatics for the thumb-typing of the BlackBerry devices. This is something only you can decide for yourself.

Internet connection

Even if you are buying a phone that is also a PDA, consider how you will connect to the Internet and get email. Units that connect via the cellular network are convenient—there is a cellular connection almost everywhere these days—but this connection can be expensive and slow. The highly touted new 3G network claims to attain speeds that rival or exceed Wi-Fi over broadband in some areas of the country, but I have yet to see anything like that in action. (I do long for the day. . . .) That's why more expensive PDAs offer a Wi-Fi connection in addition to a data plan over a cellular connection. These can end up saving you money in the long run by letting you tap into free—and much faster—Wi-Fi connections when they are available. In fact, you can get a PDA that will get you organized and handle everything but your cell phone calls very nicely. Just look for one you like that can connect to Wi-Fi.

Operating system

PDAs (even cell phones) run on operating systems the same way computers do. And, as with computers, the operating system you choose defines the add-ons (hardware and software) that you will be able to use and some of its compatibility with other devices. It also defines how things on the screen look. With many cell phones, the operating system is invisible to you and is something proprietary to the company that makes that phone. But some people start with the operating system when they shop because they have developed a passion for one or a loathing for another. There are smartphones that run on the Windows Mobile OS, the Palm OS, Symbian, Linux, and probably something new by the time you read this. The operating system is important because this interface isn't something you can change after you buy it. You don't really *need* to know much about a PDA's operating system. And if you don't want to go deep into the subject, there is no compelling reason to. But some people (myself included) do care deeply about this. At the very least, I suggest that you consider how the interface looks and acts as you evaluate devices.

Size

PDAs are all getting smaller, but smaller is not always better. I have played with some phones and PDAs that were simply too small for me. The text on the screen, the letters on the keys, and even the screen itself were too small for my once 20/20 vision. And I carry a purse, so I'm not trying to fit a PDA into my pocket. I want to be able to find it when I'm rummaging around in my purse and then use it comfortably. Maybe you are like me, or maybe you do want something that's really small. Again, it's a personal preference.

Color

I hate it when women tell me they are ashamed that they want their camera, PDA, or other gadget to be a pretty color. What's wrong with that? Men would like us to believe that we are silly for caring what color our gadgets are, but men care about the color of *their* gadgets. In fact, they care very deeply. If you doubt this, look around you. How many men do you see carrying pink iPods? Exactly. And that's why all the PDAs are black or silver. Because men care so deeply about color that they can't be swayed from buying only these safe colors. So stand up for your right to have citron green or oxblood red when you spend your money.

Screen size

This is very important and often a compromise with the size and keyboard features. If you want a very small device with an external keyboard, the screen is going to be very small. I like a nice big screen, and I don't mind if the unit is a little bigger to accomplish this. Again, this is a decision you should make for yourself based—not on technical specs—but on your personal preferences and what you plan to do with the device.

Accessories

Never underestimate the importance of accessorizing. If you have a PDA, you might as well trick it out.

Bluetooth Headsets

There may be no device that has set women so squarely in opposition as the Bluetooth phone headset. Some women tell me they wear theirs constantly, yammering away to themselves in public with a liberating sense of "Yes, I have lost my mind, and I don't care because this is just *too* convenient." Others fairly scream that they think the things are the worst invention ever, they can't imagine ever using one, and in fact refuse to consort with anyone who wears that thing stuck in their ear, making them look a silly egomaniac with a wish to join Star Trek and shout "Beam me up, Scotty!" I am dangerously fickle on this subject. I find myself agreeing with both the pros and the cons depending on how busy my day is and how I feel about someone else ranting in front of me. When it comes to choosing one, look for replaceable batteries (some actually require you to throw the unit away when the battery dies) and sound quality. There is a lot of range in quality of sound, with some units delivering echo, interference, and scratchy sounds and others giving quite respectable clarity. Some of them will work for both making phone calls and listening to music, offering a second (detachable) earbud and optional stereo sound for music. Of course, your phone or PDA needs to be able to play music for this to work.

WIRED HEADSETS

There are millions of these. They range in price from less than ten dollars to hundreds of dollars, depending almost entirely on sound quality. True audiophiles will not use wireless headsets (yet) for listening to music on PDAs or dedicated music players because this is where you see wild variation in sound quality. Even at the low end of wired headsets, you won't get interference and connection problems the way you sometimes do with wireless. The emphasis here is on the quality of the stereo sound. And of course, you get to choose how it attaches to your ears—hooking over the ear for a secure fit for running, buds that are easier to get on and off, or over-the-head models if you have no fashion agenda.

KEYBOARDS

If your PDA or phone is capable of Bluetooth, it should work with one of the Bluetooth keyboards on the market. I often bring only my PDA and a tiny foldable keyboard with me on trips or on a long day of events with the kids. There is little that I can't do with this rig, and it all fits in my purse. If your life drags you around town a lot, consider one of these.

Photo courtesy of ANYCOM
The Bluetooth ANYCOM Stowaway keyboard folds up and drops in a purse, transforming your PDA into a handy almost-computer.

MUSIC AND MEDIA PLAYERS

Everywhere I go, I see people carrying iPods. In stores, all the cases, speakers, and other add-ons are for iPods. A person might get the idea that the iPod is the only device out there that plays music and video and holds photos on a tiny device you can tote easily in your purse. But I know for a fact that though the iPod is a nice little device, there are plenty of iPod alternatives, and most of them are cheaper and richer in features than the iPod.

I love SanDisk players (*http://www.sandisk.com/*). The Sansa Clip comes in several colors, holds 2GB of music, costs only $60, and clips to your clothes. The Sansa View is not only a terrific MP3 player, but it also lets you take movies, TV shows, and other video along with you and watch on its 2.4-inch screen. It comes with several memory options, including one that will hold 48 two-hour movies. These start at $149. And a lot of people love Insignia players, which are much cheaper than the iPod and offer a lot of similar features. iRiver makes MP3 players, and Sony makes a digital Walkman. There are lots of them.

So how do you decide? I think the wild popularity of the iPod can be largely attributed to the confusion that customers face when shopping for music players. Apple cut right through all that confusion by making the iPod the most readily available option with the most accessories and compatibility. But you can save a lot of money and tap into a wealth of available content by thinking differently. Still, don't let me stop you from getting an iPod if that's what you want. The main reason I don't own one is that I like subscription music services rather than buying songs from the iTunes store, and Apple doesn't support them.

Content for Your Player

The real cost of a music player is not the device itself but the music, video, and audio books you put on it. The device you purchased defines what content—and where and how you can get it—you can put on the device, so the time to think about content is when you are shopping for a player, not after you buy one. With most music players, you need to connect to your computer before you put content on them. (A few can connect directly to the Internet without the help of a computer.) Once connected, you load the software (or website) that's compatible with your player. Then you can "rip" CDs you already own onto your computer and load them on your player or buy (or rent) new content from the Internet. If you have an iPod, you go to iTunes.com. If you have something else, you go somewhere else. Don't ignore this part of the arrangement when shopping, because your content destination is at least as important as the features of the player you buy.

A lot of people love iTunes. You can use it to buy music, rent movies, and download audio books. It's fun and fantastically easy to use. It also dominates the market, so there are lots of music and film choices. But other people get their knickers in a knot over the 99-cents-per-track cost of iTunes. And at that point, no one wants to hear me say, "That's why I like Napster." But I do like Napster. I like it so much that I insist my players (and I have several) are compatible with it. At Napster (*http://www.napster.com*), I pay $15 a month, which allows me access to the Napster To Go service (and a free basic player if I want) where I can enjoy as much music as I want on three computers and three players. I share a subscription with my kids. So I can tell them, "Go forth and download music." They don't have to save their pennies to buy a record the way I did. Music is as much a part of their lives as books, water, and the Internet. And I think that is how it should be. And I can listen to anything I want without being angry about spending money on it if I hate it later. None of that music is ours to keep (it goes away if we stop paying that monthly fee). So if we love an album, we also buy it. But we can listen—as often as we want—to nearly anything. Rhapsody (*http://www.rhapsody .com/*) works the same way.

I also pay a monthly fee to Audible.com, where I can get as many as three audio books a month. This means that every month I can download something for the kids to listen to in the car, something else for me to listen to on a flight, and perhaps some news or podcasts to listen to while I work out, for about the cost of one CD.

I have also been known to download TV and movies to my portable player from Amazon Unbox and other video download services. This is not against the law. You pay for rentals or to purchase movies the same as you do at Blockbuster, but you download them instead of hauling them home on DVD. The selection is awesome. I personally don't watch many movies on the tiny screen of my portable player, but I like having one or two movies in my purse in case the kids and I get stuck waiting in a doctor's office or bus depot. I hand the kids my player and they are occupied and happy for the duration.

So when I shop for a portable media player, I narrow my choices to those that work with the services that I want to use. Then I look for players that are cute—hey, I'm a slave to fashion too. I also look for a player that I find easy to use.

I have exactly as much patience for learning tricky gadgets as the next girl, and I've tried out some players that are simply impossible. If I have to crack the manual to use one of these, someone in the design department needs to go back to the drawing board and the player goes back in the box. And next—but this is still important—I look for memory capacity. This is usually what makes one unit more expensive than another, but it also makes that more expensive unit more useful because you will be able to cram hours and hours of entertainment—for you and perhaps a child or two in tow—onto it. Finally, battery life is another important feature, but these devices usually get the sort of days-long battery life that you expect from a cell phone.

Dear Geek Goddess,

My husband gave me an MP3 player for my birthday, but I'm reluctant to use it. I like listening to music on the stereo in my living room. My kids all run around with headsets on, tuning me out (and the rest of the world), while they listen to their iPods. That's not for me. I might like to use a portable music player to keep me entertained while I'm running, but not for regular music listening. Am I missing something?

Fuddy Duddy in Framingham

· · · · · · ·

Dear Fuddy Duddy,

I am with you, girlfriend. I have a nice stereo in my living room, and I like to use it, too. But you are missing something. Kids cling to those ear buds because they get to take hundreds of songs with them. But you can still enjoy the convenience of having hundreds—or thousands—of songs on a unit that fits in a pocket and also listen to that music on your lovely living room sound system. You just need the right cable.

To hook your music player up to your stereo, look on the back of the receiver for an auxiliary-in port. When you find it, you can plug your player into it with the right cable. Look at the back of your stereo before you go to the store to determine which kind of cable you need. Your stereo's manual or the guy in the stereo store can help you out with this if your stereo equipment is inscrutable. When you have the right cable, just plug one end into your auxiliary-in port on your stereo and the other into the headset port on your MP3 player, set the stereo to AUX, and you are listening to your music on your stereo—with no need to change the CD every 40 minutes.

Accessories

There are hundreds of fetching cases, bags, wristlets, arm bands, and lanyards available for your music player, especially if you have an iPod. You can easily find one by searching Amazon.com, Etsy (for one-of-a-kind handmade cases), eBags, or reading the reviews of particular cases at Popgadget (*http://www.popgadget.net/*). But while I support the belief that a girl can never have enough cute bags and purses, a docking station that plays your music is the real must-have accessory for your music player. You can find a docking station that connects to a stereo you already have or one that has speakers of its own. Set one on your bedside table, in the kitchen, or in your office. You can drop your player into it, charge it up, and listen to your music at the same time.

TECHNOLOGY AND THE LIVING ROOM STEREO

While covering the universe of stereo equipment is way outside the scope of this book, I do want to point out some technical innovations that might give you some ammunition in the inevitable debate over home theater equipment you will have—or are having—with your spouse, partner, roommate, or self. There have been some brilliant technical innovations in the living room in the last few years and many of them settle—or at least appease—the battle between the sexes on honking TVs and stereo wires, and how much living space should be sacrificed to them. This is an area that has grown tremendously in recent years due to the abundance of wireless home networks (see Chapter 7 for more on this). So you don't want to go out and drop a lot of money on stereo equipment, a TV, or a home theater without first stepping back and thinking about your home, the wires in it, your wireless network, and your dream entertainment system.

It used to be that to install a home stereo system that could play music throughout your house (instead of only in the room the stereo is located in) required the sort of massive rewiring that was best avoided unless you were building your house from scratch. But that's not so anymore. There are a range of devices that can shoot your music all over the house via the Wi-Fi network you are already using to connect to the Internet. This isn't exactly an inexpensive undertaking, but it is usually much cheaper than the old wires-and-plaster way. It also allows you a lot more flexibility and a wide range of music options. Why limit your home stereo to your collection of CDs (even if yours is massive) when there is a world of music out there: the subscription music services I mentioned earlier such as Napster and Rhapsody, satellite radio services (visit *http://www.xmradio.com/* and *http://www.sirius.com/*), and Internet radio stations that deliver free music from all over the world (see *http://www.pandora.com/*).

There are quite a few options when it comes to tapping into all this, and I am merely going to brush the surface. You can use a music streamer like the Sonos Digital Music System to transmit your digital music from your computer to other rooms in the house (*http://www.sonos.com/*). Or with a music server, you can access your CDs (after ripping them to the server), tap into your digital music collection, and connect to Internet and satellite radio. The solution that is right for you depends on how much digital music you have, if you subscribe to satellite radio, if you listen to Internet radio stations (or want to), how big your house is, and your budget. If this sounds like something you would like to pursue, I strongly recommend that you start at Crutchfield (*http://www.crutchfield.com/*) and read up on your options before you go to a store. It's possible that you could have a very luxurious system throughout your entire house for the sort of money that once merely bought you a nice stationary stereo system.

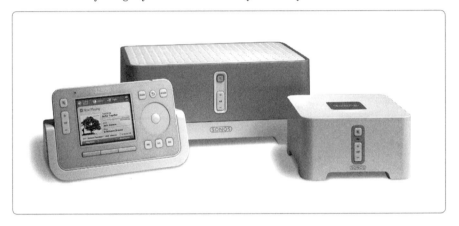

Photo courtesy of Sonos, Inc.

The Sonos Digital Music System ($999 and up) is an easy way to wirelessly stream music all over the house.

TV

Once upon a time, buying a TV was simple. Like any piece of furniture, you picked out one that looked good in your living room. Have you tried this lately? HDTV? Blu-ray? Plasma? LCD? Will it work with the DVD player you have? Is it forward compatible? Is it thin enough to hang on the wall? How much will it cost to have someone mount it? Does it require a piece of furniture to rest it on that costs more than the last TV you bought? Do you have a room big enough to house it and still sit down? Will it turn into a mirror when it's turned off?

Home entertainment has come a long way and, like everything else in the world of technology, evolution leads to acronyms. When it comes to TVs, my preference is projectors (see below), because I think all TVs—yes, even 52-inch

Plasma ones mounted to the wall—are too ugly to have in the house. But a lot of women I know let their husband pick out the TV. Don't do that! Men evaluate TVs by handling the remote control, reading the user reviews at Amazon.com, and visiting geeky sites like Newegg.com. That's why they end up with huge, ugly, overpriced monsters that you are not going to want in the living room. In fact, this is probably why a new room has emerged in American home: the Man Cave. A little intelligent shopping can save you from this fate. So let's break down the plethora of acronyms and choices that are now attached to this once-simple staple of American life so you can get what you need instead of having to live with his choices.

LCD and Plasma

These days, most people start here when thinking about a new television. LCDs and plasma screens are the flat-panel, big-screen TVs everyone seems to covet. Because they are so thin and relatively light (compared to old tube models), they allow you to stash a TV in all kinds of new places—mounted to a wall, set on a bookshelf-depth console table, or built into the wall over the fireplace. But they have a few dark secrets. For one thing, you will suffer a small amount of picture quality loss over your old tube TV, and your new TV won't have the lifespan of that old TV you had to hit with a hammer to break so you could justify upgrading. So if you are standing in the store eyeing that inexpensive but nearly obsolete tube TV, feel no shame. If you don't care that it weighs 400 pounds, will swallow half your living room, requires a dedicated piece of furniture, and won't work with the soon-to-be-all-digital broadcast TV channels unless you get a converter, buy it. It still has the best image quality (if not the largest screen) on the market. Still, plasmas and LCDs are getting bigger, better, and cheaper all the time, so if this is what you want, you are sure to be impressed with your choices. But which one? Plasma or LCD? That depends on where you plan to put it.

Plasma

The technology that goes into plasma TVs has been around a bit longer than LCD technology and has therefore evolved further. Without boring you (and me) with the technical details on this, the color is richer with plasma, and you can see the action better even when you aren't sitting directly in front of screen. Of these two options, this one will get you closer to the high-quality image you see with a nice tube TV. But a plasma TV is a fussy creature that requires a nurturing environment. It needs a room without a lot of ambient light or where you can close the curtains to shut out the light. In bright light you will have trouble seeing images on the screen. Plasmas also require a bit of babying: Because the screens are subject to burn-in, you don't want to leave a static image frozen on one for a long time unless you want to look at a ghost of that image forever. If you like to play games on the TV more than watch movies—or tend to pause images—this isn't the right technology for you.

LCD

If you want a smaller screen for a bedroom, kitchen, or guest room, this is the way to go. It is the only flat screen available in less than 40-inch screen models. If the room you want a TV in is bright, this is your TV, because the image on an LCD will still look good in a sunny room. The LCD is a good choice for a gaming machine because it is immune to the screen burn-in you'll be fretting about with plasma. If the games or programs you want to watch are in high-definition, this is also a good choice, because there are more models available in 1080p (a high-definition video format with resolution of 1,920 by 1,080 pixels—the *p* stands for *progressive scan*). And the planet will like you better if you go with an LCD because it uses less energy.

Projectors

I'm not a fan of a giant television dominating the décor in my living room—and I know I'm not the only woman who feels this way. So when projectors became a viable alternative to TVs a couple of years ago, I jumped on them. They are an infinite improvement over bulky TVs. There are a lot of important questions to ask about projectors, and buying one is not the simplest experience. Here are two important reasons to consider getting one: When you turn it on, you can get a stunning 150-inch screen, but when you hit the off switch, that screen becomes a blank wall. So one room can be both a usable living space *and* the home theater your husband is planning to convert the basement into. I believe this is a marriage-saving technology because he can get a huge-screen home theater, and she gets to keep her living room. Not only is the wall just a wall (no massive TV housing), but the unit itself, when no one is watching, is a breadbox-sized gadget sitting demurely on a table. Some projectors even come with a case, so if you aren't a big TV viewer, you can pack it away when you aren't using it.

Before you sort out the technical specs of projectors, ask first, "Do I have the right room for one?" I have a small (15 foot by 18 foot) living room with giant windows in the front of the house, a fireplace, and a flight of stairs all crammed into a room with too many entryways. But the room works perfectly as a home theater. I put a small table under the window (with seating on either side) and painted the opposite wall white. I purchased heavy curtains for the big windows. Then I bought a projector, set it on that little table, and trained it at the opposite wall. In my setup, the projector is 10 feet from the wall it projects on. That gives us a 100-inch image. That is not a typo. Our little living room is a small movie theater in disguise.

You can sneak a projector into small rooms, big rooms, tiny apartments, and big mansions, but whatever the size of the abode, the projector will need a blank wall (or a screen) six feet or more from the piece of furniture it sits on. The further away from the wall (up to a point, which will be stipulated in the specs) you set the projector, the bigger your image will be. The closer to the projection area the projector sits, the smaller the image will be. Most projectors need to be a minimum of six feet from the projection area, but a new technology is emerging—the short-throw projector—that can sit quite close to the wall. These are more expensive. You can also get around the six-feet-from-the-wall requirement by using a free-standing projector screen (rather than a wall) placed where you need it or by mounting the projector to a ceiling, but that won't be nearly as easy or elegant.

After you establish that you want to get a projector and you have the right room for one, make sure you are buying a projector that is intended for home use. There are many projectors on the market, and some of them are targeted at business users who want to hook a computer up to them for presentations. These do not have the right connections for your DVD player, surround-sound system, and DVR. You might also want to get a projector that is capable of high definition, which is not normally a consideration for business users.

Also check the price of replacement bulbs. These can be expensive ($200 or more), so the difference in the price of the bulb (which you will have to replace about once every three years) might push you in the direction of one model or another. If possible, get the salesperson to turn the projector on so you can listen to it and, while you are at it, hold a hand over it and see if it gets hot. (If you can't find one locally, check the return policy of the outfit you buy from.) Some projectors are so loud they disturb your movie and get hot enough that you can warm your fingers over them in winter. It is possible to get a nice projector for under $1,000, so, despite the impressive screen size, high-definition, and disappearing act of this option, projectors are also a bargain compared to LCDs or plasmas with half the screen size.

Rear Projection

If you are on a bargain hunt for a TV and a projector isn't an option, you might want to take a look at rear-projection TVs. These project the image onto a screen but do it in one big self-contained unit. (If you have no idea what these are, the best solution is to go to the store and ask to see one.) These massive screens once delivered a not-so-great image, but they have come a long way in the last few years. Their image quality now competes with plasma and LCD TVs, and they are not susceptible to screen burn-in. Like a standard projector, they require a new, expensive bulb every few years

A LUST FOR LUXURY GEAR

Following are some gadgets and technologies that many people would probably consider luxuries but that a girl could really get used to having around. I wouldn't part with any of these.

DVR

These allow you to easily record programs you want to watch, fast-forward through commercials, pause live TV, and generally make you the master of your TV-viewing experience. Many people allow their cable company to deliver and set up their DVR, but I think TiVo (*http://www.tivo.com/*) offers a much better service. It's usually cheaper—in the long run—to buy a TiVo machine and subscribe to that service than it is to subscribe to the cable company's expensive DVR service and lease its DVR machine.

TV All Over the House

As with listening to music, the way we watch TV is being transformed by the wireless home network. The TiVo system will allow you to wirelessly watch video from your computer on your TV simply by tapping into it over your wireless network. It will also access the movies at Amazon Unbox. The Slingbox (*http://www .slingbox.com/*) will allow you to watch what's on your TV on any computer—and even on your cell phone. There are a host of devices that let you transfer video from your computer wirelessly or by connecting a tiny device to your TV.

But a simple way to enhance your viewing options is to hook a laptop up to your TV and use your Internet connection to download movies from Movielink (*http://www.movielink.com/*), MVlib (*http://mvlib.com/*), Amazon Unbox, or any one of the many movie download services that sell or rent movies. Or if you subscribe to Netflix, you can download a limitless amount of video from the Netflix site in addition to the DVDs it sends you. I have no idea why anyone would suffer the annoyance and limited selection of a movie rental store when the best selection and pajama-friendly video rentals are available on the Internet.

The Book of the Future

I once stated rather publicly that I would never be converted to reading books in a digital format. I love books. The book is one of the greatest technical innovations in human history. But then a little company born of MIT's media lab invented

E Ink (*http://www.eink.com/*), and I changed my mind. (Note to self: Never say never.) This breakthrough technology manages to combine everything that is great about paper—its readability in many lights, lack of glare, and crisp image—with everything that is great about digital media—massive storage in a small space, search ability, and the ability to edit the data.

This is not reading on a tiny computer screen; it is reading on something very near to paper on a small device that will hold a dozen books at once. It must be seen to be believed. There are two units using this technology that are worth considering at the moment: the Amazon Kindle (sold through Amazon.com) and the Sony Reader (sold by electronics retailers). Each uses its own system when it comes to selling you the books that you will read on it, and both are expensive. This is definitely a luxury, but if you travel a lot and like to read, it might be worth it.

GPS for the Car

A lot of new cars come with a GPS unit, but you don't have to throw out your car to get one. These units use the global positioning network to give you turn-by-turn directions to your destination based on where you are—much better than looking things up on a map, even a map on the Internet. You simply type the address you want (or look up restaurants and other public places in its database), and it tells you how to get there. No more squinting at street signs while trying to drive and keep the kids from killing each other. Just sit back and let the navigator tell you what to expect, when to turn, and even when you have arrived at your destination.

These were once difficult to use and inaccurate, but nowadays I consider them indispensable. I have tried several of them and all were terrific. They made getting lost or following vague and annoying directions from your kid's friends a thing of the past. I installed one in my mother's car, and overnight she went from being almost housebound by her fear of getting lost to jetting about with her "Little Gentleman" riding shotgun and sorting her out whenever she got lost. Consider the Garmin Nuvi models, which are relatively inexpensive, easy to use, and will snap out of your car and drop into a purse for walking around. The TomTom GO (*http://www.tomtom.com/*) lets you choose from a nice selection of voices for your directions and has a host of extra features like hands-free dialing and an FM transmitter so you can use it to play your MP3 music over your car stereo. Newer devices (see the Dash Express at *http://www.dash.net/*) can perform Internet searches so you can find restaurants and movie times near where you are without worrying about your device's database obsolescence. In the future, look for models that can alert you to traffic jams in your way by using an Internet service that feeds data directly to your GPS unit.

11 | YOUR 200 CLOSEST FRIENDS

I love to get together with my girlfriends, but making it happen can be like coordinating a summit among heads of state. Recently, I went to dinner with a handful of my BFFs and we had a great time. Setting it up, though, was not so much fun. It took three weeks, several reschedules, a dozen emails, five cell phone calls, an accidental face-to-face meeting, one invitation page on my Google calendar, and grim determination. (Our determination was fueled by the realization that we hadn't managed to get together in almost a year.) Even then, half of the original group dropped out before it happened.

When those same girlfriends tell me they can't be bothered with social networks online, I have to assume they live in a parallel universe. I have lots of girlfriends I see online, and "getting together" with them is a matter of logging on and seeing who has poked or waved at me, checking out their pictures, reading their blogs, and seeing what they are up to. I feel closer to some of my online friends than I do to my local friends. But when I ask my local BFFs to join me online, they have a variety of excuses: "I spend all day at a computer; the last thing I want to do when I get home is update my page on the Internet," said Melissa. Jennifer couldn't be bothered, saying "I don't have time. But even if I did, it isn't interesting." And even Annette said, "It feels like a waste of time."

SOCIAL NETWORKING—NOT WHAT IT SEEMS

I understand the resistance, but I think it's founded on a misapprehension. I also don't believe the claim that this reluctance stems from time constraints. At the end of a work day, I want to turn off my computer just like everyone else. But I don't spend extra time online because I see my friends there. When I worked in an office, I didn't spend extra time at work because I saw my friends there, either. Having friends at work just makes the day more fun. It's the same with online socializing—seeing your friends there makes going online more fun. I think a lot of adult women see the way teenagers behave online—posting swimsuit photos, logging hours talking about nothing—and think that's what online networking is. But it isn't. Teenagers act silly, online or off. You didn't stop getting together with your friends because teenagers are annoying in groups. Why shun social networking for that reason?

"This reluctance to participate in social networking is not about time," agrees Harleen Kahlon, founder of the online social network for professional women Damsels In Success (*http://www.damselsinsuccess.com/*). "Once upon a time, I had months with nothing to do. I had left my job [as a lawyer] with no idea what I was going to do next. But you could not have paid me to use a social network," Harleen said. As she explored her career options, she found she needed to do a lot of networking and ask questions of past friends and colleagues. Much of this sort of thing happens online nowadays, so that's where she eventually went, stymied by the response times of her flesh-and-blood friends. Along the way, she came to embrace her online social network for recreation as well as for the career help it offered. Like many of us who have tried it, she found that it gave back much more than it took. And eventually, online networking became her new career.

In fact, I have noticed an interesting disparity between my online friendships and my offline ones: As I grow closer to friends I know online, a distance is growing between me and my friends who aren't online. The Pew Internet & American Life Project has noticed this too. "Our evidence calls into question fears that social relationships—and community—are fading away in America," it said in a 2006 report. "Instead of disappearing, people's communities are transforming: The traditional human orientation to neighborhood . . . based groups is moving towards communities that are oriented around geographically dispersed social networks."

Why Not Just Send an Email—or Call?

I came late to social networking. Most of my geeky friends did not embrace it immediately, either. It was for kids, we all reasoned, and oh so self-indulgent. But we all used email and instant messaging to stay in touch for a long time. I would have lost touch with many friends, former co-workers, and overseas family entirely, otherwise. Networking is much easier and less time consuming than email, which requires you to either spam the world or write individual notes to each person you want to communicate with.

My own romance with social networking started when I got a Facebook invitation from a friend I'd once worked with and had occasionally thought about looking up. I knew about Facebook, but I'd never really understood the point of it or had any motivation to join. Still, it felt rude to refuse her invitation to be friends, so I obediently accepted and created a very minimal profile at the site. While I was there, I clicked my friend's list of friends and discovered all sorts of old buddies of mine from the era of my life that I knew her from. So I invited all of them to be my friends. I even ran into my husband there, who was happily rubbing elbows with some of our friends from the last neighborhood we lived in and with my cousin who lives in England. So I friended those people, too. I poked around some more, looking up people in my address book and browsing through other friends' lists of friends until I had a rather lively little party going. Everyone had pictures of themselves up, some had pictures of their kids, and all offered some details about current work and hobbies.

To catch up with all these people via email would be a full-time job, but I accomplished much more than catching up. My Facebook friends and I almost effortlessly stay in touch. Many people post a statement about what they are doing today, thinking about, are angry about, or wishing for in their status updates. So I know that Harry (who I have not seen since we worked together nearly a decade ago) is having a busy travel day or Marian (who I have never met but liked on the phone) is enjoying a day off or that Angela (who was a BFF when we worked together in San Francisco) was kept up half the night by a toddler I've never met.

Introducing the Networks

An online network is the easiest way to join the fun. These sites have all the tools you need to set up a profile, upload a photo, describe your work or self, link to your friends, or engage in chats. There are a lot of these sites, but here is a list of popular spots you can use as a starting point.

LinkedIn (http://www.linkedin.com/)   This is a utilitarian business networking site. It is good at connecting you with clients and employers and for getting work-related questions answered. Anyone looking for a job or to advance their career absolutely needs to spend some time here.

Facebook (http://www.facebook.com/)   This site was once the sole domain of the college student (since no one else was allowed to join) but, in the way of children, it grew up. These days, everyone is welcome, and you'll see a lot of oldsters using it for socializing, work, and the gray area where the two blend. You can post a photo and status reports on what you are doing right now. These seem silly at first, but they give you a real feel for what your friends are up to.

MySpace (http://www.myspace.com/)   MySpace is certainly the biggest of the online social networks. It has gotten so big, in fact, that it isn't just for teens anymore, but it has never lost that teen feeling. With its emphasis on music and "hooking up," most adult women find it more irritating than a high school sleepover. "The only women I know who use MySpace are moms who have an account so they can spy on their kids," says Claire Celsi, a public relations professional who writes three blogs, uses Facebook daily, and met her boyfriend through the online dating site Match.com.

Bebo (http://www.bebo.com/)   This is the largest online social network in the United Kingdom, but it isn't far behind Facebook and MySpace in the United States. Like Facebook, you can post photos, videos, and blogs.

Friendster (http://www.friendster.com/)   Friendster may have started it all, but it has lately fallen out of favor. I don't use it much because when I go there, I get accosted by young, handsome (if you can judge by the half-naked photos) men with a tendency to call me *babe*. Is that a feature?

Gather (http://www.gather.com/)   This is a network where people congregate around ideas. Got an issue? You can write about it here or just comment on the writing of other members.

Pogo (http://www.pogo.com/)   This is an online casual gaming site that's popular with women because you can chat with people while you play cards. One woman I spoke to, a soldier in Iraq, was using it to get together for a chat and a game of cards with her friends back home.

Classmates (http://www.classmates.com/)   This is a social network that specializes in helping you locate and stay in touch with people you knew from high school and college.

When I want to reach out to someone, email requires that I have her email address, can think of something coherent to say, and feel like offering updates on my current life. If I send the thing off and never get a response, I then have no idea if it's because the person hates me (was it something I said in 1995?) or if she simply changed her email address. Even if I do get a response, we might fling emails back and forth for a week or so until we are caught up, but inevitably the drifting away happens again. A few months or years later, someone has to start the process all over again or the drift becomes permanent.

My online social network requires no such effort. All I do is type a one-line status report, poke someone if I'm thinking of her, or just browse the updates to see what everyone is up to. It's like having a newsfeed on everyone I know (except those friends who think they don't have time to join).

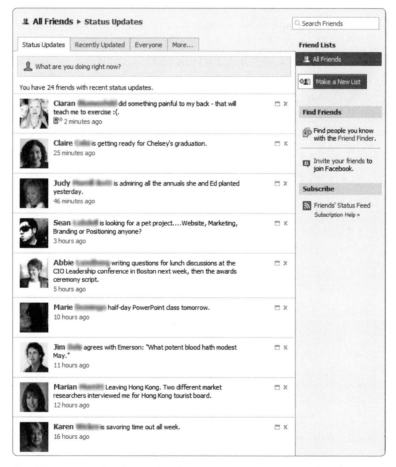

Once I have connected with a number of people, I can read a daily newsfeed of what my friends are up to or thinking about.

Social networks (and to a certain extent, blogs) are like the glue that keeps your connections alive, even if you do little maintenance beyond tending your own site. Or, to switch metaphors entirely, social networks are like soil. You plant your connections in there and they grow. While you are hanging out with your kids or reading a book, people might be connecting to your blog or your online network, getting to know you, and having the experience of being a part of your group of friends and colleagues.

What If No One Likes Me?

Everyone starts out in this with just a few friends but, somehow, without much effort, they seem to gather a crowd. People often amass huge groups, if they keep at it for a while. Don't let that knowledge invoke fears of "I'm not popular enough!" You too will amass a network of friends. Here's why: You can invite people you barely know to join your network, and they usually will. Experts, friends of friends, people you once sat near at work, someone you met once at a party, people who work at a company where you'd like a job, people in your neighborhood you've never spoken to. This isn't the same as having dinner together. These people are also suffering from "fear of being friendless" or (more likely) want a large pool of people to tap for knowledge, leads, or whatever. Imagine having 500 people you can ask for advice. You can make mass announcements, promote your company, pelt questions to the whole gang, or send individual messages to one or more members of your group. Everyone is always there (virtually) and their contact information is up to date. I might go months without seeing Jennifer or Melissa, though they both live within 20 miles of me, but I see the people in my online network whenever I want, no matter where they live.

"It is also sometimes just a bit of mindless fun," says Claire. "Sometimes I read my fortune cookie or see what groups other people in my network are joining. Or maybe I see that a friend or client has a birthday. Then I might send a note or put a comment on his Wall [a public place to post messages], or send one of those silly picture-gifts. People love it when you do that. It shows that you were thinking about them."

Working the Network

As Harleen implies with her job-switch experience, though, a fun, chick posse is not the only thing my techno-reluctant friends are missing by not going online. Sure, that's what the teenagers are in it for (along with dating), but we adults have discovered something much more valuable. Online networks—those that form around blogs or in networking sites—create a pool of experts, friends, and

Dear Geek Goddess,

I finally succumbed and joined Facebook. Everything was going gangbusters for a while there. I was catching up with people I'd lost track of and was even making new friends. Then, one day, I logged on and there was a friend request from someone I worked with a few years ago. This guy went out of his way to make my life at that job miserable. I didn't let him ruin the job, but it was a real effort. I even considered a lawsuit at the time. I can't imagine how he thinks we could be friends now, and I feel sick at the prospect of having to think about him every time I log onto Facebook. What would you do?

Mortified in Montgomery

. . . .

Dear Mortified,

It happens to all of us. Unfortunately, that guy who was so unpleasant in the office is probably just as unpleasant online. Some relationships are best left behind and that's why there is an Ignore button right next to the Accept button. Use it! I do. And so does everyone else I've asked. The person you ignore will probably never notice that you rejected him (which is probably kinder than this guy deserves) since he will simply never hear anything from you. He'll probably assume you are one of those people who created a Facebook page and never visit it. But since this guy invited you, you can go look at his Facebook profile before you accept or ignore him. This way, maybe you will learn that he is now trying to atone for past sins—or you can at least find out where he works now so you don't apply for a job there.

If you have already accepted the invitation out of a sense of misguided social nicety, you can delete the person from your friend list and be done with the entire nasty business with a few mouse clicks. Go to your friend list, locate the person's name, and click the little X to the right of it. Your so-called friend will never be notified that you've ended your online relationship. And if you two ever patch things up, you can always re-invite him to be your friend again.

confidantes who are immediately available and willing to help. Plenty of women (and men) consider their network an essential part of their work day, not just their social life.

A good network is an invaluable resource for anyone who is looking for a job, a client, advice, answers, friends, or anything at all. "I tap my network if I want to get the answer to a question quicker, faster, and better than anyone else,"

Dear Geek Goddess,

After 10 years of marriage, my husband and I have decided to split up. I'm sitting here staring at my Facebook profile: Under Relationships, it says I'm married-to him. Well, the divorce may not be final yet, but I desperately want to click that handy Cancel Relationship button. (Why don't they have one of those for the real world?) But this feels an awful lot like a public announcement to 500 people, quite a few of whom are more like work associates. I haven't even told my mother yet, and I'm certainly not ready for a flood of emails asking me what happened. Got any ideas?

Single in Sarasota

. . . .

Dear Single,

This is a bit dicey, isn't it? When you change things in your profile, make friends, and join networks, those changes show up as announcements in your friends' newsfeed. This is one way friends can stay up to date on you without you doing much of anything. Usually it's fun, but in this case, not so much. So, yes, to change that status might be letting the cat out of the bag about your split with

explains Diane K. Danielson, CEO and founder of DowntownWomensClub.com, a social network for businesswomen. "You have a Baby Boomer and a Generation Xer in the same meeting. Someone throws out a problem and asks for a solution. The boomer takes some notes and walks back to her desk to make some phone calls. The Xer sends a text message to her entire network while still in the meeting. The Gen Xer has the answer before the Boomer has even started looking."

"I use social networking first for business purposes," agrees Sandra Fathi, president of Affect Strategies, a strategic marketing, communications, and public relations firm. "I am the mother of two children and I run my own company, so the time I invest has to yield results, whether for personal satisfaction, for my family, or for the growth of my business. These are tools that help me promote my company and services, meet clients, and get the answers to questions I need my peers to assist me with. It's an incredible resource."

Sandra had a client who asked her to recommend a public relations specialist in Germany. She didn't know a soul there, so she posed the question to her online network. "An hour later, I had ten personal recommendations—all from professionals I respect," she says. "That allowed me to offer my client a real your husband. Even if you change your status from "married" back to the default without selecting any status at all, a little broken heart will appear next to your name and your mini-feed will announce you are no longer listed as married. But the material that shows up about you in your friends' newsfeed is determined by your privacy settings. So if you aren't ready to go public, I suggest that you start by editing your privacy settings so that changes to your relationship status are no longer broadcast to your friend list. Click **Privacy** from any Facebook page. Then click **Edit Settings** to the right of News Feed and Mini-Feed and uncheck the box next to **Remove My Relationship Status**. Like the following:

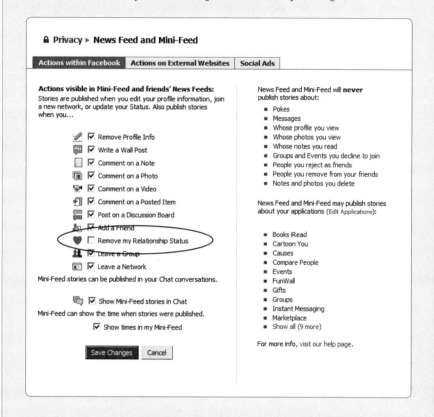

No announcement will go out now if you change your status, but anyone who goes looking at your status may well notice that you've changed your marital status to single, so maybe you should choose It's complicated or simply return it to the default, Select Status (no relationship status will show up on your profile if you choose this), until you are ready to talk about it. Of course, when you are ready to announce your new freedom, this is an easy way to do it.

service for very little effort on my part." She has also used blogs and networking tools to get health information, recruit staff, become a notable voice in her industry, connect with potential clients, and make friends.

I have used my online social network to get advice on dealing with an evil elementary school teacher, get feedback on decisions about my kids' health, market my work, find new clients (and remind old ones that they like me), locate and stay in touch with friends I haven't seen since college, get answers to technical questions, and get help with a project I'm working on. Having a diverse, intelligent, and concerned crowd of people on tap at the other end of my mouse has been much more valuable to me as a knowledge resource than the golf course, cocktail party, or book group ever was in the real world.

OF BLOGS AND BLOGGERS

Social networks are the starting place for online relationships, but a fair number of communities build up around blogs as well. People go to a blog because it addresses a subject that interests them. While there, they post a comment. Those comment sections can often turn into a heated discussion, and friendships and associations spring up from the exchanges. This may seem like an odd place to meet someone, but many profitable meetings of the minds have happened this way. The online Web tool Basecamp (created by 37signals) was born as the result of a comment by David Heinemeier Hansson on Jason Fried's blog. They liked each other and ended up working together. It seems as if I hear another story every day of people who have met this way.

"I think blogging has created a different category of friendship," says Kristin Park, a freelance journalist and mom who writes a blog about postpartum depression (*http://ppdsurvivor.blogspot.com/*) and has tapped into an online community as a result. "The blogs connect to each other. That is how you drive traffic to your blog. And so we bloggers communicate with each other and link to each other. This creates a community that allows you to have voice and an audience that wants to hear that voice. It also brings people to you because of that voice."

Nichelle Stephens embraced blogging back when the idea was cutting edge, and she has benefited enormously from writing in a public forum. She isn't one of those famous bloggers who is redefining the publishing and news industries (for better and for worse) by reporting from the trenches or the political landscape by spouting opinion without the intervention of corporate media or even editors. Instead, she uses these tools as an effective way of staying in touch with her clients, friends, family, and fellow hobbyists.

Nichelle is a bookkeeper, comedy producer, freelance publicist, and cupcake enthusiast, among other things, who lives in New York. She is very busy but

BLOG THAT!

Do you find yourself hankering to name and tame your own little corner of cyberspace? Do you want a site for your new business? Or maybe your hobby hankers for a more public forum than your garage. Are you looking for a way to sell the jewelry or furniture you make in your free time? Or maybe you share a hobby with some friends and want a place where you can all send photos, video, or text on your hobby.

A great way to stake out some Web space is with a blog. They are often free, require no special skills, and can be up and running in as long as it takes you to write a description of your endeavor and upload a few pictures. "If you are launching a business, a blog can be your whole website," says Diane.

At Blogger (*http://www.blogger.com/*), WordPress (*http://www.wordpress .com/*), Vox (*http://www.vox.com/*), LiveJournal (*http://www.livejournal.com/*), TypePad (*http://www.typepad.com/*; not free), and other hosted blogging sites, you simply choose a name for your blog, pick a template, and start writing. You can set your blog to be open to the entire Internet or only for the eyes of people you invite. You can write the blog yourself or work with a group of contributors. These days, many of these tools allow you to upload and share video (video blog, or *vlog*), podcasts (audio you record and send out via your blog; like having your own radio program), photos, and your favorite music. Some tools let you write in a word processor and post directly from there. Some encourage you to post directly from email or via text messages you send from your phone. Some even make adding commerce to your site easy, allowing you to sell your goods online. The features you want will, naturally, depend on why you want the blog.

If you are launching a business and easy commerce is what you are after, you might try the sites that specialize in this. Etsy (*http://www.etsy .com/*) allows people to easily sell handmade goods, and eCrater (*http://www .ecrater.com/*) helps you build an online store in minutes. Since people come to these sites already to shop, they save you the trouble of trying to drive traffic to your site.

finds the time to write four blogs and use several social networking sites. That may sound like something far from the experience of the average woman, but it really isn't. She has a job, a couple of hobbies, some work she does part-time, and friends and family. And she has decided to give each of those things a blog instead of a notebook or a phone tree or a meeting night. Altogether, she spends about an hour each morning on all of it—or so she says.

Her bookkeeping blog, Keeping Nickels, provides a service to her small business clients and allows potential clients to get a sense of her business and skills before meeting her. Her cupcake blog, Cupcakes Take the Cake, is part of a hobby she shares with a couple of friends. It has become, according to Nichelle, "the Google of cupcakes." It's fun (and a bit profitable) and brings her together with friends and fellow cupcake enthusiasts around the country. Her personal blog is for her friends and family. It keeps them up to date and in touch, allows her to share her current interests easily, quickly, and with a sense of fun—without pelting friends with vacation photos or emails. People can check in with her when they have time. They can comment and read the comments of her other friends, thereby bringing everyone in her life together, however ephemerally, in one spot. She also uses several social networking sites, each with a profile pointing to her other endeavors, to connect to colleagues, friends, and clients. Nichelle has maintained her blogs and online communities for years. It is a strategy that has worked for her. She has gotten clients, friends, readers, and has even been interviewed for *The New York Times* because of her online presence. "If you have a freelance profession—or if you are a stay-at-home mom—where you don't go into an office every day," says Nichelle, "this online network becomes your community. I know way more people now because of my online network than I did when I had a nine-to-five job."

I have used blogs for this sort of community gathering myself with great success. When a large group of my husband's family decided to go en masse to Ireland, we used a blog to organize it all, post photographs and travel plans, and share information for the six months before the trip. After we all returned home, we posted our photos to it and shared our unique travel stories and random, post-trip longings for the Old Sod. And when my father, an expatriate Irishman with family and friends scattered across the globe, died, I set up a memorial blog. Even though this diverse crowd could not gather for a real-world wake, we have managed to keep a lively one going online for months, complete with stories and photographs. The blog serves as a memorial as well as a virtual gathering place.

OH, BEHAVE!

Your mother told you never to talk to strangers, yet here you are on a social network swapping diet tips with someone named "Big_beautiful." It's a sure thing that isn't her real name, and it's possible that nothing she's told you is real either. In fact, she may not even be a *she*. Is this dangerous? To a certain extent, yes, it is dangerous. Perhaps it's not physically dangerous, unless you are prone to reckless abandon when it comes to getting together with people you have met online. But it can be dangerous to your reputation. In fact, online indiscretions have

a better name for your blog

The time may come when you are no longer happy with the Web address your blog got when it was born. When you name your blog at a hosted blogging service (such as Blogger) the service's name is part of your Web address (URL). So if you called your blog *myblog* and you built it at Blogger, your Web address is probably something like *http://www.myblog.blogspot.com/* rather than simply *http://www.myblog.com/*. Getting the Web address you want is possible, but it's more trouble and will cost you a bit of money.

There are two ways to go about it. Either one means you have to first choose and register your domain name (at Register.com—*http://www.register.com/*—or a number of other sites that handle domain registration) and pay an annual fee to keep that name. Once you own the name, you can either buy space on the Internet to host it or, if your service allows it, continue to host it at your blogging service. Since it's much easier to let a place like Blogger host your site than to go out on your own, I will explain that first and, since Blogger allows it, I'll use it as an example.

Follow the link at Blogger (within the editing tools for your blog) to the step-by-step instructions for hosting your blog with a custom domain name by clicking **Custom Domain** from the Publishing menu within the Settings tab:

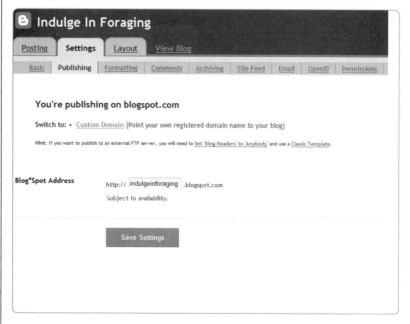

(continued)

First, Blogger will help you search for and purchase an available domain name, and then it will help you through the detailed steps of hosting that domain. You will start here:

Blogger will ask you to create a CNAME record (that is so geeky that I'm not even going to define it, since knowing the definition won't help) and tell the domain name service (DNS; sort of like an online post office, only without the people) where to find your new site. You do not have to understand any of this (I certainly don't), and hopefully you will never have to do it again. Just follow the specific directions from your blogging service, step by step, and do not deviate. You may feel as if you are going deeper into computer lingo than you ever wanted to (and you, no doubt, are) but ultimately, it is not hard. It's not programming. It isn't even algebra. It's just very detailed. It might take an hour—less if you are good at following recipes or can do those projects in *Martha Stewart Living* (I can't).

If you get deep into this, the day may even come when you outgrow your blog-hosting service. Maybe you want more than a blog on your website, or maybe you will get such huge traffic to your blog that the hosted services can't handle it anymore. You will have to move to a site that you host (and perhaps build) yourself.

Hopefully if any of this happens, you will have an entire staff of cola-drinking geeks to do your bidding, and you won't need to know any of this. But just in case you want to do it yourself, I should tell you that you could—it's probably not harder than that home-remodel project you took on. Sure this is a somewhat advanced activity, but many things are. And there are many options that make building your own website easy enough for any determined person to take on. Like anything hardish, if you break it down into steps and solve them one at a time, it becomes less hard(ish). Each step involves decisions, and each decision will ask you to choose between how much control you have over the result and how easy it is to get to that result. If you don't have the chops (or the determination to slog through) and you keep choosing control over ease, you will probably end up hiring someone to finish things for you. So if I haven't talked you out of it yet, I suggest that you go to *http://www.wordpress.org/* (not the free blogging site at *http://www.wordpress.com/*) and read and learn. There you will find all the tools and instructions you need to build and host your own blog. All you will need to bring is your own intelligence, strength, and fortitude.

become the Scarlet Letter of the digital age and an entire industry has sprung up to help people cope with it. Michael Fertik is CEO of ReputationDefender, (*http://www.reputationdefender.com/*), which offers a service (for a monthly fee) that helps its clients control what's being said about them online. "Much of the time, the harm we see begins in inadvertency, not malice," he says. Some inadvertency is worse than others, of course. Fertik has seen people discuss health problems, eating disorders, intimate relationships, and other matters they would not otherwise discuss in a public forum (which this is) because they have an illusion of anonymity. They don't realize it is often quite easy to link people's real identities to what they have said online. But even people who are being relatively circumspect do run into trouble simply because what they did yesterday does not reflect who they are today. The Internet has a long memory. As a general rule, if you would not say it in front of a PTA meeting, you should probably not say it in your social network. But even then, you might find your online image sullied simply because you aren't who you once were.

"There you are with your boyfriend, out and enjoying yourselves at a party," explains Fertik. "You take some pictures with your cell phone and post them on your social network. They aren't intimate or embarrassing. They are just photos. Later, though, you move on. You aren't with this boyfriend anymore. But because you two posted a lot of photos, your online image is dominated by this relationship," Fertik explains. This may not seem like a big deal at first, but someday it might be. In this day and age, anyone with more than a passing interest in you is sure to google you. And you may not want your reputation forever tied to this guy you broke up with.

So should you live in fear of social networking? I don't think so. I'm very shy about posting photos of myself, and I would never post one where I was drinking, under-dressed, or with someone I'm not sure I will always respect. I'm also careful about what I say online. I don't gossip or reveal anything I wouldn't tell a casual friend. But I'm also comfortable with myself and write a lot of material that gets posted online. So when I do a search on myself, the results are a rather random assortment of projects I've been involved in. It's not an accurate representation of what I'm doing now, but it is all me, and I'm not ashamed of any of it.

"I post my phone number and all sorts of information about me online," says Claire Celsi. "Why not? That sort of information is already available in the phone book, which is online." In fact, this sort of openness is rather essential to anyone who uses the Internet for work. Contact information is an important part of doing business online, and if social networking and a blog are an extension of your job search or business networking, you can't be too secretive about it. It certainly goes against the sort of online skills I teach my children (who, at ages 11 and 9, know better than to post the name of their school or anything else that locates them in the real world), but children aren't usually running a business or trying to reconnect with college buddies.

I post a great deal of information about myself online, including photos (flattering and circumspect ones), a phone number, and a physical address, but I also take a lot of precautions. I use avatars more than I use photos; that physical address is a PO box, and the phone number is a GrandCentral or Skype phone number that has no address information attached to it. So even if someone does a reverse search on it, they won't get my home address. But these are precautions I have taken for years on my business card and in professional databases in order to keep my work separate from my family. They are simply old rules applied to a new medium.

"I don't think this stuff is changed all that much by online social networking sites," says Claire. Women promoting their businesses give out business cards with their photos on them, take out ads in the Yellow Pages, and even put their pictures on billboards. "Except that now if I have a stalker (and I do), I can find out who he is," Claire says. She is being harassed by someone who sends her rude emails and posts hostile messages to her blogs and social networking sites. She could use the block feature on any of these tools to limit how much of this person's energy she has to see, but she has also used his posts to get his location. She got his IP address (a unique address that every computer connecting to the

Internet has) from one of his blog comments, and she used that to find his ISP and contacted that ISP to report him. Their fraud department now knows who he is and has him on their watch list. "I even know where he lives now, which is much better information than I could get if I had a real-world stalker," says Claire.

PEOPLE HELPING PEOPLE

I personally find it frustrating that so many women shun blogs and social networks. Part of my frustration is born of my selfish desire to see my friends more often, but most of it lies in knowing how much richer their lives could be for it and that it is perfectly suited to them. A network of female friends provides women with "support and comfort," according to Dr. Nancy D. O'Reilly, PsyD, a psychologist and the founder of WomenSpeak.com. "Women need someone to bounce thoughts and ideas off of. A network of female friends can provide comfort, safety, assistance, and a shoulder to cry on." But our busy lives and children often make it difficult to find the time to connect with that network. And if we move away from our network, it can be difficult and isolating to try to find a new one. An online network is there even if you can't leave the house or get away from the office.

And the great thing you quickly learn about people when you join a social network is that they want to help and will take time out of their often very busy day to answer your question, simply because you are in the network and you asked. I see it every day. People ask technical questions, for detailed business advice, for restaurant recommendations, for help getting through a personal crisis, or for leads on jobs. And they get answers, often terrific ones. I have seen all sorts of questions asked, from the frivolous to the insanely difficult, and not one has gone unanswered. "I think women in business especially," says Sandra Fathi, "are about karma, mentoring, and helping each other. Social networks are perfect for that."

For example, I have a friend, Ginger, whom I met in a chat room for a writing class a few years ago. I would not recognize her if I passed her on the street, but we have nonetheless been invaluable to each other. We know a great deal about the other's creative struggle, time challenges, and the particulars of our work—things I don't normally discuss. I know what state she lives in, the ages of her kids, and her name, but beyond that, I know little about her day-to-day life. Still, I have read her works in progress, offered criticism and encouragement, and cheered for her when she got an agent and sold a novel. She has done all of that for me, too. She has read my work long before friends I know in the flesh-and-blood world have heard me mention it. She and I provide a support system for each other, specific to our particular, similar projects, because we understand this aspect of each other's lives better than anyone else can.

I don't actually know my friend Tracy in person, either. We met during a work project, communicated via various online forums after that project ended, and asked each other professional advice for a while. Somewhere along the way, we became friends. We are more like colleagues who work in the same building, only we don't: We live in different time zones. One night while she was at home (in the Netherlands) and her husband was out of town, she woke to a loud noise in her kitchen and got up to investigate. There in her kitchen, at 3 AM, was a knife-wielding man. She screamed the sort of blood-curdling, horror-movie scream that brings in the neighbors and flipped her kitchen table over in his direction. Fortunately, he fled and the neighbors responded. But after the neighbors had left and the kids had gone back to sleep, Tracy was shaken and in need of human contact. It was the middle of the night where she was, but in my time zone it was early evening, and I was in my office catching up on work. She sent me a message, and we talked via Skype for 30 minutes until she was calm enough to go back to bed. She said it helped to know she wasn't alone, even if she physically was.

GET THEE TO THE PARTY

Another great thing about social networks is that you don't have to put on your little black dress and heels to go to the party, though you can if you want. And you shouldn't worry about being late. (As in, everyone else has been doing this for years and I just heard about it.) Just go.

In fact, just like a party, it might be more fun to show up late. Everyone is already relaxed and chatty, and you'll find more people you know already there. You might have to hang around and listen to get up to speed, but at least you didn't have to sit through the awkward beginning phase when they were still looking for a bowl for the chips. Just choose a network (see "Introducing the Networks" on page 274 for suggestions), send out invitations to everyone you can think of that you'd like to see online, and sit back and wait. People will start to accept your invites, and you will start to get invites from people who have found you. Soon enough, if you tend your network even nominally, you will find yourself at the heart of a vibrant online community that you value and turn to frequently.

If, after you get hooked, you find you are enthralled with your online extension of the real world, you will be happy to know that this is probably just the beginning. Hard-core networkers post hourly (or even up-to-the-minute) updates on their whereabouts via text messaging from their cell phone to Twitter (*http://www.twitter.com/*) or by camera phone photo to groovr (*http://www.groovr.com/*).

Devotees feel this allows them to stay connected to many people at once. And when they do see people in the flesh, there is no need to ask, "What have you been up to?" They have been following each other through the minutiae of their lives, all day, every day, and already know about the vet's appointment and the car wreck. So they can skip over all that and ask, "How's the cat?!" I use Twitter not only to announce projects and ask for help but also to follow news headlines, keep up with friends doing interesting things, and alert people to the many giveaways I do on my blog, GeekGirlfriends.com. And I have heard women say they have used it to track friends down at trade shows or locate people who have failed to show up for important events.

Even more popular among the young and wired are the online immersive gaming worlds such as Second Life, which are really social networks built around highly graphical environments. In this online virtual world, you can wander around and meet new people or meet up with people you already know. You can go dancing or even build yourself a house or business. I don't have the free time for this sort of gaming, but in the short time I spent here, I met an adorable Frenchman whose English wasn't very good. And it was worth it for the kissing. (Virtual sex is apparently part of the draw, but we didn't get that far: Genitals cost extra.) Maybe, someday in the future, if you and your girlfriends can't manage a real-world drink together, you could have your avatars do it for you. Note that you will need a very healthy computer to run the software.

It is likely that as high-powered computers increasingly become household appliances, more social networks will become immersive, graphical environments, and we will each develop an online version of ourselves.

Here is my online persona, Xyna Tomorrow, visiting an Australian Spa in Second Life—and wondering where my Frenchman went. I have lost my children for hours at a time to their world of online friends at RuneScape (*http://www.runescape.com/*), Club Penguin (*http://www.clubpenguin.com/*), and similar sites, so I know that when they are my age, they will think nothing of dressing their avatar in party clothes and heading out to hook up with their online friends, leaving their flesh-and-blood body at home in its jammies. Is this a good thing? I don't know. A survey done by the Pew Internet & American Life Project reports that a majority of Internet leaders, activists, and analysts predict that by 2020, "Virtual reality will be compelling enough to enhance worker productivity and also spawn new addiction problems." That makes perfect sense to me. It is both good and bad.

Residents of Second Life (in the form of avatars) can already do just about anything you can do in your real life, including own land, run businesses, and earn a living. Trade happens in Linden Dollars, and the annual economy of Second Life rivals that of some real-world towns. There are a fair number of people dropping out of the real-world workforce (or supplementing their income) to open night clubs, sell real estate, or otherwise become full-time Second Life entrepreneurs. Many real-world businesses feel it is viable enough as a marketplace that having a storefront there makes business sense.

Whether this move to socializing online, either as an avatar or not, is good or bad is probably not as important as knowing that this is a thing that cannot be stopped or denied. I honestly (and sadly) believe that those who don't embrace it, at least to some degree, will increasingly find themselves home alone, wondering where everyone went. The Pew survey was dire in its prediction that "Tech 'refuseniks' will emerge as a cultural group characterized by their choice to live off the network."

I enjoy the human contact that the diverse and far-flung posse of female friends in my virtual network brings me, so I have a lot of trouble understanding why anyone would avoid the experience. Then again, I can't understand why my kids won't try Thai food. I know they are missing out, but they persist in pressing their lips shut and shaking their heads, sure I'm trying to poison them. One day, they will try it and see how silly they were being.

12 THE SEXY GEEK

On her blog, Sabila K. details her New York City dating experiences: blind dates, failed efforts at romance, her mother's concern about her failure to marry, and her own neurosis on the subject. All of it provided Sabila with plenty of tragically comic stories that her readers—especially those also trying to survive the dating world—could relate to. One day, she noticed that one of her readers spent a lot of time on her blog and left interesting and well-written comments. "So naturally, I started stalking my stalker!" explains Sabila. "At this point I didn't know if he was a guy, girl, straight, gay, or serial killer," she laughs. But she was intrigued. When he posted a list of book recommendations—all of which she loved—she posted a response announcing, "I love you!" And this began an open flirtation on her blog, which her readers deemed "better than TV." Eventually—after a year of anonymous back-and-forth—he posted his email address in a comment so the two could communicate privately. Her readers instantly grabbed the email address, posed as Sabila, and tried to pick up her mystery man. Eventually, the mystery man managed to sort the real Sabila from the imposters and suggested they meet. "We hit it off immediately," she says, and the two are now discussing marriage. So because of her blog about dating, Sabila is no longer in the dating scene—though she still blogs about her life (*http://www.revengeofthenerddd .blogspot.com/*).

People often think of technology as cold, isolating, and inhuman. So I think it is one of the great surprises of our technological age that we most often use technology for warm and human purposes: connecting with people we care about, meeting new people, finding romance, and sharing our hopes, dreams, and darkest secrets with people with whom we feel a connection—even if we've never met them.

When it comes to online dating, a lot of people are doing it. The Pew Internet & American Life Project's survey (in 2006) found that 63 million people say they know someone who has used a dating website and that 26 percent of American adults—53 million people—say they know someone who has gone on a date with a person they met through a dating site. "We estimate the number of overall online dating marriages to be more than 100,000 a year," says Joe Tracy, publisher of *Online Dating Magazine* (*http://www.onlinedatingmagazine.com/ news2006/eharmonymarriages.html*). While researching this chapter, I received so many messages from women who met someone special online that I started to believe these estimates.

I also heard from women who use technology to do much more than find a date. Women wrote to tell me how they use technology to develop existing relationships, keep emotional attachments alive over great distances, and explore issues in intimate relationships that are often difficult to broach in person. Women are also using technology to explore their own sexuality through pornography or in virtual worlds, to learn about sex and their bodies, and even to engage in "virtual sex" with their husbands, boyfriends, and people they don't even know. Because of the way women are integrating technology into their lives, the romantic relationship has taken on a new dimension, one that extends across space, fits into small increments of time, and allows for a free flow of ideas and fantasies that were never possible in face-to-face reality. I was so awed by the creative ways the women who wrote to me were using technology that instead of answering letters in this chapter, I'm letting these women tell their stories.

HOOKING UP

There are so many ways to meet people online that it makes the big-city dating scene look as empty as the American prairie in the 1800s. Is your dream date someone who shares your love of running, scuba diving, Scrabble, all things Goth, or golf? Then check out one of the thousands of dating sites specific to a particular interest. There is at least one for just about anything you can dream up. Is your perfect man Jewish? Catholic? Baptist? Buddhist? Perhaps you will fare better at one of the sites that focus on religious preference. Are you deaf, blind, elderly, a midget, bald, a millionaire, a geek, very tall, or just hankering to meet someone who meets any of these descriptions? Google your special circumstances and you are certain to find a dating site to meet your needs. If you have no idea what you are looking for and you just want to meet someone living in your area, go to one of the big online dating sites such as Match.com or eHarmony. (I have provided a far-from-comprehensive list to get you started.)

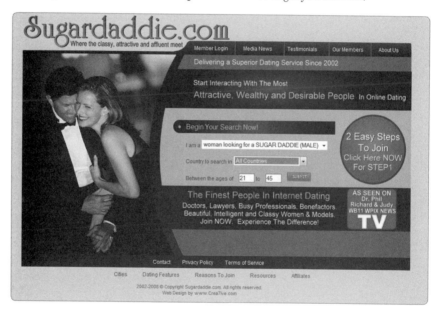

Even if you aren't ready to spring into the "Hey, baby!" world of online dating sites, there are plenty of low-key options for discovering friends online. This is, after all, what online social networks were created for. I have made plenty of friends through Facebook, LinkedIn, Plaxo, Twitter, and others. There is no reason—if both people are of the same mind—friends made there could not turn into something more. In fact, this is such an effective way to flirt and discover new friends that Diane Falzone, host of a Maxim Radio show and "The Diana Falzone Show" on Paltalk.com, considers them dangerous to monogamous relationships. "If you are in a serious relationship and don't need a Facebook or MySpace page for work, get rid of those pages," she suggests. "It opens up temptation. I have heard so many stories where women have told me 'I thought I was in a happy marriage, and then I discovered my husband was poking some woman on Facebook.' Just don't do it."

Even though I'm not single and haven't been since before the launch of online big dating sites, I signed up to see what it was all about. My husband wasn't exactly happy about this, but it was all in the line of duty, right? And until I tried it myself, it all seemed a bit murky. Sure you can "meet" people, but what does that really mean? How well can you get to know someone in this sort of forum? And can it be anything like the heady thrill of meeting someone in the flesh and blood?

After a day or so, I began to understand. There was a sense of adventure to the experience, a sort of private elation that did not in any way resemble my

When you meet someone at eHarmony, you get only a sketchy description—all of which could be lies—a fuzzy picture, and the opportunity to ask some formal questions. Your imagination is free to create the man of your dreams to fill in the rest.

memory of dating, which was either very forced or happened by accident. So what was this new, private thrill?

The answer came to me while I was watching my daughter play with her toys. Even though her toys are inanimate, for her they have names, personalities, friendships, relationships, and aspirations. It is because they don't contradict her by having personalities of their own that she is able to imbue them with intricate lives and emotions that are evocative for her. And, in much the same way, the people I met online were not real enough to limit my imagination. At the beginning stage, I had little more than a sketchy profile, a location, and perhaps a blurry photo. The rest—the gestures, motives, context, hopes, history, and personality—my imagination filled in on its own—exactly as I would have it. And this leads very quickly to affection.

I don't mean to say that relationships that eventually evolve out of these connections are imagined. I just think the environment creates a delightfully warm and safe way to start out. And by the time two people who have met this way decide to meet for real, each has already built a romance in the mind. So if the person who turns up for that first date meets expectations at all, true love can easily ensue.

And there, too, lies the rub. What happens if that person disappoints? What if the whole thing was a con? What if he said he was 6' 2" and he's only 5' 9"? "When you converse with someone online, you hear the conversation in your own voice; you internalize it," explains Lucy, who spoke to me on the condition that I not use her real name. She learned this the hard way when an online relationship she thought was perfect broke her heart—and his—when it failed to deliver in real life. "It's not like the phone where you hear the other person's voice and context. You can be reading emails in a dark room with candles and a glass of wine and everything he says sounds romantic. Maybe he only meant to say, 'Hi there!' during a break in the football game he's watching."

A Lie by Any Other Name

Remember the movie *Roxanne* or its predecessor, the play *Cyrano de Bergerac*? The message in them (and most romantic literature) is that love starts with language. In this story, a man with an enormous nose and a terrific command of the language writes love letters for a girl on behalf of another man who, while easy on the eyes, possesses no literary gift. Along the way, the poet falls for the girl. When the farce is revealed, the girl follows her heart—which was seduced by language—not her eyes. There is a lot of this sort of wooing through language in our history.

meet the dating sites

Trying to decide where to start your online dating adventure? There are so many sites, I can't include them all, but here is a list to get you started. Don't let this limit you, though. If you have a particular hankering, google it.

American Singles (http://www.americansingles.com/)   Despite the name, this site is not just for Americans, but it does offer good communication tools, including a chatroom where you can meet up with people online for a bit of party conversation before you go one-on-one.

eHarmony (http://www.eharmony.com/)   The lengthy sign-up process weeds out less serious daters and helps make matches who share your goals, aspirations, and political and religious leanings. Many men don't even want to commit to the sign-up process. In short, there are more women than men here. Not the place to go if you are gay.

Chemistry.com (http://www.chemistry.com/)   A recent launch from Match.com, this site claims to use a sophisticated personality profile to match you to people you will not only be compatible with but with whom you will find that all-important yet hard-to-quantify chemistry. The matchmaking system is designed by world-renowned biological anthropologist Dr. Helen Fisher.

JDate (http://www.jdate.com/)   Ever wonder what happened to the Yenta? The traditional Jewish matchmaker has been reborn as a dating site, only now she lets you determine what you want in a mate, search your own geographic area, leave video messages, and—if you meet someone nice—participate in instant chats.

Match.com (http://www.match.com/)   This is probably the first place people think of when they think about online dating. Many women I spoke to had success here, but others called it Bootycall.com or LetsScrewTonight.com. It's easy to sign up, and the emphasis on browsing for attractive singles means you will likely encounter your fair share of hounds among the millions who use this site. There are so many people here, though, that you will certainly find someone to interest you.

Paltalk (http://www.paltalk.com/)   Once you download the Paltalk Scene software, your computer becomes a virtual party scene where you can chat (on video if you like) with other Paltalkers, watch shows like wrestling, comedy, news, music performances, and celebrity shows. You can join video chats with up to 10 people and hang out in video chat rooms.

PlentyofFish (http://www.plentyoffish.com/)   Log in, take the personality test designed to measure self-confidence, family orientation, self control, and social dependency . Then browse your matches. One big hurdle that most other sites put you through has been eliminated here: You don't have to enter your credit card number. This site is completely free.

True (http://www.true.com/)   A compatibility test helps sort through the possibilities to hone in on those who might suit you romantically, sexually, by personality, by interest, or in terms of commitment. The site also screens communicating members against criminal records and offers plenty of coaching on dating successfully.

Yahoo! Personals (http://personals.yahoo.com/)   It's easy to set up a profile and get going here. This popular site offers lots of free trials, so you can find people who match your criteria and are in your geographic location.

GET WHAT YOU WANT

At first glance, all sites may look the same, so how is a girl to decide? This depends largely on what you are looking for and what you are comfortable with, but there are some things that everyone should ask.

How much and how often do you pay?   Each site varies. Some let you set up a profile and go public but make you pay up before you can communicate with anyone. Some will only let you communicate with other members who have paid. Some give you a completely free trial for a certain number of days. Some charge by the month. Some sell credits that you spend making contact with new potentials. Some automatically renew your membership by charging your credit card every month. Some politely remind you before they do this. Look into the payment options before you get too attached, and choose one that seems the most comfortable for you.

How much privacy?   Does the site protect your personal contact information? Does it allow protected chats and phone calls within the site so that you can talk and instant message someone while leaving you the option to disappear without a trace? Most of the big sites do, but check it out before you give out your digits.

Do you like the place?   Like a singles bar, you have to like the place to visit it often. And each site seems to attract a particular clientele, even those that don't cater to a specific demographic. If you find the design irritating, the people offensive, the ads invasive, the profiles busy and irritating, or the communication tools irritating, move on. You have plenty of options.

How do they match you up?   Some sites use very sophisticated software to sort through millions of people to find those you might like. This is why eHarmony asks so many invasive questions. And Chemistry.com purports to watch who you like and don't like so it can get better at finding Mr. Right over time. This is a numbers game, so get some help doing the math.

And it turns out to be the same online. "Most forms of communication are
first used to communicate one of two things: finances or love," says Genevieve
Bell, anthropologist and Director of User Experience within Intel's Digital Home
Group. "So it is no surprise to me that technology was immediately hijacked for
these purposes, too." When the words on the page are the first impression you
give, the way you use words becomes of the utmost importance, which is great
news for those of us who enjoy the language and another great reason to advocate
literacy in our kids. Online dating has also revived a form of romance that—for
a brief moment in time—seemed to have been killed by the telephone: the love
letter.

Even though the ability to pen prose to make a girl's heart flutter is an admirable skill in any man—and especially in an online dating situation—don't believe everything you read. Jeff Hancock, Cornell assistant professor of communication and member of the faculty of computing and information science, received a National Science Foundation (NSF) grant to pursue his study, "The Dynamics of Digital Deception in Computer Mediated Environments." He aimed to examine just how often people lie about themselves in their online profiles—especially on online dating sites. And the results were a bit staggering. Nearly all of those surveyed did not tell the whole truth.

"We actually put [the daters] on a scale and weighed them, checked their height, and we looked at their driver's license to get their age to see how it compared with their online profile," Hancock says. Does this mean that your 6' 2" online flame who makes 200K a year and writes like Byron is really a broke graduate student who looks more like Danny DeVito than Colin Farrell? Could be. Most of the lies told in Hancock's study were pretty minor, though. And, rather predictably, men tend to lie about their height and income and most often women lie about their weight and age.

Even though everyone does it, though, lying is not a sound dating practice. "I have heard all kinds of stories," says Gloria McDonald, author of *Laws of the Jungle: Dating for Women Over 40* (WAM Publishing, 2007) and owner of the matchmaking firm Perfect Partners. "I've heard of people who have put up pictures that are 10 years old. People honestly don't believe that they have changed, though they may have gained 20 pounds and look their age. I've also heard of people who have put up pictures of someone else." Do I have to say that deception is not a good idea? If you ever get to the meeting stage, your prospect is very likely to be disappointed. "You will likely be easily forgiven for what you consider to be flaws," says Falzone. "But if you lie, you look like you have a lot to hide—even if you don't. Also, there is a lid for every pot. There will be someone out there who is perfect for you. If you lie about who you are, you will never find that person." Still, the prevalence of fibbing is a good reason to meet your potential paramour in person before you let things go too far. "I recommend that people meet as soon as possible," says McDonald. "Sometimes people carry on emailing for weeks only to be disappointed when they do meet."

No One Loves Me!

"The wonderful thing about online dating is that there are millions and millions of single people out there, and they are online," says McDonald, "And the bad thing about online dating is there are millions of people doing it." That can be frustrating for anyone who imagines they will log on, fall in love, and get married by the summer. "People—especially women—have a tendency to get online and get frustrated three months later," says McDonald. If you are lucky, your number will come up right away. But chances are this will start to feel more like a part-time job than a romance novel long before you find The One. For me, this moment came pretty fast. Logging on, maintaining all the communications, and keeping track of who's who and what we've already talked about is a lot of work. Some of the sites do a better job than others helping you keep it all straight, but it's definitely work.

At first, the entire experience was a blast. I skipped right over all the guys who didn't appeal to me, even if they had sent me communications or "icebreakers," in a way that's hard to do in a single's venue—where the pushy guys tend to get a lot of face time simply by being aggressive. But Martin from Australia sounded dreamy. A documentary filmmaker with an income in the stratosphere wanted to know if I thought a long-distance relationship could work. James in San Francisco looked (at least from one fuzzy picture) to be a dead ringer for George Clooney. And everyone I met was fit, romantic, and 6' 2". Before I had even spoken to these men, I knew how many books they read in a year, what they hoped for in a relationship, what their interests were, if they wanted kids, and what they did for a living. Or at least I knew what they said these things were.

But after a couple of weeks, the thrill turned to drudgery. Communicating through checkboxes and mini-questionnaires on eHarmony was a great icebreaker. But it went on for such a long time that I lost interest in every one of these guys long before much "Open Communication" became possible. And the ones I didn't lose interest in broke up with me. At Match.com, I was overwhelmed with winks and email communications, some offering marriage before they even knew my name, many clearly looking for a booty call. On True, I was overwhelmed by men who found me "appealing" before I had finished updating my profile or posted a picture. I'm pretty sure that I was appealing only because I possessed a pulse. This careful distance—perhaps the entire online dating scene—began to remind me of middle school. In middle school, you find yourself "dating" someone you barely know. And dating doesn't mean you spend any time together. There might be a couple of notes passed. Maybe you sit together on the bus. And then, for no apparent reason, it's over. That's how it went with Martin, James, and a dozen others. One minute we were happily exchanging pre-packaged questions and answers. Then it was over. And the breakup, too, happened through checkboxes (created by eHarmony to minimize the hurt). Even though I wasn't seriously dating—and you couldn't call what we were doing dating anyway—rejection hurts. On the day that James broke up with me, I broke up with six or seven guys for no reason. Just to feel better about it. The last time I made this sort of serious emotional decisions with such casual indifference was in middle school. I'm not saying that's a bad thing. It was sort of like practice

If you are sure that you want to permanently close communication with Doug, please select from the following list those messages which best reflect your feelings at this time. After you click the "Close" button below, we will notify Doug that this communication has been closed. This match will be moved to your Closed section.

"I have decided to close communication because..."
(choose as many as apply)

- ☐ I think our family backgrounds are too different.

- ☐ I have too much happening in my life at the moment.

- ☐ I don't feel that the chemistry is there.

- ☐ I don't think our Must Haves and Can't Stands fit.

- ☐ I think the physical distance between us is too great.

- ☐ I want to pursue other matches at eharmony.

- ☐ I am pursuing another relationship.

- ☐ I'm just not ready for the next step.

- ☐ I am taking a break from dating.

When you decide to end things on eHarmony, you get to choose from a pre-packaged list of exits.

BEGIN WITH THE TRUTH

I met several people during my four-month membership on Match.com and found it to be a great tool to weed people out. I met some great guys who ended up not being The One but who are now great friends. I also met some jerks. This forum allowed me to put everything on the table without being pushy. It's an easy way to be totally honest about your expectations, to talk about life goals and ambitions, as well as what you expect from a husband and the father of your not-even-born-yet kids. If you brought that up on a first date, the man would run away as fast as he could.

And I did finally meet my husband there. We're going on two years now and have a beautiful eight-month-old son.

Rebeca

dating—the way middle school was—and who can't stand a little practice? All that virtual rejection steels your heart for the real thing.

Make Me a Match

The sheer time and energy required for online dating has spawned a new industry, or rather, a resurgence of an old industry: matchmaking. I've seen predictions that the matchmaker—someone who presorts, verifies, and provides hand-picked introductions—will be among the fastest growing job category in the next few years. I've also seen predictions that this is the next technology the online dating sites will offer as a feature. So you may bump into a Yenta—or her avatar, anyway—soon enough online. At the moment, it's a growing industry. Just google *professional matchmaker* or check out *http://www.findamatchmaker.com/* for proof. "Anyone and everyone who has ever set up a friend is now opening up a matchmaking business," says Falzone. "So you have to take a look at what you are getting." These services can offer a lot of benefits—including avoiding all those guys who are just looking for a booty call, if that's what you stipulate. But they can also be very expensive, so evaluate what the matchmaker is offering and how she defines success. Some define marriage as success. McDonald lets her clients tell her when she's succeeded. Some guarantee a certain number of dates for a price.

a LID For every POT

After *thirteen years* of online dating, I met the man of my dreams earlier this year on Tangowire.com. I am 36, plus-sized, and a business development consultant in NYC. My biotech-scientist boyfriend lives in San Diego. We each had a laundry-list of characteristics we were looking for in a partner. (He had a spreadsheet!) With the magic of the Internet we were able to check off every item on each of our respective lists!

Despite the distance—with the help of technology—we are always available to communicate with each other, and our romance is blooming. Between monthly bi-coastal visits, we send frequent text messages, emails, IMs, Facebook pictures and entries, as well as Skype and Yahoo! webcam sessions. We are constantly sending YouTube videos, Web links, and online articles to each other—including relationship advice and last-minute travel discounts. Recently, we started sharing our Amazon.com and other shopping wish lists to send each other gifts.

Andrea

But remember, in that case, she is making the same offer to everyone. So she might have a toady guy in her roster who she has also promised to match eight times. Making you go out on a date with him means she has fulfilled her promise to two people. But what did you get out of it? Some matchmakers represent hot, successful women for free just to be able to add them to their dating pool so, if you are a catch—you know you are!—explore that option first.

STAYING CONNECTED

"I met my husband in 2001," explains Lolly Johnson. "He is British. While he was visiting in Los Angeles (where I lived at the time), a mutual friend set us up. We hit it off immediately." But Los Angeles is a long way from England. That distance might have doomed a relationship like this at one time. But Lolly and her Englishman managed to carry on a romance—for four years—despite the distance. "We tried to never go more than 100 days without actually seeing one another. But it was the half hour—or more—we spent chatting on MSN Messenger using a web camera (webcam) each night that kept our relationship alive, especially through the arduous immigration process. If we had been unable to see each other this way, I'm not sure we would have made it." The two are married now and living in the United States, but her husband still uses Skype and a webcam to talk to his business partners and family in the United Kingdom.

If communication is the key to a happy marriage, then information technology may be the greatest marital aid ever created. With a few technical tools, it is possible to stay constantly connected to our loved ones, whether they are across the house or across the world. That sort of togetherness would be stifling in the real world, but in the virtual one, it's liberating.

Even when I know my husband is hard at work on something, on the phone, or not in the mood to talk, I can send him an instant message or a text message to his phone. He doesn't have to drop what he's doing to respond; he can fire back a response when it fits his workflow. And I can say things in these environments that are steamy, too mature for the kids to hear, about people who are in the room, or even too delicate to bring up face-to face. These private scraps of communication can happen even when all other forms of communication are unavailable—because of distance, time, or cost—no matter where either of us is in the world. This is a revolution in communication. But it's not the only one. It's also possible to share images, video, and places we like to go (on the Internet). It is even possible to go out together virtually, even if our physical bodies are on opposite sides of an ocean.

Instant messaging is an improvement over telephone conversations— especially for long-distance relationships—in many ways. For one thing, it is

DIGITAL marital aids

Communication technologies can bring marriages closer, whether both parties live and work in the same house or are trying to carry on a relationship across great physical distance. Here is a quick rundown of the tools with some ideas of how they can be used.

Instant messaging   A tiny software download (Skype, Yahoo! Messenger, Google Talk, and others) and an Internet connection are essential to marital communication. Instant messaging allows you to fit conversations into micro-moments—times where otherwise there is no chance to talk—to discuss things that you don't want the people around you to hear, to converse in short bursts while working on other tasks, or to explore subjects you can't bring yourself to broach in person. Schedule a little hot instant-message flirtation and see what happens. Watch out for fighting, though, which can happen by accident if you fail to use those emoticons to apply tone and mood to your comments.

Text messaging   Everyone is busy, but that doesn't mean you don't think about each other while driving the car, showering, or picking the kids up from school. Text messaging allows you to capture and share those thoughts no matter where you are—or where he is. Send a steamy text message when you know he's in a meeting or so he'll receive it when he gets off a plane. There is nothing like using the tools you have to build a little anticipation into your marriage. According to Falzone, though, this is one area where women should take the lead when it comes to being saucy. "Men are always afraid women will think they are a perverts, so they are cautious about this," she explains. "But when women get sexy, men always love it."

completely free. And it is a simple matter to connect an inexpensive webcam to your computer and suddenly see each other. "Live video and sound on our laptops almost entirely replaced the phone for us," says Lolly. A lot of women panic at this idea, fearing every bad hair day—or any risqué footage—will be broadcast around the world. Lolly worried about it too. "But I ended up loving it," she says. "You can put the camera above you or below you or whatever looks best. And you can see yourself before you connect." She insists, too, that the slightly fuzzy image and slight delay is flattering to everyone. "It makes it look like you are in candlelight."

This oddly focused form of communication led to a deep intimacy that Lolly thinks they might not have achieved without this forum. "All we could do was talk. So we both knew by the time we got married that we were in it for the long

Internet phones   If one or the other person in a marriage travels, there is no greater way to bring them close to home than an Internet phone. If both parties are using the same tool, the calls are free and offer an intimate clarity you simply don't get from POTS (plain old telephone service). You can use a computer or a dedicated phone that connects to your broadband router and talk as long as you like with no concern for costs.

Webcams   Any relationship that endures long periods of separation should make the effort to connect via webcam. These can be used in intimate ways if you are so inclined but are also great for simply sharing a new haircut or outfit, showing off a decorating project, or helping the kids see their dad.

Email   It's not a new technology, but it is certainly a great tool for keeping romance alive and communication healthy, whether the relationship has geographic challenges or not. Everyone loves to receive love letters. Email is also a great way to share information on a topic—by sending links—or to share images simply by attaching them. And the great thing about email is that it is easy to compile a virtual box of love letters. In more romantic times, a woman might stuff a love letter that she wanted to read and reread into her bodice. These days, we can wear a book-length compilation of love letters stored on a tiny flash drive around our neck. Or, as several women who wrote to me suggested, compile them and print them in a book to share with your children.

The World Wide Web   You may not think of web browsing as a form of communication, but a lot of people are using it this way. Whether you meet up together in an online virtual world to play out fantasies, take each other on virtual dates via links, or play online games designed to get you frolicking, the Internet can be a terrific marital aid.

haul, and we had already talked about the tough stuff. In real life it is easy to let physicality overshadow important things."

So many women told me fantastic stories about how they used the Internet to grow and nurture intimate relationships that I have a newfound respect for these technologies—and I was already pretty fond of them. When I was "dating" online I got dumped a lot because men thought the physical distance between us was too great. (You can usually set your own parameters on how far afield you want to system to look for a match; I wanted to browse the entire universe.) I was just playing so I didn't mind, of course, but it did make me want to tell these guys how a little technical know-how can overcome great distances.

That doesn't mean carrying on a relationship this way is for the faint of heart. "We could easily have let out entire relationship drift apart," says Carolyn Clark, who has been dating long-distance for three years. After the first year, she felt she and her boyfriend were losing touch. She spent long hours on the telephone at work and, by the time she got home, felt she had nothing left to say. Then she realized she had forgotten to tell him important things that were going on her life—trips, work events, and other things most other people knew. So she and her boyfriend came up with a plan. "We call it the question of the day," she explains. "Every other day, one of us sends the other a question through email and we both answer it. We both made a promise to each other to always answer honestly. It can be something like 'What did you wear today?' or 'Have you ever had feelings for someone else?' It has had a great impact on our relationship, and I have encouraged my friends to try it even when they live with their spouse."

The long-distance, technology relationship also demands that couples accept, even embrace, some of the basic differences between men and women. "We stayed in touch via text messages when we are home or at the gym," says Danielle Gibbs, who carried on a long-distance relationship for 11 months before she moved across the country to be with her fiancé. "If we are in the office we might use instant messaging," So even when the two were in different states they had a constant tether to each other—through their cell phones or computers. "I might even be in a meeting but if he was thinking about what we did last time we got together, he could text it to me. I could respond during the meeting. It was fun." Even with all this contact, her fiancé wanted to see her—and not just her face. "I don't need a lot of visuals—maybe because I'm a woman. I've got him in my head and that's enough for me. But I know that men do need visuals." The webcam was out though. "That's just not me," she says. But she did send him "intimate" images via email or with her camera phone. "You always feel a little funny about sending sexy photos of yourself because those things are going to live forever. But he liked it."

Even with all this communication, a big part of relationships—in the real world—happens on dates, where we do things together, enjoy meals and conversation, or go to shows, concerts, and movies. Yet, even in this, women managed to find a virtual way. "I am a military spouse and the mom of five," says Jaykada McFadden. "My husband and I met online and were married shortly afterwards. Ten years later, we still use the Internet and text messages to keep in touch when he's deployed. This past deployment, we created a date night every Thursday. On our first date, I took him to Cypress Gardens [*http://www.cypressgardens.com*; a theme park]. I sent him an email link with the location, and we both went to the site at the same time and chatted. Then we went to dinner by sending a link to Applebee's, looking at the online menu, and discussing what we were eating. When it was my husband's turn, he sent me an email with a link to a picture of an outfit that he was wearing, and I did the same. His next email was of the Hummer limo he was picking me up in. We continued to do this every week until he got back. Then we went on some of those very same dates in real life."

VIRTUAL AND VICARIOUS SEX

One step up from a virtual date night is virtual sex. This idea often evokes images of perverts and scary dungeons in the minds of women, so you might be surprised to learn exactly how popular this private entertainment is. According to the Cybersex and Romance Survey of 15,000 people done by *Elle* and MSNBC in 2004, "81 percent of men and 53 percent of women are sampling some kind of sex-related activity online, whether participating in adult chatrooms, posting to a sex newsgroup or interacting with someone on a live webcam. Porn is also popular—41 percent of women and 75 percent of men who responded have intentionally viewed or downloaded erotic films or photos." So if you've toyed with the idea of logging on for a bit of titillation, you are hardly a deviant. In fact, if you haven't, you are something of a minority. (If you are worried about the kids in your house happening onto the sites you have browsed, see Chapter 9 for tips on keeping their online experience age-appropriate.)

Okay, I know you are wondering, "What the heck is virtual sex? How the heck can sex be virtual?" Regina Lynn describes it in her book on sex and technology, *Sex 2.0*: "Cybersex, also known as 'cyber' or 'cybering,' is consensual sexual interaction among two or more adults using the Internet as the primary means of connection. I generally think of cybersex as a text-based activity because that's my preference and that's the way it's been done for decades, but cyber can also include audio chat, avatar-based communities, and webcam conferencing." So, you see, part of the beauty of virtual sex is that it is safe sex. There is no actual contact—except the conversational variety. This means it can also

sex education

"Knowledge is the food of the soul," according to Plato. And this bit of wisdom is as true in a relationship as it is in philosophy. If the spice has gone out of a relationship, you're seeing a new guy, or you just have questions you aren't willing to put to your coffee klatch, the Internet is a gold mine of information. There is no need to be seen lurking in the naughty section of the bookstore, video store, or library. No need to pay some expert hundreds of dollars so you can talk things out. No need to wait till you get your annual 15 minutes with your OB/GYN just to ask a dicey question. (Though questions that are dicey because of your health—rather than just your modesty—should always be put to a professional. There is nothing wrong with brushing up on the facts online first to make sure you are asking the right questions.) Sometimes a little online exploration is all you need.

Of course, you have to consider the source. There is a lot of rumor, silliness, and misinformation out there, but there is also a lot of terrific information. If you have a particular sex, relationship, or health question, google it. Just be wary of who is giving you're the answer. Read the About page of any site you aren't familiar with. Consider how much this source is likely to know and if they have an agenda or product they are trying to promote. Get past this hurdle, and you will find a surprising wealth of information. Here is a list to get you started.

Aphrodite Women's Health (http://www.aphroditewomenshealth.com/) This site offers lots of articles on subjects ranging from contraception to menopause, a lot of it from experts in their field. The forums are definitely worth a visit if you like to hear from real women, ask questions, and develop a sense of community.

be anonymous—something that's hard to pull off in the real world. You can send an avatar out there to represent you, and no one has to know who is pulling its strings. In fact, it's something of a debate as to whether virtual sex even qualifies for adultery if you are married. Though I doubt this argument would hold up after the fact, so if you want to play, you should probably clear it first with your partner.

If you are ready to play, you actually don't need much beyond what you already use for keeping track of your finances and sending email to your mother. If you have a partner and already use instant messaging (the most popular tool for virtual sex), all you need to do is take your IM flirting up a notch. You can use a webcam if you want to, but it's hardly necessary. Everything that is true of language and romance is also true on instant messaging—just turn the heat on your language up to high. (Talk dirty!) Put your inhibitions aside, dim the lights, find some privacy, and go for it. "Cybersex—like actual sex, now that I think about it—always looks ridiculous from the outside," says Lynn. "Yet good cybersex is so much more than the words on the screen . . . It can be such a profound erotic

The Mayo Clinic (http://www.mayoclinic.com/) This site offers a bounty of information on a wealth of health topics from the best in the business. Subscribe to a feed from the site's blog to up your health IQ, or just check in when you have questions about anything from infant care to Alzheimer's. Check out the handy symptom checker next time you're wondering if that ache is a pulled muscle or a deadly illness.

Nurture Your Nature (http://www.nurtureyournature.org/) The Association of Reproductive Health Professionals (ARHP) and the National Women's Health Resource Center (NWHRC) sponsor this site that focuses on healthy female sexuality. The goal of the site is to improve communication about sexuality between women and their health care professionals, as well as between women and their partners.

WebMD (http://www.webmd.com/) You have probably heard of this massive online health site that covers everything from ear infections in infants to the medical issues of the elderly. There is plenty of women-specific health and sex advice here, and it is a reliable source. Again, check out the forums.

Other women Who knows more about being a woman than a woman? Other women's real-life experiences can be highly instructive, even if one woman's experience isn't a statistically significant sample size. Finding women who will talk frankly about touchy subjects may be difficult in the real world, but it's not in the virtual one. Look for blogs on subjects you are pursuing, check the forums at health sites, and read the user reviews at women-oriented sex toy shops such as Babeland (*http://www.babeland.com/*) and Good Vibrations (*http://www.goodvibes.com/*).

connection between two people that they forget their surroundings and see only the interaction; their bodies respond as if they were really touching, and their emotions don't always know the difference."

If you don't have a partner, there are lots of places online to find one, whether you want to meet him in real life or not. All of the dating sites above will have some element of "hooking up" for sexy chat or instant message. If you have used these sites much at all, you have probably already rejected some of these of advances. But just because some bonehead approached with some awful come-on doesn't mean everyone is like that. Like the real thing, good virtual sex starts with a relationship. Paltalk, with its combination of chatrooms and videos, is a very popular place to find this sort of interaction. Or, if you are willing to venture into the world of massively multiplayer online role playing games (MMORPGs), there are several designed for sex play. A lot of people use Second Life for this purpose, but Redlight Center (*http://www.redlightcenter.com/*), There (*http://www.there.com/*), and Jewel of Indra (*http://www.jewelofindra.com/*) were built with this idea in mind. Here you can create an avatar, give it a name and body, and go forth to act like the slut you *never* would be in real life. You can try on different personalities, dress up in outfits that would shock your mother, and, in short, take advantage of the anonymity of the Internet to fuel your fantasies or explore a sexual identity you aren't willing to give voice to in your own home town.

And while we are on the subject of slutty behavior, you may be surprised (or not) to learn that women have become influential consumers of pornography—a genre in which the slut is the star. A big part of the reason for this is the Internet: No longer forced to shop the sleaze section at the video store, women are logging on to rent or buy DVDs via mail or even to download titillation to a laptop they can sneak off with to the bedroom. This is all good. Even though women are often consumers of the product, however, most pornography makers have failed to recognize this fact. "If you're female," says Violet Blue, author of *The Smart Girl's Guide to Porn* in an article she wrote for *GoodVibes Magazine* (where she also reviews porn), "admitting to yourself that you want to watch a dirty movie may take some—or a lot of—forethought. One of the major obstacles that we women face is the widely held notion that women don't respond to sexual imagery as men do—a notion that is absolutely untrue. In her 1994 study, Dr. Ellen Laan of the University of Amsterdam proved that women respond physiologically to sexual images, even when the women said that the porn they watched was boring or unarousing."

There is some good (well, relatively speaking anyway) porn out there, much of it directed by women who recognize an untapped market when they see it. But, as Violet Blue puts it, "Keep your expectations in check—you're not going to see anything like the mega-budget Hollywood blockbusters (but with sex included) that you're used to . . . The quality you're going to see is like daytime soap operas; with simple sets, standard lighting, digital cameras, and barely-there acting."

Even if you are willing to accept all that, finding the good stuff is a supreme challenge. The Internet is a big place. And if you have ever tried to do a Google search on porn, it might appear that the Internet is not only big but also a man's world—a scary, perverted man's world, the kind of place most women would like to pretend doesn't exist. Even if you skip over Google and go to an online porn store, you may find yourself fleeing in horror long before you find anything you would want to watch. At SugarDVD.com, which claims to be the largest online porn rental shop and offers a host of rental plans, no late fees, and downloads by the minute, just browsing the categories may tell you more than you wanted to know. It's impossible to quickly find titles that might appeal to women or couples or otherwise sort the scary from the simply not that good. Fortunately, there are some brave women out there willing to trudge through the horrific boob jobs, bad acting, and sick male fantasies and gather together the sort of smut we chicks might like. Violet Blue is one such woman. She has written many books on sex and erotica, most with a female or couple's bent, including the aforementioned *The Smart Girl's Guide to Porn*. So start with that book. If you can't wait for it to arrive, her blog is pretty good too. She has a section (*http://www.tinynibbles.com/ smartporn*) devoted to helping you sort through the scary maze of idiocy out there and hone in on films that you will find fun and sexy.

The women who operate Good Vibrations—a sex-toy store—watch, review, and filter through the universe of porn and sell only titles they have deemed women friendly. They also offer a pay-per-minute plan for downloading movies, which is a great way to try this idea out and see if it's for you—though not all titles are available this way. Blowfish (*http://www.blowfish.com/*), another sex-toy store, sells all sorts of porn on DVD, but it's easy to skip over the nasty stuff here because the site's reviewers are terrific, offering details about lighting, production values, plot, potentially over-the-top material, and strangeness so you can better avoid that which you don't want to witness. They also sort the titles into categories a regular gal can deal with such as "Couple's Videos," "By Women," "An Actual Plot," and "Documentary and Educational." (If you prefer to rent, just check out the reviews and choices at either of these sites and let them help you sort through that mess over at SugarDVD.com.) If regular people doing it sounds like more fun than watching porn stars faking it, you might want to venture into the world of amateur sex vlogging (video blogging). These sites seem to come and go but, on the whole, they work pretty much like YouTube with a focus on nudity, sex, and, well, more sex. The people are real, the sex is real, and the cameras are really cheap. Some of this is even free. Try XTube (*http://www.xtube.com/*), Porn-Tube (*http://www.porntube.com/*), or yuvutu (*http://www.yuvutu.com/*). As with all things in this realm (user-uploaded as well as sex-industry stuff) please, please, please be sure you are running good virus protection and a pop-up blocker on your computer before you surf. You may not personally catch anything by partaking in this sort of voyeuristic activity, but your computer could.

If after stepping into this world, you find it all a bit too hard-core, maybe what you are really looking for is erotica. This you can find in more traditional outlets. The movie-rental site GreenCine (*http://www.greencine.com/*), for instance, offers an erotica section that includes some pre-code films, some NC-17 material, and even some X-rated titles. And you can rent movies you can watch in mixed company here as well, of course. Better still, you will find detailed synopses and reviews by regular people who have watched the films to help you choose.

I HAVE SEEN MY FUTURE HUSBAND
(AND HE'S A TIDY TEETOTALER)

I have seen predictions that in the not-too-distant future we will skip right over relationships with humans and start falling in love with technology directly (see *Love and Sex with Robots: The Evolution of Human-Robot Relationships* by David Levy, for example). At first, this idea struck me as insane, but if you think about the human imagination and its ability to love toys, carry on relationships with people who aren't in the same geographic location, find love in chat rooms, and seek sexual satisfaction via DVD, maybe it's not so far fetched. Once you start to consider the advances in technology—bots that are trained to carry on human-like conversations, sex toys that note and remember what you like, and the ability humans have to make changes to technology (or in the modern vernacular, *mod* or *hack*)—it starts to sound downright reasonable. There are lots of things I'd like to change about my husband. But years of subtle hints, nagging, drama, and even shouting fights haven't made a dent in his tendency to discard his socks under the dining room table, leave the toilet seat up in the middle of the night, snore, drink too much beer, watch football, and curse at his computer. If he were a robot, I could skip right over the decades of nagging and fighting and simply upload some new code. While I was at it, I could add some of those "remember what I like" features, downsize the beer-drinking algorithm, and—just for fun—upload Spanish so that he could woo me in an accent like Antonio Banderas. Hey, maybe robots *are* the husband of the future? I suspect that eventually we would discover something fuzzy about love that would put a damper on the whole modding-the-husband fun. It will turn out, perhaps, that it is all the little imperfections and human flaws that endear the people in our lives to us and that we can't form strong attachments to mechanical perfection. But along the way, we would have had the chance to explore being wooed by Antonio Banderas, and whatever other whims take our fancy. So even if a moddable husband robot is not an improvement over a living husband, it still sounds like more fun than 13 years on eHarmony.

THE DARK SIDE

There are lots of hazards to sending intimate, personal, salacious, or otherwise private missives out onto the Internet, though lots of people do it and have fun with it. There are even some hazards of online dating, flirting, and virtual sex. But, like most things adults do, if you are cautious and keep an eye on your own personal safety, you can play in this world without excessive worry. Most of the hazards of this sort of activity are those involving your reputation, which is usually the case with offline romance as well. The one advantage that online romance has over the offline variety is that you can control how much of your real identity you let loose. That is very hard to do in the real world.

Develop a virtual persona   If you are planning to hit the hot singles clubs online for a bit of anonymous cybering, get yourself an avatar, a name, and a backstory. Don't tell people where you really live. Don't start chatting about your local hockey team. (You would be surprised by how much everyday banter happens in these places.) And don't mention anything else personal that might be easy to trace back to you, your hometown, your work, or your kids.

Cloak yourself   If you are dating online, you can't pretend to be someone else, and you might reasonably want to use email or the phone. But if you give out an email address, use one you can ditch—and choose a username that isn't already associated with your other online escapades. Sign up for a Gmail, Yahoo!, Hotmail, or other hosted email account to use only for this purpose. If you give out a phone number, use an Internet phone created especially for getting in touch with your online dating contacts. Skype, GrandCentral, Yahoo! Voice, Vonage (for existing customers), and others offer virtual phone numbers that are inexpensive, ring on your computer, and have no address information connected with them.

Establish trust   More than one reputation has been ruined by people carrying on over instant message, email, or other online forums and then breaking trust. There have been so many examples of people making very public fools of themselves that there is no way to claim ignorance. Be sure you trust the person you share with online. If you send naughty pictures, steamy emails, or even participate in sexy chat with someone, that person has a record of your dalliance. So be sure you trust each other, because this can get very ugly.

If you meet   Never meet anyone you met online in a private place. Always tell someone where you are going and who you are meeting. Choose a place that's easy to walk away from, like a coffee shop. And don't be afraid to bring a friend with your for a first meeting. "Have an exit strategy," says Falzone. "Arrange to have someone call you on your cell phone at a designated time so you can bail quickly by saying you have an emergency or reassure your friend all is well."

Set some privacy rules   "Everyone these days is a writer," says Falzone. "So if you fear your lover might be blogging intimate details about your relationship, and you aren't comfortable with that, tell him to stop. If he won't agree to your terms, he isn't respecting you or the relationship." Also keep in mind that it's very easy to upload video to user-generated porn sites, so be sure that's not what he has in mind if he decides to get out a camera.

index

COLOPHON

How to Be a Geek Goddess was laid out in Adobe InDesign. The font is Filosofia.
The book was printed and bound at Malloy Incorporated in Ann Arbor, Michigan. The paper is Glatfelter Spring Forge 60# Smooth Eggshell, which is certified by the Sustainable Forestry Initiative (SFI). The book uses a RepKover binding, which allows it to lay flat when open.

UPDATES

Visit *http://nostarch.com/geekgoddess.htm* for updates, errata, and other information.